JAMES POTTE[R]
(QUAKER)

*A Record of
Dissent in the
17th and 18th Centuries*

With my Best Wishes

Ken [signature]

The front cover picture is from an engraving by Robert Spence of armed Constables leading Quakers or other Dissenters away to prison for attending a Conventicle (non-allowed religious meeting), in contravention of the Conventicle Acts.

Spence captioned his engraving from Samuel Pepys' Diary of 7th August 1664 thus: 'Met several poor creatures carried by, by Constables, for being at a Conventicle. They go like Lambs, without resistance. I would to God they would either conform, or be more wise, and not be catched'.

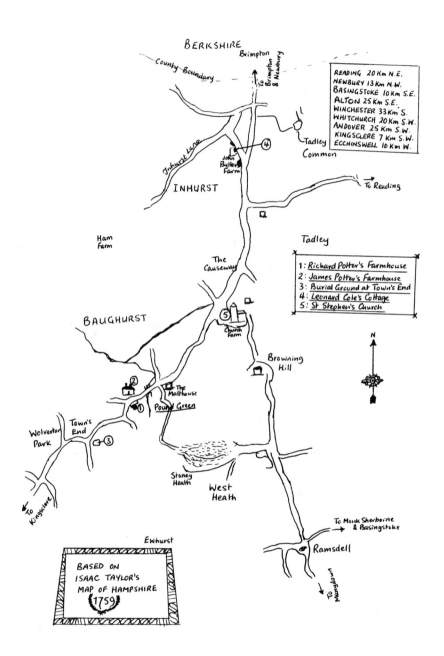

BERKSHIRE

Brimpton

County Boundary

To Brimpton & Newbury

READING 20 Km N.E.
NEWBURY 13 Km N.W.
BASINGSTOKE 10 Km S.E.
ALTON 25 Km S.E.
WINCHESTER 33 Km S.
WHITCHURCH 20 Km S.W.
ANDOVER 25 Km S.W.
KINGSCLERE 7 Km S.W.
ECCHINSWELL 10 Km W.

Inhurst Lane

John Buller's Farm

Tadley Common

INHURST

To Reading

Ham Farm

The Causeway

Tadley

1: Richard Potter's Farmhouse
2: James Potter's Farmhouse
3: Burial Ground at Town's End
4: Leonard Cole's Cottage
5: St Stephen's Church

BAUGHURST

Church Farm

N

Browning Hill

The Malthouse

Pound Green

Wolverton Park

Town's End

To Kingsclere

Stoney Heath

West Heath

To Monk Sherborne & Basingstoke

Ewhurst

BASED ON
ISAAC TAYLOR'S
MAP OF HAMPSHIRE
1759

Ramsdell

To Monydown

2

JAMES POTTER
(QUAKER)

A Record of
Dissent in the
17th and 18th Centuries

KEN SMALLBONE
B.A.(HONS.)

Sessions Book Trust
York, England

ISBN 1 85072 097 5

Initially typeset in 1989
by the late Charles Skilton
and now printed and bound by
William Sessions Limited
The Ebor Press, York, England

THIS BOOK IS DEDICATED TO MY GRANDMOTHER,
THE LATE MARY SMALLBONE, FORMERLY
MARY BROWN, WITHOUT WHOM I WOULD NOT HAVE
HAD SUCH INTERESTING ANCESTORS

IT IS ALSO DEDICATED TO
JAMES POTTER, AN EXTRAORDINARY MAN
BUT NEVERTHELESS AN UNSUNG HERO

FINALLY, IT IS ALSO DEDICATED TO THE MEMORY
OF MY FATHER AND BEST FRIEND INDEED, WHO,
SADLY, DID NOT LIVE LONG ENOUGH TO READ THIS BOOK

BROWN'S FARM, THE FIRST MEETING-HOUSE

BAUGHURST HOUSE, THE SECOND MEETING-HOUSE
(by kind permission of Mr Michael Wallford)

ROSE COTTAGE, THE THIRD MEETING-HOUSE
(by kind permission of the Misses Wigley)

CONTENTS

ILLUSTRATIONS

*The illustrations on pages 44, 56, 105 and the front cover are from
engravings by Robert Spence and are by courtesy of Friends House
Library, London.*

Winchester Great Hall.

THE GREAT HALL of WINCHESTER CASTLE where James Potter's Assize Court Trials were held.

INTRODUCTION

MARY SMALLBONE died at Basing Road Hospital, Basingstoke, on 14th August 1970. She was in her eighties, and had led a rather unhappy existence for the majority of her long years. She was a frail old lady who had gradually starved herself to death over the years in her attempt to provide proper nourishment for her unmarried sons.

She was a true Victorian in her outlook upon life, and was therefore virtually unapproachable when the topic turned to her personal life. Certain things remained unspoken for fear of emotion affecting the outcome.

Therefore, I never really discovered the real Mary Smallbone. In fact, I never asked because I always understood that her answer would be either " there's nothing to tell", or " that's no concern of yours". I have always regretted this lapse, for within a year of her departure I had become hooked upon that dreadful disease known as genealogy or family history.

All that I knew of my grandmother initially was what my father had told me. She was a farmer's daughter and their farm was at Baughurst, aptly named "Brown's Farm". I discovered in my early research that she was born there on 11th April 1883, the youngest of the six children of Thomas and Maria Thirza Brown. Later I found out that she was nine years old when her father had given up the farming business, which was fast becoming bankrupt through the stresses placed upon that industry during the latter decades of the nineteenth century, known collectively as "the Great Depression".

Mary's parents, however, were Londoners. Thomas Brown hailed from Putney, while Maria Thirza was a native of Clerkenwell, and they had married at Reading in Berkshire in 1867. I traced the Browns of Putney back to 1802 when Thomas' grandparents, John and Sarah Brown, baptised their first child in that Surrey church. John was recorded as the gardener for a Mr Drummond of Putney.

So, on the face of it, it seemed that my Browns were only recent residents of Baughurst, and that the name of the farm was fairly modern. I discovered quite early in my research that a John Brown had been at Brown's Farm until his death in 1865, when his brother, Thomas (my grandmother's grandfather), took over. Thomas Brown senior was classed as a carman, living at Putney, in 1851 and I assumed that he and John had scraped together enough money to acquire the lease of Brown's Farm in partnership.

My assumption was totally off-target. I had despaired of finding the

Browns, since in 1802 they were virtually newcomers to the Putney area, and could have come from anywhere in the south, attracted possibly by the nearness of the great city. The name Brown, for obvious reasons, did not help matters. I had almost abandoned all hope of finding them when a friend appeared on the scene with an incredible find.

I had not considered searching further back at Baughurst, simply because I was convinced that the family was new to the area around 1860. The late Don Kent was the head of the local branch of the Hampshire Genealogical Society at that time, and I used to attend the meetings regularly on the first Wednesday of each month at his home in Baughurst. Although Don's ancestors were from the Orkneys, he had an incredible interest in Baughurst and the people there. He founded a scheme in that area whereby volunteers were extracting all the information possible from the monumental inscriptions on the headstones in the local churchyards. At one such meeting he handed me a list of the inscriptions in the churchyard at St Stephen's, Baughurst, saying that there were a few Browns there in whom I might be interested.

I could hardly believe my eyes. I had already dismissed this source because of my assumption that my Browns were not homegrown. Yet Don's list of inscriptions proved that that assumption was totally wrong.

First of all there was the inscription for my grandmother's grandfather, Thomas Brown, who had died of heart disease out in the fields in 1872. On his headstone was recorded the fact that he was the brother of John Brown (this I knew already). Then there was the inscription for his brother, John, who had died in 1865. Here it was recorded that he was the grandson of John and Mary Brown! And nearby were the headstones for John, who died in 1801, and his wife Mary, who died in 1822, and another for one of their son, Richard, who died in 1849.

So, my Browns were of Baughurst extraction after all, and the name of the farm was much older than I had previously believed. As soon as possible I went through the Baughurst registers once more. I had noticed the name of Brown there before but, for the reasons I have already outlined, I never attached too much importance to them.

But there were still problems. Although John and Mary Brown had a son, Richard, who apparently inherited the farm on the deaths of his parents, and although their son John was never recorded in the registers after his baptism (he obviously moved away because of his lack of inheritance, and his age at death in the Putney register confirms that he was the John who was baptised at Baughurst in 1774), I could not find the baptism for John senior at Baughurst or in any of the surrounding parishes. According to his entry in the burial register for Baughurst, John was born in 1736 or 1737. For several months the origin of John Brown senior eluded me.

Then one day I was searching through the birth digests of the Quaker General Meeting of Hampshire and Dorsetshire. I noted down the birth entry of a certain John Brown, son of John Brown, on the 26th June 1737, but could not be sure if there was really any connection with my John Brown. Then the pieces gradually began to fit together. I remembered that my father had told me of the time when he took his mother to Baughurst and that she pointed out her birthplace to him. Furthermore, she showed him the old yew tree on the edge of the garden and alongside the road, proudly stating that there were Quakers buried there.

Further research in the Quaker digests brought forth the entry of the marriage of John Brown junior of Basingstoke to Mary Potter of Baughurst, and the birth of Richard, son of John and Mary in 1703. I later amalgamated these findings with those on the farm itself, extracted from the Court Rolls of Manydown, and a clear history began to take shape. There was an error in the birth digests. The entry, in the first place, did not contain the place of birth — only the fact that it came under the jurisdiction of the Alton Monthly Meeting. But the error was in the name of the father. John Brown, born 1737, was documented as the son of John Brown, while his actual father — and this tied in with the Manydown accounts — was Richard Brown, the son of John Brown. John Brown the grandfather of the infant was probably recorded by mistake as he often represented the Baughurst Meeting in those days, while Richard, the real father, was virtually unknown to the Alton assembly. In research of this type one must be aware of errors in the originals as well as errors in transcriptions.

So, in time, the whole story began to unfold. The Quakers were outstanding for their records, and many of these have been used as the basis of this book. Although I have related here my interest in the Browns, this book is basically the history of the Quaker meeting at Baughurst, and the main characters are the Potters, from whom my Browns have descended. This history is intended more as a social history, and is thus purposely made devoid, as much as possible, of religious intentions and sympathies. At the same time it is hoped that it is not looked upon as primarily a local history, for the Quaker sufferings were universal rather than local. It hopefully fills a gap between what is known and what is implied. The sufferings of the Quakers and other religious minorities during the course of the seventeenth century are widely known, but there has been little progress made in the attempt to detail such persecutions and to research Quaker communities. In the event their stories must be told, for they are not the histories of religious persecution as much as they are the histories of dissent against arbitrary government of any type — royal or parliamentary. The Quakers in particular stood against the laws of the land which they deemed had curtailed their rights and liberties. They were not merely protesting for religious toleration but for all those other civil rights which were denied them because of their faith. They demanded equality with all men and women, the right not to support the Church which was alien to their beliefs (that is, to refuse to pay tithes), the right not to bear arms against their fellows, and the simple request to allow their word to be their bond and thus not to be forced to swear on oath. Above all, however, they demanded the right to worship as they pleased, without interference by any other person. Eventually, they were also demanding the right to justice, which was also being denied them.

This is therefore the story of people, great and small, but one person stands out in this story, for he was the one who continuously fought for those rights mentioned above to become realities. He was a remarkable man, with a remarkable tale to tell. He would not tell it himself, so an unknown author centuries later will have to do it for him. The story itself may answer many questions heretofore unanswered, and it may even provoke rather more questions than it can answer. There is only one thing left remaining. Read it for yourself.

K. S.

ACKNOWLEDGEMENTS

A BOOK cannot be written entirely by the effort of one person alone. All too often the author or authoress needs somebody to help with the progress of the work. In most cases there are several people involved with the task of producing a worthwhile piece. It is here that I wish to acknowledge the help I have been given over the years, and I sincerely wish to thank the following:—

The Librarian, Staff and Members of the Society of Friends at Friends' House, Euston, London, and wherever they might live in the world, for allowing me the use of their historical records, which form the bulk of this book.

Miss Rosemary Dunhill, and the Staff of the Hampshire Record Office, whose assistance and efficient service were always welcomed.

Mr J. A. S. Green, the former County Archivist, and the Staff of the Berkshire Record Office, who were most helpful in their assistance.

Canon Paul Britton, the former Canon Librarian, and the Staff of the Cathedral Library at Winchester Cathedral. In particular, Mrs Barbara Carpenter-Turner, the former Assistant Librarian and renowned historian of Hampshire, for her invaluable help and guidance.

Mr Michael Wallford, of Baughurst House, who has shown considerable interest in the project, and has always found the time to discuss history and to help in any way at all.

The Misses Wigley, of Rose Cottage, Baughurst, who have been most helpful in providing clues for the whereabouts of the last meeting-house.

Mr Alan Meredith, solicitor, of Lincoln's Inn Fields, London, and his late wife, Viv, the former occupants of Brown's Farm, who had shown me the greatest of hospitality on my many visits there, and had encouraged me in my research.

And many other people whom I have neglected to mention, but, nevertheless, have helped in their individual ways to make this book possible.

Finally, I wish to thank my former wife, Linda, for advising me, correcting some of my mistakes, and generally helping me wherever possible.

Despite the long list of acknowledgements here, however, I wish to make the statement that the responsibility of the work is solely mine, and any errors or misinterpretations do not belong to any of the persons listed above, or to other persons not mentioned.

K. S.

SOURCES

THE bulk of the sources used for this book are the series of Quaker records deposited at the Hampshire Record Office at 20, Southgate Street, Winchester. They are as follows:

Deeds   Schedule of Deeds relating to the Properties of the Quakers in Baughurst, Doc. No. 25M54/61.

Conveyances   A Record of the Last Conveyances of the Meeting Houses and Burial Grounds belonging to the Quakers in Hampshire, Doc. No. 24M54/18.

Men's Minutes, Alton Monthly Meeting   The minutes to the business meetings of the Alton Monthly Meeting, Docs. Nos. 24M54/34 and 24M54/35.

Men's Minutes, Hampshire Quarterly Meeting   The minutes to the business meetings of the Quarterly Meeting in Hampshire, Docs. Nos. 24M54/1 and 24M54/2.

Sufferings, Hants   The Sufferings Books recording the persecutions of the Quakers since 1655, Doc. No. 25M54/14.

Digests   Digests of Births, Marriages and Deaths since 1662, Docs. Nos. 24M54/29, 24M54/30 and 24M54/31.

The Hampshire Record Office (abbreviated in the notes to the text as H.R.O.) also holds these valuable documents, which were consulted for this book:

Bates Coll.   The Bates Collection, which is a series of documents deposited by the late Major Oliver-Bellasis relating to the Manor of Manydown.

Dean and Chapter   Court Books relating to the estates held by the Dean and Chapter of Winchester Cathedral 1729-1868, including the Manor of Manydown.

Will of Richard Brown   The H.R.O. holds several hundreds of wills and administrations recorded on print-outs. This one is dated 1779.

The Berkshire Record Office (B.R.O. in the notes) also holds similar Quaker documents pertaining to that county. Those consulted here were:

Sufferings, Berks   These were mainly used in respect of those recorded for the Newbury and Oare Monthly Meeting, while there are also references in this book to the Reading and Warborough Monthly Meeting, some of which are in printed form.

Digests Digests of Births, Marriages and Deaths recorded by the Berkshire and Oxfordshire General Meeting.

Another major source of information was the Cathedral Library at Winchester, which holds the main documents pertaining to the Manor of Manydown and the former estates of the Dean and Chapter of Winchester Cathedral:

Manydown These are the original Court Books and Court Rolls of the Manor, some of which date back to the 13th and 14th centuries.

Parliamentary Survey There are two surveys, dated 1650 and 1660. The first was made as a result of the purchase of the Manor of Manydown by William Wither, while the second is a copy of the first with extra information added after 1661.

The final research institution in this list is the Public Record Office at Chancery Lane in London, where I consulted the following:

Lay Subsidy Rolls These record assessments of subsidies, and a few of hearth tax, and the rolls which were consulted here were for Baughurst in Hundred of Evingar in 1628, 1641, 1656 and 1675, Docs. Nos. E179. 175/521, E179. 175/550, E179. 176/554 and E179. 176/561.

Wills The wills consulted for this book were those for James Potter dated 1703, and John Harris dated 1736.

And then there were the local libraries in Hampshire and Berkshire, and the University Library in London, where I had located these very useful books:

Clark Sir George Clark: "The Later Stuarts", O.U.P., 1956. The general reference book for the period 1660-1714.

Cragg Gerald R. Cragg: "Puritanism in the Period of the Great Persecution", C.U.P., 1957. Probably the best on the subject of the non-conformists in general and their sufferings.

Davies Godfrey Davies: "The Early Stuarts", O.U.P., 1959. The general reference book for the period 1603-1660.

Browning Andrew Browning (ed.): "English Historical Documents, Vol. VIII", Eyre and Spottiswoode, 1966. The best reference work for the period 1660-1714 for statutes and other important documents.

Davidson   Florence Davidson: "The Quaker Burial Grounds at Baughurst", Proceedings of the Hampshire Field Club Journal, Vol. 7, Pt. 2, 1915. The only account on the Baughurst Meeting before this date. Very erroneous and untrustworthy.

Fox   George Fox: "The Journal of George Fox" (John L. Nickalls, ed.). C.U.P., 1952. Fox's own account of his life and journeys. Mentions Baughurst. An egotistic view of the Quaker sufferings.

Vipont   Elfrida Vipont: "The Story of Quakerism", Bannisdale, 1960. An extremely good account of early Quakers and their sufferings. Good background material.

Russell   Conrad Russell: "The Crisis of Parliaments", O.U.P., 1971. Another good general reference book for the period.

Hill   Christopher Hill: "God's Englishman", Penguin, 1972. An excellent study of Oliver Cromwell. Also recommended are Hill's "The Century of Revolution" (Nelson, 1961) and "Society and Puritanism in Pre-Revolutionary England" (Nelson, 1963).

V.C.H., Hants   "Victoria County History of Hampshire". Found in most libraries in this county, it is a general starting-point for those interested in local history.

Kitchin   G. W. Kitchin: "The Manor of Manydown", Simpkin and Warren, 1895. A good general interest book devoted to the history of the Manor of Manydown, although restricted to documents formerly held by the Rev. Reginald Bigg-Wither.

Baigent and Millard   P. J. Baigent and J. E. Millard: "A History of Basingstoke", Jacob, 1889. The best yet on the history of that town.

There are many other books which could be quoted, but the most important have already been listed.

Furthermore, I must not forget to mention the parish registers and the transcripts of parish registers and monumental inscriptions which I have consulted for use in this book.

AUTHOR'S NOTES

THE people recorded in the following pages of this book were real living persons, and the incidents described herein did actually occur. But to relate those incidents, as they were being recorded in the surviving documents utilised for this work, would hardly convince the reader that each character did breathe, walk, think, or love or hate.

Therefore, while attempting to relate the true story of James Potter and the Baughurst Meeting, I have also endeavoured to make the people in the history appear as human beings, and not merely as names recorded in documents. Thus, I have attempted to interpret the situation and the sequence of events which made up each historical incident. In the majority of the cases I have given each recorded incident what I believe is a logical sequence, based upon clues given in the sources or upon the historical background for the period. For example, the incident in Baughurst church, in the first chapter, relies heavily upon the fact that Parson Benthall was a known Calvinist, who had attained his position as the incumbent of Baughurst through his dealings with William Wither, and that he was a dominant man who used bullying tactics — as displayed by his treatment of the Quakers after 1657. None of the sequences of events are based upon pure imagination. However, for those of somewhat academic minds, who wish merely to read their history as related in the documented accounts, I have included the sources at the beginning of each section.

There will probably be, in the course of the history, certain terms with which a reader might be unfamiliar. These will, in the majority of cases, be related to Quakerism and the manorial system. Therefore, I shall briefly attempt to explain them.

In the first place, Quakerism itself was an extremely revolutionary movement when it was conceived. In many respects based upon the beliefs of individual Seeker groups before George Fox united these in the Quaker movement itself, it was totally alien to the various, yet accepted, beliefs of those times, despite all the differences that divided the other numerous groups and sects in this country. Quakerism was different because it was radically "heretical" by proclaiming that every human being was divine (the "Inner Light" doctrine), and this contravened the Blasphemy Act. Thus the Quakers were being persecuted more than other sectarian groups, and not just by the Anglicans, for their beliefs were also alien to the Catholics and the most extremist of the Protestant separatists.

The Quaker meeting was held normally in silence, and local meetings would take place once a week, but not necessarily on a Sunday. As the movement became more organised the business meeting system grew, and extended into the monthly meeting, where representatives of all the local meetings in the district met to discuss matters of religion or business, and then into the quarterly meeting, which comprised the representatives of the meetings in the county.

Because of his belief in the divinity of mankind, the Quaker practised equality and the sanctity of human life. These fundamental principles conflicted with the views of the Anglican heirarchy, who were in power, and the Quaker was further persecuted for his refusal to pay his respects to his social "betters" and to muster arms and serve in the local militia. In addition to these grave trespasses, he was also in trouble for refusing to swear on oath (as his word was his bond), and to pay tithes and church repairs (as he had no church).

The manorial system was dependent upon copyhold tenure, whereby the tenant of a manorial estate held his land by a copy of the Court Roll, which proved his title deed to the property. In order that he farmed the land efficiently for the Lord of the Manor he was legally given the right to nominate his own heirs to succeed him in his copyhold estate. "Three lives" were recorded on each copyhold warrant, thus allowing a perpetual succession to the estate. This would then guarantee that the land was being farmed efficiently, as the land itself would remain in the hands of a family or families for generations. However, the inconvenience of copyhold tenure led in more recent times to statutes having for their object the conversion into freeholds of copyholds, which nowadays no longer exist, though they survived until comparatively late.

It is not my intention, in this book, to divide the antagonists into the "goodies" and the "baddies". The Quakers themselves were as much to blame for the constant persecutions as the Anglican priests. Both sides had their radical elements as well as their moderates. The Anglicans had more of the right-wing section because, for obvious reasons, they were more populous than the Quakers. Yet, please remember, one side did encourage and motivate the other.

Furthermore, this is not intended as a religious history, and I hope that it does not appear so. If anything, this is a social history, the history of a community which was allowed to exist and to grow because of the ideals — social, as well as religious — of one man. It is also interesting to note that the community began to expire from the moment that one person had himself expired.

This is not intended as a purely local history, either, as it is just one chapter in the histories of all our nonconformist groups, and, hopefully, the reading of this story would inspire others to undertake research of other dissenting communities. It is, therefore, only a minute fraction of the whole, but enough for us to realise that we should never generalise in history concerning one large grouping which had any semblance at all of unity only through the generalised terms of "dissenters" or "nonconformists".

Lastly, this is a topic on Dissent, for whatever reason, and thus will always be a topical subject. Wherever there is mankind there is always dissent of one form or another. The reasons for dissent in this history, and the results of that dissent, are, unfortunately, taken so much for granted nowadays.

KEN SMALLBONE, B.A.(Hons.),
(Genealogist and Historical Researcher)
PO Box 7
Whitchurch
Hampshire, RG25 3NT
England.

POTTER OF BAUGHURST

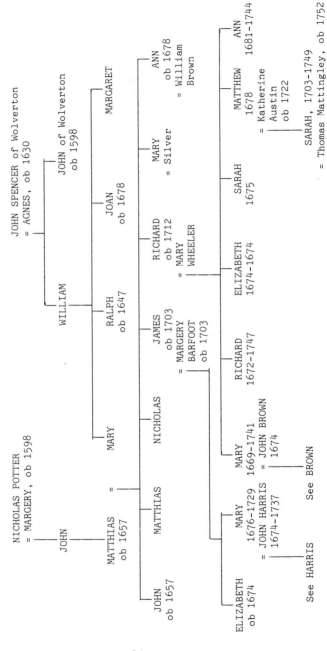

HARRIS OF BAUGHURST

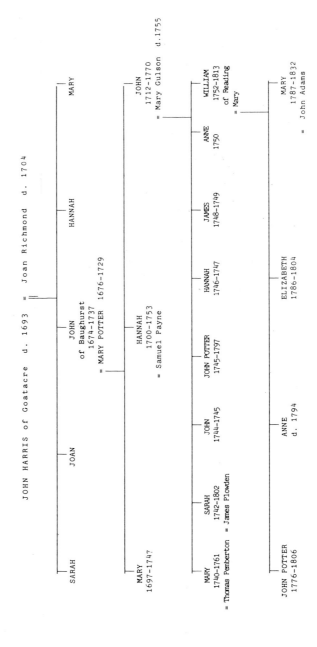

JOHN HARRIS of Goatacre   d. 1693   =   Joan Richmond   d. 1704

SARAH

JOAN

MARY

HANNAH

JOHN
of Baughurst
1674-1737
= MARY POTTER 1676-1729

MARY
1697-1747

HANNAH
1700-1753
= Samuel Payne

JOHN
1712-1770
= Mary Gulson   d.1755

SARAH
1742-1802
= James Plowden

MARY
1740-1761
= Thomas Pemberton

JOHN
1744-1745

JOHN POTTER
1745-1797

HANNAH
1746-1747

JAMES
1748-1749

ANNE
1750

WILLIAM
1752-1813
of Reading
= Mary

ANNE
d. 1794

ELIZABETH
1786-1804

MARY
1787-1832
= John Adams

JOHN POTTER
1776-1806

BROWN OF BAUGHURST: CHART 1

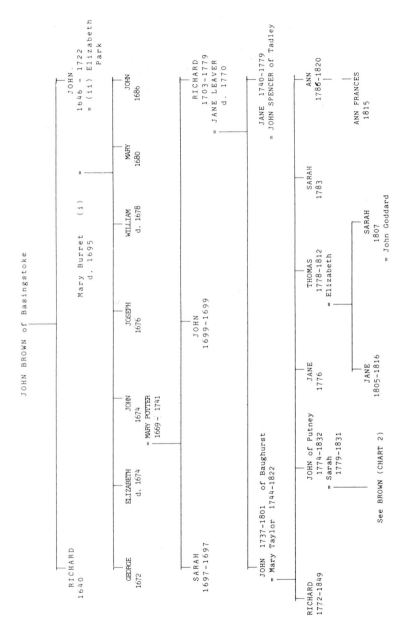

JOHN BROWN of Basingstoke

Mary Burret (i)
d. 1695
=
JOHN.
1646 - 1722
= (ii) Elizabeth
Park

RICHARD
1640

GEORGE
1672

ELIZABETH
d. 1674

JOHN
1674
= MARY POTTER
1669 - 1741

JOSEPH
1676

WILLIAM
d. 1678

MARY
1680

JOHN
1686

SARAH
1697-1697

JOHN
1699-1699

RICHARD
1703-1779
= JANE LEAVER
d. 1770

JOHN 1737-1801 of Baughurst
= Mary Taylor 1744-1822

JANE 1740-1779
= JOHN SPENCER of Tadley

RICHARD
1772-1849

JOHN of Putney
1774-1832
= Sarah
1779-1831

JANE
1776

THOMAS
1778-1812
= Elizabeth

SARAH
1783

ANN
1786-1820

See BROWN (CHART 2)

JANE
1805-1816

SARAH
1807
= John Goddard

ANN FRANCES
1815

26

BROWN OF BAUGHURST: CHART 2

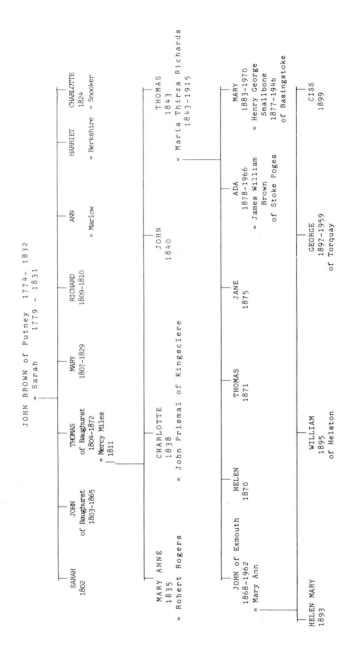

JOHN BROWN of Putney 1774- 1832
= Sarah 1779 - 1831

SARAH 1802

JOHN of Baughurst 1803-1865

THOMAS of Baughurst 1804-1872 = Mercy Miles 1811

MARY 1807-1829

RICHARD 1809-1810

ANN = Marlow

HARRIET = Berkshire

CHARLOTTE 1824 = Snooker

MARY ANNE 1835 = Robert Rogers

CHARLOTTE 1838 = John Prismal of Kingsclere

JOHN 1840

THOMAS 1843 = Maria Thirza Richards 1843-1915

JOHN of Exmouth 1868-1962 = Mary Ann

HELEN 1870

THOMAS 1871

JANE 1875

ADA 1878-1966 = James William Brown of Stoke Poges

MARY 1883-1970 = Henry George Smallbone 1877-1946 of Basingstoke

HELEN MARY 1893

WILLIAM 1895 of Helston

GEORGE 1897-1959 of Torquay

CISS 1899

Whereas James Potter of Baghurst in the County of Southton yeoman hath by Deede bearing date the fift of the month called June 1695 settled a messuage or tenement with the outhouses & Buildings w.th the Garden Orchard & little pittle of ground with the Appurtenances thereunto belonging within the said parrish upon us our heires & Assignes to the use & behoofe of the said James Potter for & dureing the terme of his naturall life. And after his decease to the use & behoofe of Marjory his wife dureing the terme of her naturall life. And after their decease to the use of us our heires and assignes our heires & Assignes for ever Provided that the said James Potter do not make another settlem.t of it in his life time, as by the said Deede may more at large appeare. Now wee do hereby declare that the said messuage with the Appurtenances so made & settled as aforesaid is only in trust for the use & Benefit of the people of God called Quakers And that it is the intent & agreem.t betwixt the said James his heires and assignes: And by our heires & assignes that they the said people shall have the use & benefit of all the said premises with free liberty to meet in the said House to do & performe any such duty or service as may tend to the honour & Glory of God, And to the good of his people called Quakers; Or to performe any other service in it which they shall see meete. And that the true end & intent hereof may bee truly performed wee do promise for our selves our heires & Assignes that if the said messuage or tenement shall descend & come into our power by the death of the said James Potter & Marjory his wife that wee shall order & dispose of the said messuage or tenement with the Appurtenances, as our ffriends of the monthly meeting now settled at Alton (or that may or shall bee settled at any other place for the service of God & of his people aforesaid thereabouts on that side of the County) shall from time to time, And at all times hereafter order direct & appoint. And if it shall come to pass (as wee hope the contrary) That any difference shall arise by or betweene the ffriends of the monthly meeting concerning the premises aforesaid that then such differences shall bee referred to the ffriends of the Quarterly meeting of the said people in the County aforesaid to bee determined by them or by such as they in the wisdome of God shall see meet to commit it unto to put an end to it. And wee do each of us promise for for our selves our heires & Assignes truly & faithfully to performe the trust therein committed to us. In witness whereof wee have hereunto set our hands the 24.th of the month called July 1696.

Whereas in the Deede of trust to Robert Mosses Nicholas Gates Jun.r Moses Neabe Jun.r Henry Streater & John Bug the tenement is settled on us for the terme of our naturall lives, wee do hereby promise that wee shall not hinder that wee shall not hinder our ffriends to have the use & Benefit of the said House to meete together in to performe that

Duty which they ore unto God And one to another But rather Endeabour
to Propagate the same. And also that they shall have liberty to
Bury their Dead in that p̃r Parcell of Ground already Planted & sett
forth for that use & service with free Ingress Egress & Regress to pass
& repass to the said House & Parcell of Ground as often as they shall
have Occasion, or see a service in it witness our hands the 24 of the
month called July 1696

                                    James Potter

And whereas there is a power reserved to mee in the said Deed that
I in my life time by will or otherwise may alter the settlment of the said
Tenemt I do hereby Promise not so to alter it as that it may bee Enverted
to any other use then is Intended or is herein after Expressed.
And whereas one motive was at the first Inducing mee thus to settle
the said Tenemt, that it might bee a place for gods People to serve & worship
him in them them Parts. And that they might not bee to seek for a Con
veencont Burying place. And also that it might bee a place if need
require to Accomodate Publike ffriends that shall bee drawne forth
in their spirits to visit that meeting or other meetings thereabouts.
So it is my desire of the monthly & Quarterly meetings to the power is
committed to which shall or may succeed when it shall please god
to remove us out of this troublesom world to Endeabour to keep an
honest friend in it of truth in it And let him have the use & Benefit
of it so far as hee shall assist & Entertaine such Publike friends as aforesd
If it should so please God (which it hoped otherwise) there should not bee any
other friend in that place that's able & so given up in his spirit to assist
& entertaine such publike friend as aforesaid. But if there shall bee
any ffriend or ffriends thereabouts Conveenient that is able & ffreely
given up in that service Then the Benefit or Rent that shall bee made
of it may goe into the Publike stock for friend of that County to bee
Imployed in the service of truth among the despised people called
Quakers, witness my hand the 24th of the month called July 1696.

                                    James Potter

DEED OF CONVEYANCE OF JAMES POTTER'S HOUSE
to the use of the Quakers, 1696 (in Potter's hand)

*Doc 24M54/1 (Hampshire Quarterly Meeting, Men's Minutes), Hampshire
Record Office, with the kind permission of the Society of Friends*

WILL OF JAMES POTTER
proved in the P.C.C. in 1703
(Public Record Office, P.C.C. 13 Ash, PROB 11/475)

PROLOGUE

1643-1657

GEORGE FOX was only nineteen when in 1643 he gave up his worldly occupation as a shoemaker to travel the roads and byways in search of "The Truth"; and only twenty-three when, after constant heart-searching, he discovered the seeds of that "Truth" which had lain dormant within himself for so long. He had wandered through the Midland counties, asking various questions on religion at every given opportunity. He had asked these of Anglican priests, learned men of letters, university lecturers, sectarian leaders. But still he received no satisfactory answer. At best he had dumbfounded his betters; at worst he was subjected to the utmost hostile treatment. Yet he still persisted, and in his persistence he created a new movement which would endure through some of the worst persecutions of the times, and would survive to become a major international faith.

Because of his dissatisfaction with contemporary views in religion, he had to find his own answers, and these he found in his outlook on life itself, comparing that with the same of his fellow men. He found many things in contemporary England that he abhorred and which seemed to him to be sacrilegious, thus depriving the accepted religion and the numerous separatist faiths of the real meaning of Christianity. In his wanderings and in his observations he did, in a sense, imitate Christ himself, who had also found much worldliness in the established religion during his time. When at last Fox had found what he had sought he then had to preach his message to the masses of the "unconverted". This was done, at times, purely by accident when, listening to a sermon or a lecture, he was stirred by an uncontrollable urge to argue the case of the "Truth".

Because of his preaching and his disputes with his "betters", Fox was to come into conflict with the authorities on several occasions. There was the time, in 1649, when he suffered his first imprisonment. By then he had gathered around him a small band of followers who had seen the "Light" of his beliefs. While this band was proceeding towards Nottingham, the steeple of St Mary's Church there had such an effect upon Fox that the building beneath it "struck at my life when I spied it, a great idol and idolatrous temple".[1] He had an overwhelming desire to go there alone to

31

see for himself what lies were being housed within that mortal edifice. Already incensed against the teachings of the established Anglican Church, it did not take much for Fox to interrupt the sermon of Nicholas Folkingham, who was using the importance of the Scriptures as his theme.

By interrupting the sermon Fox had seriously violated a strict Church law dating from the reign of Elizabeth I, and for his crime suffered a "long term" of imprisonment in Nottingham Gaol (so he says). But this incident was highlighted by the fact that he received the hospitality of the head sheriff, John Reckless, who was soon converted to Fox's beliefs, so much so that he actually went out and preached in the market-place himself.

Through his missionary wanderings, Fox was gradually building up a fairly substantial following. From Nottingham he travelled to Mansfield-Woodhouse, Barrow, Bagworth, Coventry, Atherstone, Market Bosworth, Twycross, Chesterfield and finally to Derby in 1650, attending meetings, visiting prisons, markets, fairs and churches — anywhere there were people who would listen to his preaching. Much of the time he was given a good reception, although on occasions he came into dispute with sectaries, but it was in Derby that he was to receive his next prison sentence. Arrested under the Blasphemy Act of 1650,[2] he was examined intermittently for about eight hours. During this long examination Justice Gervase Bennet of Snelston coined the term "Quakers" for Fox and his followers, after Fox had told the magistrates to tremble at the word of God.[3] (In 1650 there was no full-scale movement called "Quakers" but various bands who had accepted Fox's teachings, and at that time were only local groups of which some called themselves "the Children of the Light", others "the Friends of the Truth". But, because of the publicity that Bennet's term must have received in his attempt to degrade those of Fox's persuasion, there could have been a gradual acceptance of the name locally, as the English generally love unofficial terms to describe the full title. The nickname began to stick.)

The outcome of the investigation by Bennet and others was that Fox was imprisoned at Derby for six months. During this term of imprisonment he was given the freedom of the prison surroundings within the radius of one mile. This was not simply a generous gesture the jailer and the civil authorities bestowed upon Fox, because the real motive behind this act of compassion was the hope that Fox would escape, and therefore Derby would be rid of a thoroughly confounded nuisance.

But to the authorities' surprise, Fox did not attempt to escape. How could he? This imprisonment was a form of martyrdom for his beliefs. In the event, his prison sentence meant that he could carry on his work converting the other prisoners. He came into contact with mutineers from the Parliamentary Army who instilled in him a total abhorrence of war. Towards the end of his sentence in 1651, Derby was full of soldiers heading for Worcester, where there was to be a great battle against the Royalist Army of the son of King Charles I. It was at this point that Fox's experience of leadership was probably realised by the authorities, who, through the insistence of some of the soldiers, offered the convict a captaincy in the Army. Fox resoundingly refused this "honour" because it contravened his beliefs of non-violence, and for this he was immediately thrown into a dungeon "amongst thirty felons in a lousy, stinking low place in the ground without any bed".[4] Here he was confined for almost another six months, occasionally being allowed exercise in the garden.

After his release Fox continued his wanderings. His reputation was, by now, increasing, and as he journeyed throughout the north, his following grew larger. He not only gathered around him common people, but also former adherents of other faiths, justices and other officials, and the occasional Anglican priest.

The majority of the people who were being influenced by Fox's teachings were those who could loosely be termed "Seekers". These had no formal doctrines, but consisted of scattered bands throughout the country who could not adhere to any of the religious beliefs, orthodox or unorthodox, of the day. In their frustration they were condemned to search for the truth in religion, which they deemed to have eluded both Anglicans and sectarians alike, who had constantly become more worldly in their outlook and had denied Christendom of its Christianity. Fox himself was also a Seeker, and his work became much easier as he found groups of these religious misfits scattered around the countryside. It was Fox who united these groups, while also allowing former adherents of the other faiths to swell their ranks, and, in so doing, did not eliminate the individuality of his followers. Because of this, the united movement which became Quakerism could embrace several different attitudes while professing the teachings of its founder. Fox gave to the Seekers a new lease of life while, at the same time, he borrowed many institutions which they had themselves innovated, e.g. the silent meetings. So, as 1651 merged into 1652, the Quaker movement was about to be born in reality — the faith was there, all it needed was organisation.

"From the days of the first publishers of the truth until our own time, the year 1652 had been regarded as the birth-time of Quakerism. The preceding years had witnessed a slow process of development to which the eventful weeks of 1652 gave an irresistible impulse."[5] For, that year, Fox climbed Pendle Hill in Lancashire, and saw a vision of a world awaiting the "Truth". Not long afterwards he visited Swarthmore Hall in

Cumbria, the home of Judge Thomas Fell and his young attractive wife, Margaret. During this first visit, in the absence of the judge, he converted the willing Margaret to Quakerism. This was enormously significant, for Margaret Fell was to become the nursing-mother of Quakerism, while Swarthmore Hall was to evolve into the nerve-centre of the organisation of the new movement. Fell himself was at first very distressed at his wife's adherence to a fanatical religion, but as time passed, and under his wife's influence, he became less hostile, eventually allowing his house to be used for meetings, while, at the same time, reserving justice for Quakers in his court, without becoming one himself. After Fell's death, Margaret was to become Fox's wife. Therefore, 1652 looms large in Quaker history, and it was from Swarthmore Hall that Quakers sent out missionaries to set up meetings all over the country. Quakerism as an organisation was born, and now the movement could grow. Within five years it would capture the imagination of countless people throughout England, Ireland, Europe and the West Indies. It had been awaiting organisation and, now that had come, there was no stopping the spread of the Word.

The "Word" being preached was fundamentally Fox's, although somewhat adapted to individual taste. At a time when there was so much religious discontent, when the world was being "turned upside down", Quakerism was deemed revolutionary — in this sense rebellious — even among the most unorthodox faiths. Ever since the time of Henry VIII's break from the Roman Church, the first stage of the Reformation in England, religion had been the main cause of hostility throughout the nation as a whole. Since Elizabeth I's reign, Calvinism had penetrated the Anglican Church itself, where many had entrenched themselves in order to "purify" the Church from within. Of the Calvinist faiths which were based upon predestination (that is salvation for the elected few, the "saints", but utter rejection for the masses), the Presbyterians became the dominant group, while the Independents and Baptists were becoming equally important as the years passed. These people were now being termed as "Puritans" by their opponents and gradually religious views coincided with political views to form the nucleus of strife in Parliament. The Church had, by the second decade of the seventeenth century, accommodated many varying doctrines and beliefs within its national set-up. But by the end of that decade, the whole religious issue had become explosive after Charles I attempted to set up a High Church policy in line with his proposed royal absolutist programme. The Church, under the King's patronage and the leadership of Archbishop Laud, became Arminian overnight.

The new religious policy led to critical conflict with the Puritans, whose simple religious tastes opposed those of the Arminians with their ceremonials and idolatry. The Puritans detested the Arminian Church and compared it with Romanism. Under Laud, Calvinism was outlawed and the extreme persecutions which its adherents suffered became the roots from which the grievances sprang, heralding the causes of the ensuing civil wars. After the fighting had ended and a republic had been established under the victorious Parliament, toleration then became the latest policy in religion. Once the shackles of Arminianism had been snapped, religious sects freely sprang up almost everywhere as attempts were made to imitate the holiness of the early Christian communities in contrast with the worldliness of the former national Church. Even during the war new groupings were appearing as the stranglehold of persecution was subsiding owing to more urgent distractions. On the religious side the world was certainly being turned upside down. Yet even under such a noble policy as toleration there was no subsidence of religious tension. The toleration programme had allowed the reversal of a national Church policy which was meant to unify the people. With the abundance of so many new orders there were many whose fanaticism appalled decent minds. Therefore the religious arguments continued, but more over ideals than doctrines. While opinions varied, there were bound to have been beliefs which absolutely astounded traditional views of the majority of the population. These beliefs spilled over from religion and into socialism and politics, and were termed not only fanatical but also rebellious and treasonable.

Minds weaned on the tradition of a spiritual omnipotent being, who resided in a kingdom beyond the limits of the earth's atmosphere, were totally appalled by the suggestion that each person held within himself a "divine spark". This seemed to be a fantastic theory at best, and quite repulsive and unholy at worst. Yet this was the sole basis of Fox's newly established faith, which had its seeds in his quest for the "Truth" among the scattered bands of Seekers in the northern and midland counties.

Quakerism centred around the belief that man possessed the "Inner Light" deep within his body — that immortal and divine spark of good which may be termed by some as God and by others, less religious in their outlook, as the Soul. This one concept was central to the whole faith and around it evolved all the other Quaker doctrines. As each man was there-fore "divine", then no man could claim his superiority over his fellow humans. This bred the belief in equality, which often caused conflict since no Quaker would submit to any authority under God. A Quaker was considered disrespectful as he would not remove his hat in the presence of those in authority. He would instantly become recognised as a rebel through his usage of the words "thou" and "thy" instead of the formal

35

terms "you" and "your", reserved for the officials of seventeenth-century England. He had to pay for this disrespect most severely and was marked by his insistence on equality for all men.

Therefore, the Quaker would not even accept an authoritative leader at his meetings. As each man possessed the "Inner Light", then there was no need for a minister to lead the service, as Fox himself discovered that God's ministers were not made at Oxford and Cambridge, but were the people of the world. Meetings were normally held in silence so that each person could probe the divinity within himself, but could speak when the spirit took him or remain silent if his spirit did not move him to utter a word. The meeting house itself was of no special construction, merely an ordinary dwelling with plain furniture, for worship needed no special trappings. In Fox's words, "the Church is not the building, but the people inside".

The doctrine of "The Inner Light" meant that human life was sacred, and that killing was a sin no matter for what reason. Therefore Quakers refused to serve in the militia or to perform an act of violence. Because of this they were subject to intense persecution, while others attempted to pile all kinds of abuse upon them, knowing full well their doctrine of non-resistance. They therefore passively subjected themselves to all kinds of treatment, bravely taking their punishment fully and without complaint. They would never swear on oath, for their word was their bond and no honest man needed to embellish it. And it was simply this refusal that made them into "traitors" against the realm. For the oaths which were being forced upon them were the Oaths of Abjuration and Allegiance — the first in order to renounce Catholicism and the second to profess unswerving loyalty to the State. Quakers were undoubtedly enemies of Romanism, while, at the same time, among the most loyal of Englishmen. They refused the oaths purely because of their principles, but their unwillingness was often interpreted as disloyalty. The oaths framed to expose Jesuits were constantly being used against the Quakers and therefore they were being treated as Jesuits, or being mistaken for the same. Many abusive terms were thus being directed towards the people who called themselves "Friends" and the "Children of God". They were condemned for the most fantastic crimes, ranging from obscenity to witchcraft, as well as professing allegiance to the Bishop of Rome.

Understandably, the Quakers attracted many misfits into their society. Their strong belief in equality for all men allowed former Levellers to infiltrate the movement. The Levellers were a political sect under the leadership of John Lilburne, but had been exterminated by Cromwell when their leader had made it abundantly clear that he aspired to the Lord

Protector's power. With the extinction of the Leveller Movement, some of its former adherents would have wandered the byways and highways in search of other groups with beliefs similar to their own. In many ways the Quaker Movement would have answered their prayers. The same democratic principles would have allowed Winstanley's Diggers to have found common ground with Quakerism. Therefore as less enduring sects faded out of the pages of history, Quakerism grew stronger by attracting those who held common principles dear. At the same time, however, Quakerism was also gaining notoriety because some of its latest converts were of dubious character and had little or no principles at all.

Oliver Cromwell himself employed Quakers in his domestic service, despite their refusal to grant him the dignities of which his office was worthy. Since 1656 when he first interviewed George Fox, after Fox's arrest by Colonel Hack, the Lord Protector and the Quaker became particularly good friends, exchanging views on religion among other topics. Yet Cromwell's tolerated view of this sect was not shared by the majority of the officers and members of the Republican government. And in 1657 they were proved right in their assessment of this strange new sect. The trouble stemmed from the infiltration of that fanatical group known as the Ranters into the Quaker Movement. James Naylor, Fox's main rival for leadership, was moved by the overtures of the Ranter element in his area in the west of England. Amid ecstatic Ranters women shouting their "hosannas" and strewing palm leaves in his path, he entered the town of Bristol astride a donkey. This incident horrified the authorities to such a degree that there was a reinforcement of the laws aimed at curbing the fanaticism of the sectaries. Naylor himself suffered for his blasphemous act by being flogged, pilloried, branded, and then by having his tongue bored before he was imprisoned indefinitely. He suffered real pain for his impersonation of Christ, without the martyrdom of crucifixion. Despite attempts to dissociate themselves from Naylor's activities, the Quakers themselves suffered a temporary setback as more accusations were being flung at them. They remained serene and took their punishment without complaint.

Thus the Quakers were often treated with contempt by their fellow countrymen. In this, however, they were not unique, as many of the more fanatical movements knew times of dire persecution. In due course they were branded with a multitude of crimes by those who grossly misunderstood them and their beliefs. They were hauled before the magistrates by those who feared their socialist and religious attitudes, for persecution was born of fear itself. John Evelyn, the diarist, wrote in 1656: "I had the curiosity to visit some quakers in prison; a new fanatic sect, of dangerous principles, who show no respect to any man, magistrate, or other, and seem a melanchony, proud sort of people, and exceedingly ignorant".[6] So much were those principles dangerous, that the records show that in Hampshire alone thirty-four Quakers were imprisoned and almost £300 in value of goods were taken by distress in fines between the years 1655 and 1660, while after that latter year a further three hundred and fifty-five persons were imprisoned (of whom six died in prison) and over £1,500 levied in fines until 1792.[7]

The crimes themselves consisted of non-payment of tithes, for refusing to pay towards church repairs, for not attending church services, for refusing to muster arms, for meetings for worship, for not respectfully removing their hats before those in authority, for vagrancy, for visiting fellow Quakers in prison, for refusing to swear oaths, and for keeping schools. They refused to pay tithes simply because these were Church taxes, amounting to approximately one tenth of the yield or profit of the parishioner, and these supplemented the clergyman's income. The refusals to help repair the churches and for not attending church services were obvious. These buildings were held in derision by Fox's followers, who called them "steeple-houses", while "the sight of a church steeple brought to him (Fox) the mockery of the religion which seemed to revere the temple made with hands at the expense of the living temple".[8] The refusal to muster arms was based on the doctrine of non-resistance, that of not removing their hats on their inherent regard for equality, and the oath refusals for their belief in their own honesty, which was exemplary. All other "crimes" were purely in line with religious policy at any period in history before toleration was put into legislation through the parliamentary process, and the attendance of the populace for church service had been compulsory since the reign of Elizabeth I.

As government in those times was mainly parochial, the onus therefore rested upon the local magistrates and, in religious cases, the parish priests. They were in an unenviable situation, for they had, despite the odds, to maintain law and order, either through the civil or the ecclesiastical courts. If they became outwardly radical in suppressing Quakerism, it was generally for good reasons. Local government in Commonwealth England was in a particularly crucial position: with numerous bands of discontented Royalists roaming around the countryside they could not afford to sympathise too much with the revolutionary ideals of fanatical new sects like the Quakers. Therefore they had to come down hard upon suspected violators of law and order, reinforced especially by the Quaker disrespect for their authority. In this way the Quakers quite often got what they deserved, for if Fox's followers were out to reform the social order, the authorities had neither the time nor the inclination to allow them to do so. But in the main, this was not what the Quakers intended to do. They wished to be allowed to worship as they pleased, without interference. If they preached social equality within their beliefs then there could be little harm in that. They were definitely not out to provoke riots nor to bring down the government of the land. That in itself was against their religious principles. And they were a religious group, not political. But this fact could not be recognised by those who had a particularly difficult task to perform in maintaining law and order throughout this divided country. Therefore it became an accepted fact that each side had to provoke the other into action, and a course had to be maintained that would bring about a headlong collision. The Quakers provoked the magistrates and ecclesiasticals to deal severely with them, while the officers themselves provoked the dissenting community by constantly persecuting them. Neither side could give way owing to their principles and matters of faith. So for many years the conflict continued.

Even at the height of the persecutions the records show that the same individuals were being persecuted often, which is conducive to the argument that the officials were mainly provoking certain Quakers for definite reasons other than merely religious principles. In many cases it was the more affluent Quaker who bore the brunt of persecution, for there was actual financial gain from persecuting the farmers and the wealthier elements. The poorer members were also being persecuted, but less often. They were then left alone for a while as there was no gain in plundering an empty casket.

Persecution for financial gain, however, was a later development of the situation. When Quakerism was still in its infancy there was much opposition due to the fact that it was supposed to have bred treason and that the doctrines of the faith were wholly alien in an unsympathetic world. Because they were grossly misunderstood by the authorities and by the commonalty as well, the early Quakers were regarded both as enemies of the State and of God. Therefore it was so very easy for a so-called "Friend" to fall foul of the law, even if he was only attempting to spread the "Word". A Quaker was an obvious target, a scapegoat for the Jesuits and other destructive forces, and, better still, he did not retaliate physically.

From Swarthmore Hall the "Word" was spread. Fox was on his travels again, but this time his work had been reduced and he was no longer alone in spreading his version of the "Truth" to all and sundry. From Swarthmore Hall Quaker missionaries were extending the message to all parts of the country, converting numerous people into the faith. It did not take long for the apostolic missions to penetrate the capital, where Francis Howgill and Edward Burrough established a Quaker meeting-house at Aldersgate. From Aldersgate newly recruited evangelists were sent into the Home Counties, and gradually the movement spread into the neighbouring southern regions.

As Quakerism grew stronger in the southern counties, it is not surprising that malicious rumours grew around the activities of this new sect, and their unusual ways caused much alarm wherever they wandered to promote the message of Fox. The authorities were being alerted to the danger of sedition which the Quakers were often being accused of causing, and generally the cry of "Jesuits" preceded them.

Thus when John Stubbs and William Caton arrived at Maidstone in 1655, they were almost immediately recognised as Quaker missionaries and were subjected to the most savage treatment after being accused of vagrancy, the only effective charge against them at the time. They were stripped naked, put in the stocks and then whipped until they bled. Finally they were set on their way home, under the Vagrancy Act, to travel under a warrant from parish constable to parish constable, until eventually the constables grew tired of them and set them loose to wander as they pleased.[9]

The incident involving Stubbs and Caton was quickly relayed throughout the southern counties. Even at Basingstoke, in Hampshire, the magistrates soon heard the news. There were already Quakers in the town, but these were mainly peaceable and very few in number. The authorities could keep a check on the followers of Fox quite easily, and could persecute them at will if the need arose. The most imminent danger would obviously come from without the borough limits. Therefore close attention was being paid to strangers entering the town.

On the 18th July of that year two men halted their horses on the brow of Norn Hill, overlooking the town, viewing the buildings nestling in the valley below with the River Loddon winding its way through the narrow street. Across to their right stood the ruins of the medieval chapel which, when it was in its full glory, dominated the skyline above the town. Its place had been taken by the parish church of St Michael's which stood immediately to the south of it. Thomas Robertson and Ambrose Rigg sat for a while discussing the whereabouts of the house of William Knight, whose name they had been given as a fellow Quaker. Knight's house stood at the bottom of the hill from the chapel, at a point where the track leading down into the town was bisected by the street through which the Loddon flowed.[10] As they rode down Norn Hill and towards the town they stopped briefly in order to ascertain the location of Knight's house.

William Knight made the two strangers extremely welcome, offering them hospitality for as long as they wished to stay in Basingstoke. Quickly he prepared to make arrangements for a Quaker meeting at his house within the next few days.

In the meantime the news of the arrival of the two strangers had already reached the ears of the parish priest, and he made himself busy spreading scandalous rumours and laying false accusations upon the two men whom he had never met. It was William Knight who brought these lies back to Robertson and Rigg. They immediately sent word for the priest to come to Knight's house and to lay his accusations directly before them. When he was confronted with this message the ecclesiastic refused the request and was said to have replied that he might soon have the two Quakers thrown into prison.

Soon afterwards the Quakers of the town were congregated in Knight's house for a religious meeting, with Robertson and Rigg preaching before newly converted members who had been told briefly of the movement in the market-place or around the town. There were a number of people gathered in the room, and the door was opening and closing continuously as the curious entered to see for themselves what happened at a Quaker meeting. The Quakers were certain never to lock their doors while a meeting was in progress because they believed that their meetings were open to everybody. Suddenly, from the area around the doorway, came the question: "By what authority do you come to speak here?", to which came the reply that their authority was from the Lord. Back came the first voice again, saying "I have the authority to try you". With this Knight recognised the men standing by the door. They were town officials, and with them was the parish priest. The man who had been talking was Edmond Pitman, the justice. Pitman relayed word to others standing outside and stood aside as armed troopers entered the building and made their way towards Robertson and Rigg, arresting them and escorting them away, with Knight following in pursuit.

The Quakers were then taken inside Pitman's house where he charged them for being Jesuits and, in front of several witnesses, including the priest and Knight, he offered them the Oath of Abjuration. Robertson and Rigg refused to swear the oath, but made a solemn declaration instead saying that they stood as witnesses against all popish supremacy over the Catholic Church in general. Not being content with this Pitman then proceeded to accuse the two of entering Knight's house against his will. Knight, of course, denied this himself, despite the fear of reprisals which would most certainly follow. Pitman, having failed at this, promptly ordered the constables present to transport the two Quakers to the town prison where he would examine them again — only this time they would be separated and examined individually.

On the third day of imprisonment without food they were asked if they had been whipped in Kent (referring to the incident of Stubbs and Caton, mentioned above). Not being believed when they denied this, they were then forcibly stripped in order that their captors might see if there were any weals on their bodies. This treatment raised an objection from some of the officers present, and, encouraged by this, the Quakers demanded justice from their accuser. Having been denied the satisfaction of finding marks on their bodies, Pitman once more offered them the Oath of Abjuration. Their second refusal thus condemned them, and they had to remain in prison.[11]

Meanwhile, an associate of Robertson and Rigg, named Robert Hodgson, had run into similar trouble in the town of Reading, sixteen miles north of Basingstoke, in the county of Berkshire. Earlier that year he had arrived at Reading and begun preaching his Quaker beliefs inside St Giles' Church. He was bodily thrown out of the church and thereafter escorted closely through the town, preaching as he went. He was attracting a fairly large crowd around him and, made confident by the extent of the large following, his preaching grew more intense. Eventually, they reached Justice Frewin's house and Hodgson was forced inside. The Justice was annoyed by the Quaker's refusal to remove his hat, so he struck it from his head. Immediately, Frewin began to examine Hodgson. "Do you own ye Scriptures to be ye Word of God?" asked the Justice. To which Hodgson replied, "In ye beginnings was ye Word and ye Word was with God, and ye Word was God". Frewin was not satisfied with the answer and continuously pestered the Quaker for a less evasive reply. Finally the Justice grew tired of the cat and mouse game and had Hodgson thrown into prison. The Quaker was then offered the Oath of Abjuration. His refusal condemned him and he spent twenty-one days in prison.[12]

After his release, Hodgson then travelled to Basingstoke in search of Robertson and Rigg. He went to Knight's house and that evening attended a meeting there. During the course of the meeting there came a resounding hammering on the door. Within seconds Justice Pitman entered and had Hodgson pulled roughly out of the house by his accomplices. Under examination the Quaker explained that he had come from Reading in order to see his two friends in prison. The magistrate then replied, "Then you shall go and see them". Pitman had both Hodgson and Knight imprisoned on the account that they had refused to swear the Oath of Abjuration. The four Quakers were finally set free at the quarter sessions

42

following, after Robertson and Rigg had served fifteen weeks in confinement, and Hodgson and Knight thirteen.[13]

No more was heard of Thomas Robertson in Hampshire. Knight remained in Basingstoke where he lived, and for the next five years appeared to have been left in comparative peace by the magistrates. In 1660 he served a second term of imprisonment — this time for eighteen weeks — on the same charge, that is, refusing to swear on oath, and was to suffer much more persecution after that.

Hodgson, after his release from Basingstoke Gaol, wandered northwards again into Berkshire and was soon in trouble. In the November of 1655, he was at Newbury, where he was hauled before the mayor of that town. On examination he was subjected to the oath and again condemned by his refusal. In consequence he was delivered into Reading gaol for the second time. This man continually came into conflict with the authorities in Berkshire, until finally he had to emigrate to America in the ship *The Woodhouse*. Even there he found no peace. Persecuted in New Amsterdam (later New York), he wandered through Maryland, publishing "The Truth".[14]

It was in 1657 that George Fox made his first and only visit to Basingstoke. He was not impressed, calling it "A very rude place, where they had formerly very much abused Friends".[15] He attended a quiet meeting at William Knight's house on the evening of his arrival, and as it drew to a close, Fox removed his hat to pray to the Lord, "to open their understandings". He received a polite yet unanimous salute from the gathering who proclaimed him to be a very good man. Overcome by this praise the Quaker founder once again removed his hat — a rare tribute — in order to bid the assembled Friends a good night (which was never really in his heart).

After leaving the meeting, Fox retired to the George Inn in London Street where he was abused by the rude and drunken landlord. The following morning he complained of the landlord's behaviour, before setting off on his way to Bridport.

A mixed band left Knight's house that evening and travelled their separate ways home. Yet they held something which united them spiritually as they walked out into the cold night air. Some, however, could only just grasp Fox's message for a few brief moments before letting it drift away into the night forever. Others were resolved to become Quakers and to practise the faith sincerely until their dying days, only to fail in that resolve under the surmounting persecutions of subsequent years. Then there were the handful who had heard Fox's message and had

43

accepted it in the faith in which it was given, and it was these people who nursed it and cherished it and lived by it no matter how many obstacles were placed in their paths, no matter how much suffering they would undergo and no matter how often they would be shunned or molested for it. These were to become the true martyrs of Quakerism. They would successfully pass the test of their faith or die in their attempt.

[1] Fox, p. 39

[2] It was an offence to declare oneself to be God, or to be equal with God, or to say that God was solely to be found in man, or to claim divine authority for grossly immoral actions.

[3] Fox, p. 58.

[4] Fox, p. 58.

[5] Vipont, p. 35

[6] Quoted by Davies, p. 196n

[7] Sufferings, Hants

[8] Vipont, p. 24

[9] Vipont, p. 47

[10] Knight's house later became the "Rose Inn" on the corner of Chapel Street and Brook Street. It was demolished during the redevelopment of Basingstoke in the 1960s

[11] Sufferings, Hants

[12] Sufferings, Berks

[13] Sufferings, Hants

[14] Sufferings, Berks

[15] Fox, p. 286

GEORGE FOX speaking
with OLIVER CROMWELL.
From an engraving by Robert Spence

CHAPTER ONE

1657

"1657 James Potter of Baghurst was committed to the comon Goale at Winton by William Wythers, and Richard Kingsmell (called Justices) for reading a ffriends paper in the Steeplehouse of Baghurst, after the priest had done, and at the Assizes following was by Judge Nicholas fined ffive pounds for wearing his hatt, and there kept prisoner five yeares and two weekes, and then sett free by a Committee of Parliament."

(Sufferings, Hants.)

I

THE SOUND OF Edward Benthall's voice echoed through the twelfth-century church until even the thick walls appeared to shake with fear and the ancient pillars which supported the roof seemed to tremble at each accentuated tone. Benthall had such a way with words and such a forceful mode of delivery that his congregation of common yeomen and labouring stock could actually feel the wrath of God fall upon them. The awe in which they held this man was such that they fell into an attentive silence as soon as their priest opened his mouth to speak.

His sermons left his flock in little doubt as to how the true path of Christian virtue should be trod. They were rather noisy affairs, accentuated by the thumping of Benthall's heavy fists upon the pulpit rail, which he considered a necessary action in order to deliver his lectures on hellfire and damnation in the most convincing way to his "children".

Benthall had served his apprenticeship fully in the ways of the Lord. As an itinerant preacher imbued with the ideals of Calvinism, he had delivered his sermons on village greens, by market crosses and by the side of the road. Under the Laudian Church he had been persecuted regularly, and had seen the interior of many a prison, mainly as a convicted vagrant. His hostility towards the royalist government was forced into him by way of

45

his rough treatment at the hands of the High Church officials. It is not surprising that he would support the rebellion against Royal Prerogative when it came at last. Nothing had seemed more rewarding to him than when his pulpit was some broken-down cart and his congregation was made up from the young men who filled the troops of Parliament. He could goad these willing disciples into action by mere words, and could instil into them a supreme confidence that they were fighting on the side of God. He obtained real satisfaction and pleasure preparing his soldiers for action, and they responded by fighting all the more fiercely having been "blessed" for the battle.

But that war had been over now for more than eight years. The new England which had emerged from the chaos of civil war was indeed a different country from that which Benthall and his contemporaries had known. The victory for Parliament was also a victory for the dissenting factions who had been persecuted under the Laudian Church. Religious toleration was now the policy of the republican government, and this policy opened up the floodgates to allow cranks with all kinds of belief to roam the countryside at will. In turn the more numerous and more powerful sects began to persecute the lesser denominations, which led Cromwell himself to criticise the Presbyterians in Parliament by saying: "What greater hypocrisy than for those who were oppressed by the Bishops to become the greatest oppressors themselves as soon as this yoke was removed?"[1] Fear of a different kind filled the air — not the fear of persecution so much, but that any new sect could now challenge the position of those more entrenched in their own petty kingdoms. With the abolition of the monarchy and the High Church itself, with all its trappings and hierarchy, many benefices became vacant and were then filled by those who had been persecuted by the outgoing clergy.

Edward Benthall was one of those Calvinist "Puritans" who had benefited from the ejection of the Arminian ministry. Being a staunch Parliamentarian, he had found favour with William Wither, Lord of Manydown, and had, under Wither's patronage, secured for himself the benefice of Baughurst, a tithing of the sprawling manor which Wither had purchased in 1650.[2] Benthall had found that Baughurst, having a predominantly farming community, earned him a comfortable income. Equally important, the parish held its own peculiar court, which meant that the priest was virtually independent of outside interference in ecclesiastical affairs and enjoyed the right and control over the proving of wills, which earned him an extra income.

Therefore Benthall was master of his domain, except, of course, in his dealings with the Manor of Manydown. He was now content with his life, serving the spiritual needs of his flock. This contentment had mellowed him in his advanced years, and, although he still breathed fire into his Sunday sermons, there was definitely something lacking. He needed a crusade in order to invigorate his lectures — something that had been missing since the days when he used to urge on the troops of Parliament. Gradually, this sense of urgency was returning as he heard of new religious disturbances flaring up in the district all around his citadel. It was only very recently that the Quaker "Messiah", Fox, had dared to preach his scandalous views in the nearby town of Basingstoke. So, with renewed vigour Benthall was able to pound out his sermon against these false beliefs, inwardly shaking through the fear that his bastion might one day be besieged.

At last, the rantings of the volatile minister had subsided and his heavy frame lurched forward as he came to rest with his large hands placed on the front of the pulpit, supporting his shaking body. The silence was deafening in itself as the humbled congregation hardly dared to breathe for fear of disturbing the uplifted soul of their shepherd. That is, until a young man in the midst of the assembled worshippers arose from his pew and turned full-face to address the aging minister who was now standing in his pulpit with his hands clasped together in prayer, facing heavenwards.

II

HIS WHOLE BODY trembling, James Potter stood there staring at the old minister. Hushed whispers of amazement were all around him, and his brother who was seated next to him was agitatedly tugging at his sleeve. On his other side, his sister Ann was smiling encouragingly at the young man. Benthall, still in the attitude of prayer, was gradually becoming aware of the disturbance in his congregation. The old priest opened his eyes to see James Potter standing in the midst of his seated parishioners and smiled expectantly at him for the praise he believed to be forthcoming.

But now, young Potter had produced from his tunic a pamphlet, which he was starting to read nervously. At first Benthall could hardly hear the quiet, halting voice, but Potter's convictions grew stronger as he progressed through the pamphlet, and his voice grew louder. There was a mention of the temple being the people and not the building, and the regular repetition of the words, "Fox said". Before long the cries and the gasps of the outraged community were drowning Potter's words. Benthall, meanwhile, was growing angrier and angrier, until he could not stand any more. Furiously, he ordered the young rebel to stop, but Potter continued to read from his pamphlet.

The whole congregation was in an uproar. Many hands were reaching out for Potter and he was roughly dragged from his pew and thrust into the aisle, yet still the young man was spouting the ideas which had incensed the people. Benthall had descended from his pulpit and Richard Potter was now by his side, begging forgiveness for his brother. The old man ignored these pleas and slowly proceeded towards the now prone figure of the blasphemer.

Benthall glowered down into the still defiant face of James Potter. For a moment there was complete silence. These simple country people had never experienced anything like this before. They had been forced to witness an astonishing event which had left them totally confused and they anxiously looked for direction from their priest.

The brooding silence was at last broken by the sound of Richard Potter's voice again pleading for mercy on his brother's behalf, but to no avail. Benthall was definitely not in a forgiving mood. He ordered forth the tithingman to have the young rebel bound and then placed in the parish lock-up. As James was being escorted out of the church by the villagers, closely followed by Richard and Ann Potter, the minister called back his servant and took him aside to speak quietly with him. The servant then hurriedly departed and now Benthall was alone in the vast echoing consecrated building, left to think out his next movements carefully. Finally, having pondered over the situation and reaching a satisfactory conclusion, he walked purposefully towards the vestry door, stopping briefly to stoop down and pick up the tattered pamphlet which had been lying forgotten on the floor of the aisle where it had fallen from Potter's hand in the confusion.

By the time that Benthall had reached the churchyard outside the clamour had subsided to a mere murmur in the distance. The tranquillity of the countryside had been restored just as if nothing had occurred at all to shatter the stillness of the air. The birds had already begun their evensong anew as the dying rays of the sun cast long shadows across the grassy slopes of the cemetery. The priest stood there for a while deep in anxious thought as the light began to fade, while the setting sun was disappearing behind the old yew trees. The world was once more in danger of being turned upside down, and the old man was now beginning to wonder how long it would be before he himself would be toppled from his pinnacle of authority. Despite the success of the constitutional rebellion, authority was still being challenged by the new religious sects, just as the older

"Puritan" groups had opposed the former royal system of government. At last, Benthall shook himself out of his pensive mood and proceeded towards his rectory house, his mind fully made up over his next actions.

III

EARLY THE following morning, trussed and gagged, James Potter was roughly manhandled into the ancient tithe-waggon. Only a handful of spectators witnessed the scene as the majority of the menfolk were already busy at work in the fields. The tithingman then mounted the high vehicle and sat himself down on the bench alongside the driver; the driver cracked his whip and the two cart horses strained into action, slowly heaving the heavy cart into motion behind them. The waggon descended the hill and turned left on to the Brimpton Road.

The main highway from Brimpton in Berkshire runs through the village of Baughurst. Heathlands abound the border district, and in the seventeenth century they were areas where the writ of law hardly intervened. Notorious as havens for footpads, vagabonds, gypsies and felons, they were useful in the sense that fugitives from the law could regularly "hop" from one county to the other as the need arose.

South of the border district was the small hamlet of Inhurst which was attached to the manor of Wolverton to the south-west. Wastelands divided Inhurst from Baughurst and this latter parish, formerly in the possession of the Dean and Chapter of Winchester Cathedral, and now an apanage of the Withers of Manydown, was abundant with rich farmlands, interspersed with commons and copses. Small homestead farms appeared at intervals along the road, in particular the Causeway, copyhold estate of the Dickers. Just to the east of the Causeway stood the splendid parish church dedicated to the early Christian martyr, St Stephen. Alongside the church was Benthall's rectory house and close by were Church Green and Church Farm. Several sheep enclosures were easily seen as the tithe-waggon proceeded southwards.

Religious dissent was not new in Baughurst and James Potter was making the same journey for the same reasons as had John Marsh, in the time of King Charles I, when on his way to trial for recusancy.[3]

Approaching Pound Green the tithe-waggon rounded the bend in the road as the Malthouse came into view. The Malthouse stood at a junction and as the waggon began to turn left along the track which led away from the village, it was brought to a halt. A large procession had been gathering behind the vehicle and as the distance increased the farmworkers were leaving the fields and joining the throng. The villagers were jostling and jeering the bound occupant of the cart. When the waggon came to a stop, so the crowd surged forward shouting invective at the unfortunate young man lying in the cart. At the junction stood Richard Potter, holding the reins of his horse; beside him was his sister, Ann.

As the tithingman alighted from the waggon to speak to Richard, Ann pushed her way through the crowd to stand at the tail of the cart smiling encouragingly at her brother. After a few minutes she was helped into the waggon and sat down on the boards pillowing James' head on her lap. The tithingman resumed his position on the bench, while Richard mounted his horse. The vehicle was goaded into motion and continued its journey to Manydown House.

As the vehicle progressed along the road, James had forced himself up into a sitting position in order to catch a final glimpse of the farmhouse which had been his home. After it had disappeared from view between the trees he sat there for a while facing his sister, tears trickling from both their eyes. Eventually, as the strange procession reached the parish boundary at Stoney Heath, the two parts separated, the wagon pressing onwards with the catcalls and jeers of the crowd following them, mixed with the barely audible well-wishes of a few honest friends.

The final stage of the journey took over an hour as the waggon slowly lumbered its way towards Manydown. Across the flats of Stoney Heath and West Heath, the driver hardly spoke a word as he nervously egged on his horses, for fear of attack from marauding bands of royalists who blighted rural England in those days. The tithingman sat by his side fully alert and watching here and there the skyline and the distant woods for movement, with his faithful blunderbuss perched between his knees. Ann Potter sat in the back, her hand comfortingly stroking James' hair, while Richard brought up the rear of the party, his eyes scanning the horizon one moment and then concentrating on the track ahead. At times he was deep in a pensive mood and quietly weighing up the situation.

After trundling its way through the hamlet of Ramsdell, the waggon negotiated the long upward climb towards Woodgarston, passing on the way the chalk pits where labourers were digging out vast quantities of the mineral and loading it onto the waggons for a copyholder to haul to Manydown, as was his customary duty to the lord of the manor.

On the top of the hill at Woodgarston, the waggon halted for a while. Wither's leasehold farmer was soon there demanding water from his servant to quench the thirsts of the tired travellers and their horses. From their perch high on the hill, beside the grassy motte and bailey which served as the only visible sign of the former Norman castle, the occupants could see the parish church of Wootton St Lawrence nestling in the valley below. To their right stood the cottages of Upper Wootton. South of that hamlet could be seen Fabians, the residence of Richard Kingsmill, and beyond that Manydown Park — their destination. The travellers thanked the farmer for his hospitality and then the driver cracked his whip and the waggon lurched into motion once more.

Before long the party was proceeding through the gates of Manydown Park and up the winding drive. The waggon halted in the courtyard where waiting servants hustled James away to incarcerate him in the stables, where he would await his summons to appear before the magistrates.

IV

THE YOUNG prisoner, flanked by two of the retainers who had guarded him while he was occupying the stable, stood nervously in the open doorway while another retainer announced their entry. The tithingman stood at the back of the group, silently contemplating the outcome of the examination. Only a few minutes earlier he had pleaded on the behalf of Richard Potter to allow him to be present at his brother's inquisition, but without success. The tithingman had promised both Richard and Ann that he would personally relate the whole ordeal to them.

Swallowing heavily, James Potter was pushed bodily forward into the drawing-room by one of his escort. Once inside the oak-panelled chamber he was horrified to notice that he was physically trembling with fear; he had never experienced the trauma of being hauled before the magistrates until this day. As if by a natural reaction, he attempted to compose himself and stood bolt upright, displaying a look of defiance upon his face. However, the aching in his wrists made him look down to his bound hands, which were now white through the tightness of his bonds.

He heard someone order his wrists to be freed, and almost immediately one of his escort was before him and releasing his hands. Then he heard his name being spoken. With a start he looked up again at the three gentlemen seated behind the oaken table just in front of him.

William Wither occupied the high-backed chair in the centre of the group behind the table. He was in his thirties, having succeeded to the Lordships of Manydown, Woodgarston, Worting and Andwell on the death of his illustrious father four years earlier. William Wither the Elder had been a Member of Parliament since 1631, and had espoused the Royalist cause at first, subsequently changing sides before the outbreak of hostilities. Appointed a Commissioner by Parliament in 1642 whose duties were to seize warlike stores for the Parliamentary Army, he was also a member of a committee of three appointed in 1649 to supervise the demolition of Winchester Castle. He had purchased the Manors of Woodgarston and Worting in 1619, and was, by inheritance, the Lessee of Manydown Park and the Demesne Lands under the Dean and Chapter of Winchester Cathedral, Lords of the Manor of Manydown. However, in 1649 with the abolition of the deans and chapters, the Manor of Manydown fell into the hands of the Parliamentary Commissioners whose object was to sell the manor to the highest bidder. Subsequently, Wither was successful in his bid, and he bought the property in January 1650 for £6,550 14s. 4d. James Potter's father, Matthias Potter, was one of the copyholders who assented to Wither's purchase of the manor. Wither died at the age of sixty-nine and his thirty-year-old son became the new lord, whose total lands stretched from Baughurst in the north to Pardown in the south, and from Hannington in the west to the boundary between Worting and Basingstoke in the east, save for the island around Andwell Priory near Nately Scures. Wither was an extremely wealthy man and it appeared ironic to James that his father's assent had aided this family to their present position.[4]

To the right of Wither sat Richard Kingsmill, a member of an equally illustrious family which had their seat at Sidmonton Court near the Berkshire border, and had thus allowed them to interfere with the jurisdiction of both counties. This Kingsmill, however, was a member of a junior branch of the Sidmonton family, and resided officially at Fabians, just to the north of Manydown House, as Wither's most important lessee, and at Malshanger in the parish of Church Oakley, to the west of Fabians.[5]

Both the gentlemen were dressed in the puritan style of attire, with their plain wide collars almost covering their drab tunics. The third gentleman in the ensemble sat a little way to the left of William Wither, and had no need of introduction to James Potter. He was Edward Benthall — the accuser and sworn enemy of Potter! And lying on the table before the two magistrates was the Quaker pamphlet which James had brought into the church at Baughurst on that day of incident.

The examination began at once. Both Wither and Kingsmill were thrusting questions at James, while Benthall himself added several interjections. The pamphlet was being used as evidence of Potter's guilt — a guilt which had in effect been assumed by his interrogators from the start. He had little chance of defending himself, for he was allowed very little at all to say. Finally, he was offered the Oath of Abjuration, which he declined as a matter of faith. Time had stood still and what may have been minutes seemed to James to have been hours. All that was left were the formalities. He would be transported to the common gaol at Winchester and at the next assizes would appear before the judge who would then give him a "fair" hearing. With that the magistrates rose and James Potter was led back out of the room to be detained in the stable until such time as an escort could be provided to take him to Jewry Street Gaol in Winchester.

When Richard Potter was told of the hearing he wept openly for his brother. Richard knew that James had been convicted as sure as if the assize judge had found him guilty himself. It was a mere formality now. He was refused leave to see his brother until such time as he was incarcerated at Winchester and only then after the trial. Therefore, there was nothing that Richard and Ann could do for the moment but return home with heavy hearts.

V

THE GROANING of the heavy wooden doors as they were slowly pushed open was greeted by an ear-splitting roar from the crowd waiting outside. Beads of perspiration were trickling from the brows of the two attendants who were struggling to free the oversized wooden gates from the press of the crowd. From the prison courtyard emerged two mounted dragoons, their helmets and swords glinting in the morning sunlight, who used their horses to force a pathway through the surging crowd. Their rough handling of the immediate citizens caused loud curses to intermingle with the already overbearing noise.

It was the first day of the assizes, and Jewry Street had once more become alive with jostling spectators, many armed with the most rotten fruit and vegetables that they could lay their hands on. They had come to jeer and deride the wretched felons who were now having to make their way precariously through the streets of Winchester, in order to hear their own particular fates being sealed by some remote justiciar who was not concerned in the least whether or not they were guilty.

The roar increased in volume as from the courtyard there now emerged the prison waggon, loaded with the dregs of human society in chains. Flanking the waggon and bringing up the rear was an escort of armed and mounted dragoons, and as the tumbril slowly rumbled its way over the cobblestones, the soldiers forming the vanguard of the escort were hard pressed to force a way through the crowd. At times the whole procession came to a complete standstill until the spectators would succumb to the forceful thrust of the escort's swords.

The occupants themselves looked a sorry lot. Murderers, conspirators, Royalist traitors, harlots, thieves, debtors, counterfeiters and religious criminals were chained together as strange companions indeed. Some appeared frightened by the violence of the crowd, others were too deep within their own thoughts to take much notice, a few were crying while one old man took the opportunity to preach a sermon to the uncontrollable and disinterested mob. The air was filled with missiles of all kinds and to this the troopers were forced to retaliate as they themselves also became targets.

James Potter was ducking instinctively, but when he saw that the old preacher stood unperturbed, he found inspiration which quelled his fear. He stood upright alongside the old man, his inner nervousness portrayed only by his holding his hat firmly on to his head, while he then looked the crowd full in the face unflinchingly as rotten food bombarded them from all sides. This stand of defiance did not go unnoticed by the old evangelist, who gave James a reassuring smile and put his arm around the young rebel's shoulders before rendering his sermon more boldly and with stronger diction.

The waggon and escort moved slowly out of Jewry Street and began the ascent of Castle Hill, passing the George Inn where an old harridan cackled gleefully as she leaned from an upper storey emptying the contents of a chamber pot over the miserable prisoners in the cart. She quickly retreated from view as screams of abuse arose from bespattered members of the crowd and escort. The procession wound its way slowly up the hill towards the West Gate, from which gentlemen debtors were viewing the proceedings from their barred windows. As the entourage passed under the West Gate the less fortunate debtors could be seen through the gratings of their cellar prison. Eventually the waggon turned into the courtyard of the Great Hall, which was all that remained of the old castle destroyed by Cromwell. Here, the escort was reinforced and the prisoners were quickly despatched to the cells.

Soon afterwards the prisoners were standing in the Great Hall, which was now the courtroom. With the exception of the legendary Round Table hanging on the wall above the bench, the chamber resembled more a common market place than a hall of justice. The noise was tremendous and Judge Nicholas, seated on his high throne, was barely audible above the tumultuous throng as he attempted to dispatch "justice" on those unfortunates brought before him.

James' clothes were tattered and filthy from the dampness and poor conditions during his long wait in the county's common gaol. They were flecked with the stains from the rotten food with which he had been pelted. Yet, despite his poor appearance, he retained an arrogance which disquieted the justice when James' turn came for judgement.

Nicholas noticed that Potter was still wearing his hat, which should have been removed as a token of respect towards his office. Sarcastically, the judge demanded the Quaker should remove his headwear in his illustrious presence. James' reply that no man has a superior beneath God, brought forth a titter of amusement from the jury, thus further infuriating the judge. For his pains Potter was fined £5[6] and the rest of the trial was a mere formality, as the outcome was now clear. He was accused of reading a Quaker pamphlet in church and of refusing the Oath of Abjuration, to which the throng responded with jeers and cries of "Jesuit". The jury found him guilty and the judge sentenced him to an indefinite term of imprisonment in the common gaol. Justice had been served according to the harsh rules of seventeenth-century English law.

When the assizes had finished for the day the prisoners were loaded back into the waggon and, with their escort, returned to the prison. As the waggon rumbled down Jewry Street, James' thoughts were on Baughurst and his family.

While the waggon was passing into the courtyard of the prison a sense of heavy despair had already descended upon the occupants. What little hope that had filled their minds as they were departing that morning had now vanished completely as they returned to the prison-house in Jewry Street. Even the once vociferous preacher was unusually silent. The realisation that some of the lives would soon be terminated in the name of sweet justice had sent a shockwave of stark horror through the group, and each occupant had retreated into his own personal thoughts, for even those with less severe sentences were now being deprived of their liberty for at least a matter of months. As if they were almost unconscious of what was happening to them they were manhandled from the waggon and shoved into the prison-house, which would be their home for as long as the law required it to be so. Once the door to the chamber was finally slammed shut and they were enfolded in semi-darkness, some of the convicts let loose their emotions. The others just stared blankly at the surrounding walls, a few muttering inaudible prayers.

[1] Hill, p. 178.
[2] Benthall had been the elected Parliamentary Registrar for Whitchurch from 12th July, 1655 until 8th April, 1656 when he was offered the benefice of Baughurst by Wither.
[3] A recusant was a person who refused to attend Church of England services. John Marsh was recorded as a Catholic recusant: Lay Subsidy Rolls, Baughurst 1628. Public Record Office.

[4] Rev. Reginald F. Bigg Wither: "A History of the Wither Family" (1907); V.C.H. Hants.

[5] Since 1622 known as Tangier Park (after Charles II's marriage to Catharine of Braganza — Tangier was part of the dowry).

[6] Equivalent to about £250 today.

AT AN ASSIZE COURT.

From an engraving by Robert Spence

CHAPTER TWO

1657-1662

"Matthyas Potter by Coppy dated 12° September 8°
Jacob holds a messuage the toft of a messuage and one
yard land and a halfe wth th appteancs in Baghurst
containing by estimation 39 acres and 3 rood for his lyfe
under the reserved yearly rent of 21 shillings But is worth
upon improvement over and above the said rent £18 19s p
ann _____

> John Potter sonne of the said Matthyas by the same
> Coppy for his life in the premises after his said
> ffather
> Richard Potter brother of the sd John. by Coppy dat.
> 20° Septem 7° Car reverconer for his lyfe in the
> premises after his said father and Brother."

(Parliamentary Survey of Manydown, January 1650)

I

ALTHOUGH James Potter had already spent several weeks in the
common gaol while awaiting his trial, and had grown accustomed to
the noises all around him, he found that he could not sleep at all that night.
He had found a small space in the corner of the cell where he barely had
room to lie down, but after heaping up a pile of dirty straw he settled
himself on the floor, propping his back against the damp wall. His body
needed rest but his mind was abnormally active that night as he thought
and rethought in detail the incidents leading to his conviction. As he
analysed the situation he became more aware that his imprisonment for his
beliefs was meant to have been. He, like his teacher Fox, had to suffer the
martyrdom of incarceration for his Quaker ideals.

But as the night wore on his thoughts wandered towards his family who
were at home in Baughurst, and from them to his home and his parents,
both now dead. The farmhouse where James was born and bred was

situated in the area of that parish known as Pound Green, that is, to the south-west of the church and alongside the road stretching from Brimpton in Berkshire to Wolverton, where the parishes meet at Townsend. The house was typical of a larger yeoman's cottage of the time. It was a two-storeyed house, excluding the large attic which normally housed the servants in wealthier farmhouses, under a thatched roof. The frame of the house was constructed from thick tarred timbers, fashioned into crucks by the carpenters who originally made them in their shops, identifying each timber with a Roman numeral. A similar mark was made for the adjoining timber so that the whole could be constructed on site easily and readily by hammering strong wooden pegs or iron bolts through the holes in each timber. When the framework was constructed then the floors could be added by being lain and fixed to the bearing beams which extended from one cruck to another. The inner walls were then joined and nailed to the same crucks, and these wattled walls were later roughly plastered. Before the middle of the sixteenth century the wattled walls formed the outer walls of many yeoman's cottages, while others would have covered these with wooden planks. However, in later Tudor times brickwork became more fashionable for the yeoman classes as well as those above them on the social ladder. Therefore the farmhouse where the Potters later lived was faced with bricks made at the neighbouring kiln in Ramsdell. Only the interior of the house allowed one to see the exposed timbers which supported it.[1]

Each floor inside the house consisted of one room, based on the medieval design. But as the family grew then each room could be divided by nailing panels to the main beam of the ceiling. This was a highly practical scheme as each panel could be removed easily when the family grew up and left home, allowing their parents to live in comfort in their spacious single-roomed house.

The open hearth of the Potter dwelling was on the south wall, while the door to the outside occupied a portion of the east wall. Therefore it was more often a necessity to keep a panel nailed to the beam in order to prevent draughts during the winter, which caused the fire to smoke excessively. The newel ran to the right of the hearth leading to the upper floor, while a handmade ladder stood near the eastern wall of the first floor for access through the trapdoor to the loft above, which was spacious enough for sleeping quarters. The size of the house in floor space was approximately twenty-four feet by seventeen feet and each room measured about six feet three inches from the floor to the beams which ran from the north to south of the house.

To the south of the house itself stood an old barn, bricked and beamed in a similar style as the house. Here was the so-called " toft " or site of a house which was described in the later deeds to the copyhold estate. The barn was at times converted back into a dwelling again for certain members of the family, and never ceased to be an important feature of the farm.

The extent of the farm was almost forty acres in the mid-seventeenth century — a considerable estate for a humble yeoman. It was held by copyhold tenure from the Manor of Manydown, which since 1541 was in the hands of the Dean and Chapter of Winchester Cathedral, as a gift from Henry VIII. Matthew, or Matthias, Potter had been granted reversionary interest in the estate in 1582, and on the death of his grandmother, Margery Potter, in 1598, he was admitted as the customary tenant under that manor of his family's copyhold farm.[2] He would have been barely twenty-one years old at the time.

In 1611 his son, John, was granted a warrant from the Court Roll as Matthias' heir to the estate.[3] Then in 1628 another of Matthias' sons, Richard, was granted the right of succession to the farm as the " third life " in the copyhold tenure.

By this time Matthias' name was being recorded on the Lay Subsidy Rolls as one of those in the parish who were being assessed for taxes. He appeared on the Subsidies for 1625 and 1629,[4] in company with William Deane, John Mearsh (a recusant convict), Mary Spencer widow, Richard Crosse junior, Richard Diker by "the Causwaie", Lawrence Nott, Elizabeth Marsh the wife of John Marsh, Mary Coale (the last two being recorded as recusants), Richard Diker, and Thomas Harmsworth. The total assessments for the parish, at that time, amounted to three guineas, of which Matthias' contribution was four shillings. He was also paying twenty-one shillings a year as rent for the land on which his farm stood, which did not increase even in 1650 when the Parliamentary Survey was made.

Parliament did not sit from 1629 until 1640, after Charles had alienated the Scots by his introduction of the Prayer Book to that northern kingdom. While there was peace, the King could govern without the need of parliamentary subsidies, but the dispute with his Scottish subjects had erupted into the Bishops' Wars and the dire want of extra income in order to fight successfully against the rebels. Now Parliament had the upper hand and expressed emphatically that redress of their grievances would be followed by the much-needed subsidies. Charles, however, issued promises to keep his English subjects' representatives at bay, and before long Parliament was ordering the collection of poll tax once more. In 1642, on the eve of the Civil Wars which wracked the nation, Matthias Potter was being assessed for eight shillings in taxes, or double the assessment of 1625.[5] Whether or not the impending war upset the arrangements for actual payment is not known, but the extra expenditure of the Treasury which meant doubled taxes for the taxpayers would obviously have been unpopular among the people.

Agnes Spencer held her copyhold farm next to that of the Potters, but on the opposite side of the road. At over forty-seven acres, it was slightly larger than Matthias'. She had died in 1630, after holding the tenure since her husband's death in 1582. As her son, William, had predeceased her, her grandson Ralph Spencer became the next copyholder tenant of that farm. Ralph died unmarried during the winter of 1646/7, and his spinster sister Joan inherited the family farm. Matthias Potter had married a sister of Ralph and Joan, and the Potters were now farming Joan's lands for her. Matthias died in 1657, shortly after his eldest son, John, had expired. By the time that Matthias' executrix, his daughter Ann, had proved his will in London on 4th February 1658, her younger brother, James, was in prison.

With the end of the Civil Wars and the abolition of the monarchy and the Episcopacy, the Dean and Chapter of Winchester Cathedral were deprived of their livings, including the Manor of Manydown. Their manorial lands therefore came temporarily under the supervision of the Parliamentary Commissioners. The manor was then sold to William Wither, himself a former Commissioner, who added the large Manor of Manydown to his hereditary acquisitions of the Manors of Andwell, Bighton, Woodgarston and Worting, and the Hundred of Chuteley. Prior to the sale a survey was made of the Dean and Chapter's former estates in order to assess the lands, valuations, rentals and prospective increases in rents as well as listing the current tenants and their heirs.[6]

On 26th December 1649, however, an agreement had to be drawn up with the tenants of Manydown purely for their assent to Wither's purchase of that manor.[7] Matthias Potter placed his mark (a curiously shaped "W") to this agreement, while other names included on that document were those of Elizabeth Marsh, the wife of the recusant John in 1625, and Joan Spencer. Then on 2nd July 1650 a warrant was issued by the "Guardians of England" to restrain certain tenants of the Manor of Manydown from cutting, felling, or destroying any tree or timber in that manor under a penalty of £1,000 to be levied on their goods and chattels.[8] The certain persons mentioned were Hugh Hack, Richard Dicker, Thomas Dean, Matthias Potter and Ann Soper.

The last appearance of Matthias Potter's name on a document was that of a rental agreement in 1652.[9] Within five years both he and John Potter were dead, and his wife had died some years beforehand. Now in 1657 Matthias' son Richard was the tenant in possession of the farm and also farming Joan Spencer's estate for her. Ann Potter, his sister, was living in the Spencer's house with Joan, while poor James, his brother, was a convict languishing in Winchester Gaol. The Potters and Joan Spencer were now renowned as religious rebels or recusants. For them there was the assured future of constant harassment from the minister of Baughurst. At least James was now safe from further persecutions from that man. But although he had made his stand and was willing to suffer martyrdom for his actions, he now had the time to ponder over the dangers to which he had exposed his family and friends. Time and time again he would consider what his revolt had meant to his loved ones, and his conscience could never be quieted even by their assurances of support. Yet during those early days of imprisonment he was not to know that they were just as staunch in their Quaker beliefs as he was.

II

"Once the prison door had closed behind him, the prisoner found himself amid conditions which varied all the way from comparative comfort to indescribable squalor. Some men were well satisfied with their treatment, and felt that they had little cause to complain."

(G. R. Cragg: "Puritanism in the Period of the Great Persecution", p. 89 (C.U.P., 1957)

IMPRISONMENT in the seventeenth century was a matter of application. It was particularly arduous for those whose living standards were normally quite comfortable if not wholly affluent, yet might appear astonishingly pleasant to the many who knew abject poverty outside its walls. For others it was merely a home from home.

The prison house was filled with offenders of all kinds — notorious felons like murderers, thieves and malicious thugs, and lesser criminals such as debtors and religious convicts. Terms of imprisonment ranged according to the crime and the behaviour of the offender. The most important feature determining the treatment of the prisoner depended upon the relationship between the captive and his gaoler. In most prisons the gaoler reigned supreme, almost an autocrat in his own particular sphere of influence. He was able to supplement his wages by charging his "guests" for extras such as food, beds and bedding, and could influence their social life by refusing them visitors. If one fell foul of the gaoler then prison life was made extremely unbearable, though in many prisons because of the gaoler's influence the hardened felon was made more comfortable than the unfortunate lesser offender. Prison life, therefore, was a matter of the survival of the fittest and, in particular, the strongest.

The prison itself also varied from place to place. In some towns it was no more than a foul-stinking hole where the convicted were hard pressed to find standing room, let alone floor space to rest their weary bodies. Where a castle overlooked its dependent borough its dungeon often served as a gaol for the district and would often have been a damp dark basement where one's health would quickly suffer. Yet there were also some county prisons which afforded more luxurious apartments for the prisoners, where dangerous felon and lesser offender were separated unless they met occasionally in the courtyard when exercising daily. In a number of towns the less dangerous criminal was also allowed the freedom of the prison's vicinity, and in a few the whole radius of the town was within his bounds, but they would have had to return to prison during the evening so as to spend the nights in confinement. Normally these were for special prisoners and not the common offender. George Fox himself experienced a wide variety of prisons during his life.

Life in Winchester Common Prison was probably no worse than that of the average large prison. The site measured approximately three hundred feet by eighty feet, and would have had two storeys. During times of political and religious persecutions the building would have been overflowing with inmates, while normally all the prisoners could have been lodged quite comfortably, with the upper storey being reserved for the more dangerous elements. Of course, the murderers did not stay long as they were executed as soon as possible after conviction.

James Potter spent just over five years in that prison but never once recorded how he utilised his time there, although as the Clerk for the Hampshire Quarterly Meeting in later years he would have had the opportunity to do so. As a long-term prisoner he would have become involved with the other convicts. As a Quaker he would have interested himself in their conditions and the injustices which they had suffered. Also as he was literate he would be the prime candidate to represent his fellow convicts at every given opportunity, whether by letter or personally as their advocate. Indeed Winchester Prison proved to be an apt training ground for his later career.

He was an extremely intelligent man who would allow little to escape his notice and had the ability to confound the authorities. At every given opportunity he would also espouse the Quaker cause and lecture the inmates on Fox's teachings. Indeed he proved to be a thorn in the flesh of the prison authorities and the justices would not allow him an early release for fear that he might spread his dangerous views around the countryside. James was so active in prison that the authorities made sure that he was not allowed his freedom. During his term of imprisonment no fewer than forty-eight other Quakers shared his cell temporarily, yet no other of that faith served anywhere near as long a sentence as James.

James' devotion to Quakerism was obviously increased through the influx of other Friends into Jewry Street Prison. Of the forty-eight fellow Quaker convicts, six spent more than one term there.[10] In 1657 Stephen Beavis from Southwich was already there serving a sentence lasting eighteen weeks for attempting to convert an Independent pastor to Quakerism.

That same year Humphrey Smith, William Bailey and Anthony Milledge were arrested at Ringwood on a charge of vagrancy and imprisoned at Winchester for one year and two months. Smith returned there again in 1662 for attending a meeting at Alton but died after serving only six months of his sentence.

In 1658 William and Richard Baker, the servants of Henry Streeter of Bramshott, were detained in Jewry Street Prison for twenty-four weeks because they had agitated against the parish priest, John Corbett, for stealing a cow from Robert Biddleworth, possibly in payment for tithes which Biddleworth owed the priest. Soon afterwards Streeter's wife, Elizabeth, accosted Corbett on the public highway over the same offence and for her servants' unjust imprisonment and for her pains she was taken away from her suckling child and thrown into the common gaol for twenty-one weeks. She and her servants were eventually released by order of a parliamentary committee, probably instigated by her outraged husband and supported by a Quaker deputation. However, Elizabeth Streeter was back in Winchester Prison three years later for refusing to muster arms and this time spent fifteen days there although she had been sentenced for only ten. This was after her husband had died in the common gaol on 1st April 1661 while serving a sentence for attending a Quaker meeting at Alton.

Again in that same year of 1658 Daniel Baker, John Day and Winifred Newman from Brixton on the Isle of Wight were detained in the common gaol at Winchester for nine months, seven months, and eleven weeks respectively for arguing religious matters with Robert Dingley, the parish priest. The woman was released after being found not guilty at the following assizes.

That same year also John Page of Buriton was committed to Jewry Street Prison for refusing to pay his tithes and was released after serving five weeks, only to return there in the January of 1661 as a member of the

Alton meeting which was broken up. He witnessed poor Henry Streeter's death in the prison house three months later.

No further Quaker convictions occurred in Hampshire until after the Restoration of 1660. Fanatical sects such as the Quakers were now being termed rebels and traitors, and as such were being labelled as seditious. More and more attempts were made to clamp down on these seditious sectaries, and the atmosphere grew increasingly tense as the year progressed. A spate of Quaker arrests followed which proved that the authorities were growing more nervous of these unorthodox worshippers.

John Bishop of Gatcombe on the Isle of Wight spent twenty weeks in the common gaol at Winchester for his refusal to pay tithes.

Philip and Martin Bence were brothers who lived at Ringwood. In 1660 they were visiting prisoners in the common gaol, and for their pains were cast into the gatehouse overnight and then sent back on their way home. Martin Bence spent a further eight weeks in the prison as one of the members of a meeting assembled at Poulner near Ringwood in 1661.

Another visitor ended up as a prisoner there again in 1660. Edmund Jessup from Bramshott had visited the prisoners and was handed a letter from them, probably written by James Potter, complaining of their conditions and treatment, with the instructions that Jessup was to deliver it personally to John Hook, the justice. Jessup entered Hook's house but once there was refused admittance to the magistrate and was beaten up by his servants, escorted to the prison and detained there. He was freed by the end of the year, but returned again after his arrest for attending a meeting at Petersfield in the January of 1661. Six weeks later he was released when he appeared at the assizes.

John Pidgeon of Crawley had been administered the Oath of Allegiance, but refused. He was then imprisoned at Jewry Street in October 1660 and remained there for eleven weeks before the Quarter Sessions took place. Although his name appeared on the roll he was not summoned before the magistrates and remained in prison. The gaoler, however, being quite a compassionate soul, had allowed Pidgeon out of the prison to "take a little air". For this act the gaoler was fined £5 and ordered to keep the Quaker a close prisoner. Consequently the gaoler thought twice before he gave further Quaker captives special concessions.

In November 1660 Samuel Pidgeon was likewise imprisoned at Winchester for refusing the Oath of Allegiance. In his absence his house was ransacked by neighbours to the value of £500. Drunkards then took over the building and in so doing frightened away Pidgeon's young servants.

On 2nd January 1661 an Order in Council was issued forbidding large meetings in secret places, and at unusual times, of Anabaptists, Quakers and other sectaries, and restricting their assemblies to their own parishes — such was the fear that the authorities had of these so-called seditious sectaries, who were supposed to have been former Cromwellian soldiers. More and more, religious discontentment was being interpreted in terms of political conspiracy. On 6th January Venner's abortive rising had erupted on to a scene that was already filled with acute nervousness. This was the last attempt by the fanatical Fifth Monarchist sect to establish the "Monarchy of Christ" in England. Although, in reality, it may have been no more than a mere outburst from a declining religious group, its implications were regarded as highly dangerous by the government. It was seen as part of a much wider rebellion embracing the treacherous views of all the dissenting groups. Recrimination was bound to follow. On 10th January a Royal Proclamation was published prohibiting all unlawful and seditious meetings and conventicles under the pretence of religious worship. The authorities in every parish and county were now forced to act in order to trample upon the activities of the dissenters. The prisons of England were starting to fill as religious meetings were being broken up. Yet this was only the beginning of religious persecution. There was much more to come.

Ambrose Rigg, who had run foul of Edmund Pitman in Basingstoke back in 1655,[11] had again suffered imprisonment at Southampton in 1657. Now, on 11th January 1661, he was arrested at Petersfield and offered the Oath of Allegiance, which he naturally refused. From there he was taken to the common gaol at Winchester wherein he remained a close prisoner until May of the same year.

On 13th January a Quaker meeting was being held in Alton, when a group of soldiers broke into the house and arrested the seventeen male members assembled there for worship. The assembly were then forced to walk to Winchester, staying for three days and three nights under guard at an inn in Alresford *en route* to the county capital. Finally Henry Streeter, Robert Biddleworth, William Valler, Edmund Heath, Henry Wake, Nicholas Eades, William Blamshott, Robert Terry, James Collier, Henry Elliott, Nicholas Lamie, John Lack, John Wigg, John Page, John Marshall, James Tampling, and John Harvard were all imprisoned in the common gaol in Jewry Street. It was here that Streeter died on 1st April.

On the 17th of that same January William Buckland was imprisoned for refusing the Oath of Allegiance. Then on the 20th another meeting was broken up, this time at Petersfield. Edmund Jessup, William Churchman and Nicholas Finkley were held in prison until they appeared at the Assizes of 5th March. They were then found not guilty and were released immediately after serving over one month's imprisonment.

At the same assizes three other Quakers were released. Thomas Ham and Stephen Gloss had been in prison since the 21st January, while Henry Mullins had been detained there since the 2nd February.

Meanwhile, Thomas Walter of Waltham had been arrested on the very same day as the members of the Petersfield meeting, but because he appeared on charges issued out of the Exchequer, probably because of his refusal to pay tithes, he was detained in the common gaol until 13th April.

On 24th January 1661 James Hunt, James Miller, James Hide, Martin Bence, and John Pritchett were imprisoned for eight weeks for attending a meeting at Poulner near Ringwood.

In that same year William Knight and Nicholas Rabbetts were placed in Jewry Street Prison under a ban of excommunication after continuing to hold Quaker meetings at Knight's house in Basingstoke [12] despite attempts by the local authorities there to stop them. Already Knight had served two sentences in prison at Basingstoke, and James Potter would remember this man, for it was at his house that he first saw and heard George Fox.

So, during those dark days James never lacked the companionship of his fellow religionists, and constant contact made him even more convinced that his beliefs were right. He had become inspired by the sufferings of his companions, and encouraged by the constant visitors who had brought some relief to the lives of the miserable inmates. Because of his attempts to represent his fellow convicts while in detention himself his imprisonment was more prolonged. Yet, although he was out of the way, he was still aware of events outside the prison walls, brought to him by relatives, friends and other Quaker sympathisers. He knew, therefore, that his family had also suffered acutely while he was lying in prison, and this troubled him immensely.

III

"1657 Anne Potter of Baghurst was imprisoned by Edward Benthall priest of Baghurst for Tythes, in the Prison called Cheny Court Prison neer Winton and there was kept Prisoner, Twenty eight weeks."

(Sufferings, Hants.)

"1659 Richard Potter of Baghurst for Tythes had his gate thrown off the hookes, and had taken out of his

Backside, by the said Edward Benthall priest himselfe, and his wife, and two of his sons, and Thomas Cradick, of Winton Bayliff, and two more with them, Three Cowes Two heifers, and a calfe vallued at 17 lb, and at an other time had taken out of his house two peices of pewter, for the use of the said Priest, by Walter Swan of Tadly; all of which was taken away for 5 lb Tythes which the said Priest demanded of his Sister, for which he had at that time imprisoned her, he having nothing against the said Potter from whom he took the goods."

(Sufferings, Hants.)

EDWARD BENTHALL'S vengeance was quick and sharp. No sooner had he made sure that James Potter had been locked away safely in prison, than he embarked upon a persecution programme against those in his parish whom he suspected of Quaker sympathies. He believed that he was the shepherd and that his flock should practise in the same faith that he readily preached. There was no room at all in his parish for rival doctrines, least of all for such a fanatical sect as the Quakers, who conflicted with his authority as well as his religious ideals.

His prime target was, naturally, the Potter family which had not openly defied his ecclesiastical authority, but the recent imprisonment of James had removed from the immediate scene his most dangerous opponent in this quarter. James' removal had also made the Quakers of the district somewhat cautious. Because of Benthall's instant action at nipping the movement in the bud once he had found evidence of its activity within his realms of jurisdiction, further suppression of the faith would probably be more acute. The Quakers, therefore, continued their activities, but under the cover of darkness. Benthall was well aware of the fact that he had not destroyed the movement in and around Baughurst, but was willing to bide his time and to concentrate his actions solely upon the Potter family for the moment.

Before long the parson had approached William Wither again in order to find support against the Potters, but Wither was now reluctant to aid the priest further in his persecutions, as technically Richard Potter had not committed any crime himself, and was also a good tenant of the manor, fulfilling his duties towards Wither as lord of Manydown in a satisfactory way. Wither then advised Benthall that any further oppression against the family had to come directly from the Church and through the ecclesiastical courts, unless, of course, the civil laws of the land had been infringed.

However, Benthall's opportunity came soon enough. Ann Potter, the sister of Richard and James, had already made her own particular stand in support of her faith and in objection to James' imprisonment. She had refused to pay to Benthall the tithes which had been assessed for her in her own right.[13] By the end of 1657 these had amounted to five pounds, and the parish priest was now ready to collect them.

He proceeded to Winchester where he obtained a summons out of the Exchequer against Ann Potter and consequently she was arrested and then transported to Cheney Court Prison just outside the southern wall of Winchester, alongside the River Itchen. Here she remained a prisoner for twenty-eight weeks, and soon afterwards, in 1658, Benthall had another Baughurst Quaker, Richard Dean, imprisoned in the same place and for the very same offence.

Therefore, for just over six months Richard Potter was the only member of the family at liberty and at home in Baughurst. He had escaped Benthall's wrath simply because it could not be proved that his profits from farming were enough in order to have tithes deducted from them and, in any case, Wither would obviously object to such treatment against one of his tenants for, from the manorial point of view, it would mean that important farmlands would have been left untended for some time.

Richard Potter would have made the occasional tithe payment to Benthall when the occasion warranted it, for he was extremely aware that the survival of Quakerism in the district depended now solely upon his freedom to encourage its growth there. Therefore he was careful not to provoke the priest too much in this direction. Yet he was often absent from the parish, either visiting his brother and sister in their respective prisons, or attending meetings at Basingstoke or at Brimpton Mill where Samuel Burgis the miller would accommodate Friends. All the while he was similarly contemplating opening his own farmhouse for the occasional meeting for worship.

Despite Ann's prison sentence Benthall would not allow the matter to rest there. Two years later in 1659 she was back in Cheney Court Prison for the same offence, and while Richard himself was absent on one of his visits, his farm was broken into and several animals stolen.[14]

Edward Benthall arrived at the farm, accompanied by his wife and two of his sons, with Thomas Craddock the bailiff from Winchester and two of Craddock's accomplices. The occasion was in order to deprive Potter of goods to the value of the five pounds owed by Ann, and the bailiff was required for the sake of legality.

The gate had been chained to its posts, and before the tithe-waggon could be driven into the farm it had to be opened. The chains held fast and eventually Craddock's men had to resort to pulling the gate away from its hooks altogether in order to allow the waggon free access into the farm. When the party reached the rear of the building the whole farm could then be surveyed. From Potter's livestock Benthall selected three cows, two heifers and a calf, and after rounding them all up the accomplices herded the beasts down the track leading to the gate and the road beyond, followed closely by Benthall and his wife and the bailiff in the waggon. Without bothering to replace the gate the party then drove the cattle along the Brimpton Road and into Church Farm, where Benthall had his own holding.

When Richard Potter returned home and found that his gate had been damaged he immediately went to discover the extent of his loss and found that his livestock had been drastically depleted. He immediately sought out the tithingman, who had already been informed of the proceedings by the bailiff. Therefore, Richard was advised to approach Benthall personally, and this he did, but to no avail. Benthall answered that he had acted according to the law and that the bailiff had accompanied him to make sure that the action was not excessive. He maintained that Potter's sister had owed him a debt that was not fully recovered and that he had now discharged that debt from her next of kin. It made no difference at all if Potter's dispossessed goods were valued at seventeen pounds while the debt was for only five, for Benthall could easily sell the cattle for the same amount of money which had been outstanding. In that way the debt would be cleared without profit for the parish priest.

But that was not the end of it. According to Benthall the debt had not been fully recovered, despite Ann's imprisonment and Richard's loss of livestock. Soon afterwards he commissioned Walter Swann of Tadley to enter Potter's house itself, which, of course, was totally illegal, and to deprive him of further smaller goods. Swann broke into Richard's house while the Quaker was again absent from home and stole two pieces of pewter which he delivered up to the parish priest. And Richard could do very little about it as Benthall denied such an offence.

So, while James Potter was languishing in prison, his family was being persistently oppressed by their adversary. They were generally suffering for the crime which their brother had committed and was now still paying for his actions. Yet they were also guilty of that same felony, and were paying for their involvement in Quakerism. Such payments became the more attractive to their adversaries as the years progressed because in many instances Anglican priests would welcome the idea of Quakers in their parishes as they were a major source of financial gain. More often than not the value of the goods which were impounded in respect of tithe debts were double or even treble the value of the debts in the first place. The clergy would grow rich on the spoils from Quaker persecutions.

Yet the fear remained of a rival faith within the jurisdiction of the persecuting priest which openly defied all authority — whether civil or ecclesiastical. Rebellion was contagious, and had to be put down whenever and wherever possible. It was the responsibility of the justices and the Church together. But, even as Benthall persecuted the Potters and other Quaker families in the area, and while James Potter was still detained in prison, the movement was growing and the circle of Quakerism in that small parish and in the surrounding countryside was growing wider and wider and appeared to threaten the existence of the Church itself.

IV

" And because the passion and uncharitableness of the times have produced several opinions in religion, by which men are engaged in parties and animosities against each other, which, when they shall hereafter unite in a freedom of conversation, will be composed or better understood, we do declare a liberty to tender consciences, and that no man shall be disquieted or called in question for differences of opinion in matter of religion which do not disturb the peace of the kingdom; and that we shall be ready to consent to such an Act of Parliament as upon mature deliberation shall be offered to us for the full granting that indulgence. "

(Declaration of Breda, 4/14 April 1660)

" Whereas of late Times certain Persons under the Names of Quakers, and other Names of Separation, have taken up and maintained sundry dangerous Opinions and Tenents, and (amongst others) that the taking of an Oath in any Case whatsoever, although before a lawful Magistrate, is altogether unlawful and contrary to the Word of God; and the said Persons do daily refuse to take an Oath, though lawfully tendred, whereby it often happens that the Truth is wholly suppressed, and the Administration of Justice much obstructed; And whereas the said Persons, under a Pretence of Religious Worship, do often assemble themselves in great Numbers in several Parts of this Realm, to the great endangering of the publick Peace and Safety, and to the Terror of the People, by maintaining a secret and strict Correspondence

amongst themselves, and in the mean Time separating
and dividing themselves from the rest of his Majesty's
good and loyal Subjects, and from the publick Congregations and usual Places of Divine Worship."

(The Quaker Act, 13 Car II, Cap. I (1662))

OLIVER CROMWELL died in the September of 1658, and with him the
hopes and dreams of a lasting republic. He was indeed the keystone of the
Interregnum, for he ruled with an iron fist over the Army which
maintained it and the Parliament which represented it. His rule over the
State affairs of the country brought much-needed prestige from abroad.
He was loved by some, hated by others, yet feared and respected by all as
one fears and respects a strong autocrat who is severe and just. He was
sincere in his beliefs and as a true Englishman attempted the best for his
people, yet his views were too premature for his contemporaries. He was,
in many ways, ahead of his time because his government lacked the
constitutional instrument which would allow it to continue during a time
when the monarchy was still shrouded in the mystical conception of divine
right, and medieval values of Church and State still dominated the government system. Above all, Cromwell was still remembered as a regicide —
the singular most important member of the committee which had tried
and sentenced to death the late king. Therefore his reputation was scorned
and his memory would be damned forever. But while he lived and ruled as
Lord Protector he gave to his country a stronger government than it had
known for some time.

But now Cromwell was dead and as his body was being interred in
Westminster Abbey, the dispute over his successor was being determined.
Cromwell's iron rule would have been maintained if only his son-in-law
Henry Ireton had not predeceased him. Ireton was Oliver's nominated
successor, but, alas, it was now too late to find someone else of that stamp.
Finally Oliver's son, Richard Cromwell, was selected to fill the vacant
position, but although the name continued there was in his younger son
little of Oliver's ability to govern. Richard did try, however, but lacked the
strength and determination of his father, and would have been much
happier at home on his farm. The Protectorate lasted another year as the
younger Cromwell's power gradually slipped more and more into the
hands of the factious military. Finally in 1659 Richard Cromwell resigned
his title in favour of a Council of State which still had no authority over
the bickering generals and the corrupted Parliament. The country plunged
further and further into the anarchy which had been prevented by Oliver
Cromwell back in 1653. Even now hardened republicans could see that the

country needed a stable government to unite it, and more and more people were talking about the recall of the exiled son of the late martyred King Charles I.

In February 1660 General George Monck took the initiative and, at the head of his Coldstream Regiment, entered London and declared the Restoration of the Stuart Monarchy and allowed the purged members of the Long Parliament to return and to take up their seats in the House once more. Negotiations began between Monck and the exiled Stuart government in the Netherlands, culminating in the Declaration of Breda, by which was promised an amnesty to all except those specifically named by Parliament, safeguards for the purchasers of the estates of delinquents, religious tolerations as granted under Cromwell, and the payment of arrears to the Army. All these conditions were subjected to the assent of Parliament.

In May 1660 Charles Stuart entered London triumphantly and was crowned as King Charles II in Westminster Abbey the following year, and for a while both king and subjects celebrated a belated honeymoon. Unfortunately, this joyous interlude was short-lived, owing to the sudden revival of the Anglican-Royalist fortunes.

Towards the end of 1660 the Convention Parliament passed the Act of Indemnity and Oblivion, which meant the return of former royal and ecclesiastical estates to their original owners, while other lands had to be settled with, according to their merits on the basis of whether they were purchased or confiscated. Prior to this act retribution had been made upon the surviving regicides and Cromwell's body had been exhumed and hanged at Tyburn. The Convention Parliament played little further part in the legislation beyond preparing the way for the Restoration Settlement. All successive enactments had to be made by a fully constituted parliament elected under summonses from the King.

In December 1660 Charles dissolved the Convention Parliament and took the opportunity to issue a Declaration of Indulgence based upon the condition made at Breda by which he promised religious toleration. However, this royal document immediately caused controversy as it was suspected that the King was intending to liberate his Catholic subjects, who had been most loyal to him and his father during their trials. Charles had to withdraw his declaration through pressure from his judges, among others, as he was felt to be encroaching upon ground which was beyond his ecclesiastical prerogative and encompassed within constitutional issues.

Attempts, however, were made to settle the religious issue which was seen to be dividing the nation. The agreement made at Worcester House, the home of Charles' chief minister, Edward Hyde, now Earl of Clarendon, made way for the Savoy Conference, attended by the leading clerics and sectarians of the country. The aim was to produce a religious policy which would enable the dissenting groups to become part of the Established Church system, but it ended with complete division of interests as the radical Anglican group represented the majority view at the conference. In the meantime the Convocation was set to work to produce a revised Prayer Book based mainly upon the Anglican doctrine. Consequently the dissenting groups were now alienated completely from the Church, and even the Presbyterians, the most moderate of the sects, could see the gradual erosion of "comprehension", which would have meant that they could have been accommodated into the Anglican Church system.

In the meantime the dissenting congregations were being condemned as enemies of the State by the Royalist-Anglican majority which now formed the nucleus of the squirearchy and the ruling classes of the nation. The suspicions were confirmed by Venner's rising of January 1661, and amid the alarm which spread through the countryside as the aftermath of that futile revolt, the elections for the new Parliament were called. The result was that the new Parliament was packed with a strong majority of radicals supporting both the Royalist cause and the High Anglican Church. This was the so-called "Cavalier Parliament" which remained in session until the next election of 1678.

The Cavalier Parliament now had the responsibility of legislating in favour of Anglican supremacy over the dissenting factions, in order to bring about a Church settlement. In this they were in agreement with the King's wishes, but were bent on furthering the cause of the Established Church by the legalised persecution of the nonconformists. They attempted to turn the dissenting minorities into Anglican conformists through legislation, and could not echo their royal master's sentiments towards "tender consciences". Parliament, therefore, was bent upon the destruction of dissent rather than religious toleration, which they deemed as a totally defeatist attitude. The Anglican Church would reign supreme throughout the land and they would legislate towards this aim, despite the fact that some of the members of the Cavalier Parliament held Presbyterian or Independent views.

Thus in 1661 Parliament embarked upon a series of enactments known since in history as "the Clarendon Code", the aims of which were to deprive the dissenting congregations of offices in government and church, of their meetings and their ministers, and any other influences beyond their own assemblies. That year they legislated in response to the nonconformist element which held high positions in local and national government, by passing the Corporation Act. This act prevented dissenters from holding or gaining government offices, and one of the victims of such an act would have been William Wither of Manydown.

By the end of 1661 the Quaker Act had been passed which was now aimed primarily against a particular sect which was seen to have been most seditious. After 8th May 1662 any person refusing to take an oath, or assembling for worship in a meeting-house or in any other place than the parish church, would be liable to a first fine of five pounds, and subsequent offences by a fine of ten pounds and thereafter transportation. It has been estimated that after the Quaker Act had come into force about 1,300 Friends were in prison[15] out of an estimated Quaker population of perhaps 40,000 in 1660.[16] Persecuted during the Interregnum as those of the most dangerous principles among many unorthodox beliefs, their plight had become much worse now that the Royalist-Anglican party were in power. They were again being aligned with the Catholics as the most disturbing influence among the separatists.

Yet, later in 1662 they were not alone in their sufferings. Now the Cavalier Parliament launched a bitter attack upon all nonconforming ministers by the passing of the Act of Uniformity. The Prayer Book had been revised by the Convocation and was now to be used as the instrument for depriving of their livings the dissenting ministers who had filled the vacant pulpits of the ejected Laudians after the Civil Wars. The Prayer Book had to be used by the clergy for Anglican services; all clergymen and teachers had to be episcopally ordained, to abjure the Solemn League and Covenant and to take the Oath of Non-resistance. The usage of the Prayer Book meant a struggle with his conscience for many a Puritan clergyman, especially if he were Presbyterian and looked towards the day of " comprehension" with the Church; the oath against the Covenant confirmed his beliefs that "comprehension" was now only a dream for those Presbyterians who could not face the reality of the situation; episcopal ordination meant that no clergyman suspected of dissenting views could hold office in the restored Church. In order to remain in the ministry which the Puritan had held for so long now he had to conform completely. Those unwilling to do so were to be ejected from their livings when the Act came into force on St Bartholomew's Day, the 24th August 1662. In the event about 2,000 clergymen were ejected that year, and those who remained in their pulpits were uncompromising Anglicans.

The Corporation Act had deprived William Wither of his role in local government, and in 1662 the Dean and Chapter of Winchester Cathedral were restored to their lands at Manydown, with no compensation to Wither whatsoever. This was the condition of the Act of Indemnity and Oblivion of 1660, although The Dean and Chapter had allowed Wither some time to wind up his affairs in the manor and then to allow him to remain as their leasehold tenant on the demesne lands, while he remained in Manydown House itself as the squire of Wootton St Lawrence. So Wither was not treated too badly. His position merely reverted to that of his father prior to 1650. For Benthall it was a different story. He had until the August of that year to remain in his rectory. After that his future was insecure and he would be put out of his house to wander the countryside as a penniless refugee from the law. He was to become persecuted as he himself had persecuted others.

Benthall's last act as the Rector of Baughurst was an attempt to accumulate as much money as he could before he became dispossessed of his living. Therefore he revived his battle against the Potters, and travelled to Winchester to obtain a warrant from the Exchequer against Richard Potter.[17] Richard had to appear in court at Winchester where he was indicted on the word of the parish priest of Baughurst. Richard offered his defence admirably, citing the value of the losses which he had sustained at the hands of Benthall, and of the two terms of imprisonment which his sister had suffered for the same offence. The case was dismissed and Benthall had been utterly defeated in his last attempt to fight the Potter family. Soon afterwards he would be trudging the road out of Baughurst, shunned by all there and without the support of his former master, Wither of Manydown.

As Benthall was preparing to leave Baughurst there were others in that parish making preparations for a homecoming. On 26th October 1661 Joan Spencer had nominated James Potter as her heir in her copyhold estate.[18] Now that the Dean and Chapter were once more in possession of the manor, she could complain rightfully that while her heir was being detained for a long period in prison owing to a sentence which he had been given by former "illegal" magistrates, her lands were in danger of being left untended.

Furthermore, Quaker delegations were lobbying both Parliament and the King for the release of religious prisoners. George Fox and Richard Hubberthorne wrote a letter to the King on behalf of the Quakers still in prison. They stated that out of the 3,173 Quakers who had been imprisoned for their beliefs, seventy-three had been incarcerated since the time of the Commonwealth and that during the same period no less than thirty-two people had died there. But since the Restoration Quaker imprisonments had totalled no less than 3,068 persons.[19]

The letter had its desired effect. Quaker delegations continued to pressurise the officials and before long a parliamentary committee was set up to investigate their complaints. The Committee was merciful to those whom it had thought had suffered severe sentences, and by order of that same committee several Quakers were released, including James Potter who had now served a sentence of five years.

As James was travelling northwards towards Baughurst, a free man at last, his adversary was preparing to leave. But James was in no mood to gloat over his opponent's misfortune. When he arrived home he found that things had altered significantly. The small community which he had left five years before had grown and he found that while he was away there were several Quaker families living within the area who now had a real need for a meeting closer to home. Yet for the moment there were the arduous tasks of tending his future copyhold estate and helping his brother to replenish his stock which had been decimated in the earlier raids by the tithe-gatherers. James had found peace again, but as he set about his duties he was constantly aware that peace could not prevail for long for those with unorthodox views in Restoration England. He would wonder just how long such a respite would last.

[1] Now Brown's Farm, Baughurst, where the original building described above still survives as the lounge of the house. The old house was extended in 1693.
[2] Dean and Chapter Court Books, Winchester Cathedral Library.
[3] Parliamentary Survey, 1650 (H.R.O. and Cath. Libr.).
[4] Lay Subsidy Rolls No. E179. 175/511 and 521 (P.R.O.).
[5] Lay Subsidy Rolls No. E179. 175/550 (P.R.O.).
[6] Parliamentary Survey 1650 (H.R.O. Doc. No. 11M59/59493, also a version in Cath. Libr.).
[7] Kitchin, p. 176.
[8] Bates Collection, H.R.O. Doc. No. 21M58/M11.
[9] Bates Collection, H.R.O. Doc. No. 21M58/E8.
[10] Sufferings, Hants.
[11] See p. 40-3 of this book.
[12] See p. 40-3 of this book. Rabbetts was sometimes recorded as Roberts.
[13] Sufferings, Hants.
[14] Sufferings, Hants.
[15] Clark, p. 22.
[16] Clark, p. 18.
[17] Sufferings, Hants.
[18] Warrants of copyhold and the 1660 Survey of Manydown, Cath. Libr.
[19] Fox, p. 423. Compare these figures with those of Clark on p. 74 of this book.

CHAPTER THREE

1662-1668

I

"The traditional burial ground in the garden of Brown's Farm (Richard Potter's old home) is, always has been, a grass-grown part of the regular garden, with an old yew tree and shrubs in it. It lies next the division hedge on the Baughurst and Newbury road. Confirmation of this being an old burial place has been the discovery of a bricked vault, by the present occupier, who dug to see if he could find traces of burial here. And there is an entry in the parish register on November 26th, 1742, which further confirms the fact of burial in the farm grounds: Ann Potter, a Quaker, was buried 'in her brother's garden.'"

(Florence Davidson: "The Quaker Burial Grounds at Baughurst", P.H.F.C., vii, 2, 1915, p. 42)

FOR SEVERAL months Baughurst was without a parish priest, that is, until such a time as Benthall's replacement was able to enter into his living there. During the ensuing vacancy the Quakers of the district were naturally far from inactive. After James Potter had fulfilled his immediate responsibilities towards his family and his copyhold inheritance, he turned his attention to the advancement of his faith. At the business meeting which followed that of religious worship he would put forward plans to establish a local meeting in Baughurst, and with the agreement of his brother advocated the use of the Potter copyhold farmhouse for such a purpose. The proposal was subsequently accepted and plans were drawn up in order to initiate the new Baughurst Meeting, including the nomination and the appointment of trustees for the meeting-house. Of course, no such notice was given to the Lords of the Manor of Manydown — the Dean and Chapter of Winchester Cathedral — for the most obvious of reasons. The machinery was then set into motion as the news was spread to the surrounding meetings by word of mouth, and by the early months of 1663 Baughurst had its own Quaker meeting in progress.

Thus, because Baughurst had remained particularly quiet owing to the absence of a residential Anglican priest throughout those few months, the Quaker meeting there was allowed to become organised. Before long it would flourish considerably enough to be able to attract a fairly substantial gathering of regular worshippers, and by the April of 1663 it was deemed necessary to set aside a portion of land next to the meeting-house for the use of burying the Quaker dead. On the 23rd of that month the first burial of the Baughurst meeting took place. Elizabeth Kent had died at her home in Tadley a few days beforehand and her will had been that she would be buried next to the meeting-house where she regularly worshipped. Therefore her body was transported the few miles from Tadley and, under the cloak of darkness, was put to rest in the meadow alongside the Potters' house.[1]

The burial of Elizabeth Kent of Tadley, however, remained a singular event in the history of Quakerism in Baughurst for a number of years, as it was not until 1668 when the next interment took place in that same cemetery. For the same duration of time the meeting itself was allowed to flourish with little hindrance and almost a total lack of repression from the authorities, lay and spiritual, which would appear rather ambiguous inasmuch as severe legislation was being enacted against the dissenting groups during that time, and being strictly enforced by the majority of magistrates and law officers in every part of the country. The reason for the outstanding lack of oppression against the Baughurst Quakers was quite simple — the fate of the local Quakers was dependent upon the character and the nature of the person who filled the vacancy left by Benthall.

II

" And all such person and persons as shall take upon them to preach in any unlawful assembly, conventicle or meeting under colour or pretence of any exercise of religion, contrary to the laws and statutes of this kingdom, shall not at any time from and after the four and twentieth day of March which shall be in this present year of our Lord God one thousand six hundred sixty and five, unless only in passing upon the road, come or be within five miles of any city, or town corporate, or borough that sends burgesses to the Parliament, within his Majesty's kingdom of England, principality of Wales or the town of Berwick-upon-Tweed, or within five miles of any parish, town or place wherein he or they have since the Act of Oblivion been parson, vicar, curate, stipendiary or lecturer, or taken upon them to preach in any unlawful assembly, conventicle or meeting under colour or pretence of any exercise of religion, contrary to the law and statutes of this kingdom, before he or they have taken and subscribed the oath aforesaid before the justices of peace at their quarter-sessions."

(An Act for restraining nonconformists from inhabiting in corporations – "The Five Mile Act," 1665 (7 Car II, cap 2))

GEORGE MUSGRAVE entered into the living at Baughurst in 1663. He was a rather kindly old man and, despite his pure Anglican beliefs, he was reluctant to oppress those who did not share his devotion to his faith and the Established Church. Before long he was to discover that there was a fairly strong Quaker meeting within his new parish, but once he had recovered from this particular shock he would go about his business as usual, attempting to ignore the presence of the alien views which conflicted with his own religious sensitivities. At times he would meet some of his dissenting parishioners along the way and would then treat them with courtesy and a limited respect, while discussing theology and other interesting subjects. The Quakers held a high regard for this man, who would refuse to persecute them despite their unlawful practices, and nothing was recorded by them which would have been detrimental to his memory.

Perhaps Musgrave was a rarity among the Anglican ministers of those days of bitter hostility against dissenting communities. He was indeed completely the opposite of his predecessor, who had appeared to have personally delighted himself with his persecutions against the Potter family and their acquaintances. Musgrave was reluctant even to gather in his tithe dues from that family, although these were his main source of earnings.

Yet while George Musgrave was serving as the spiritual shepherd to the Baughurst flock, Parliament would pass another two oppressive statutes against the dissenting population of the realm. In 1664 the notorious Conventicle Act was made law in an attempt to prevent the clergy ejected by the Act of Uniformity from forming their own congregations. It forbade conventicles of more than five persons (other than meetings for family worship) except in accordance with the Book of Common Prayer. This Act, however, was specifically to be enforced for three years and, therefore, due to expire in 1667, in the belief that all illegal conventicles would have become extinct well before then. In many places, however, the Act had largely been ignored before its date of expiry, owing to the reluctance of several magistrates to prosecute local offenders, and neighbours to inform upon friends who were not seen to be dangerous conspirators. This was so in Baughurst. Despite the existence of the Quaker meeting there and the influence it was generating in the area, there were very few who would wish to see these normally peaceful rustics threatened and persecuted as they had been under Benthall. Although the Baughurst meeting should have been a prime target for the persecuting element, there was to be no danger of this while Parson Musgrave remained in his ecclesiastical office.

Then in 1665 another Act was passed in Parliament which had more bearing on the history of the Baughurst meeting than the previous one. The Five Mile Act gave to the Baughurst meeting its greatest impetus to extend its activities and, therefore, to enlarge its membership. This Act struck at the ministers who had evaded the conditions of the Conventicle Act (especially so in London during the Great Plague where nonconformist preachers were to remain amid the depredations and fill vacancies left by the fleeing Anglican clergy). Nonconformist ministers were forbidden by the act within five miles of a corporate town or a place where they had previously preached, unless they would take the Oath of Non-resistance. At the same time dissenters were forbideen to teach in any public or private school. Yet the Five Mile Act did not actually reduce the numbers of the nonconformists, even in the towns. But it did increase the influence of the meeting-houses and nonconformist chapels in the outlying rural areas. Now, unless they wished to suffer persecution under this Act, urban dissenters were being forced to travel to other places of worship outside the stipulated limits enacted. The Five Mile Act, therefore, in effect transferred the responsibility of nurturing the dissenting faiths from the urban conventicles to those of their rural counterparts. From Lady Day 1665 it was the countryside which would provide the bases upon which the nonconformist sects could strengthen their faiths and which would allow them to survive until religious toleration was granted in 1689, although the Five Mile Act itself was not repealed until 1812.

The 1665 Act thus aided the growth of the Baughurst meeting precisely at the time when religious oppression there was virtually non-existent. Because it was situated at an important position between the boroughs of Kingsclere and Basingstoke, and amid rolling countryside and sprawling woodlands, Richard Potter's house on the south-western edge of the parish of Baughurst was deemed a prize site for the Quaker meetings, as it was easily accessible to the recently ejected Quaker communities of the neighbouring boroughs and retained a certain isolation for them from the prying eyes of persecuting Anglican dignitaries. Equally as important was its location just below the county boundary with Berkshire, and thus it was within easy travelling distance from the corporate boroughs of Newbury and Reading, both of which held a substantial Quaker population. Therefore Baughurst equally served several Quaker communities recently deprived of their own illegal assemblies. The marriage and burial records show that people had journeyed to the Baughurst meeting from Sherfield-upon-Loddon, Pamber, Ecchinswell (in the parish of Kingsclere), Tadley, Basingstoke, Silchester, Froyle, Kingsclere, and Alton, in Hampshire; from Swallowfield, Midgham, Brimpton, Aldermaston, Newbury, Reading, and Thatcham, in Berkshire; from Dorchester, Whitchurch, Sibford, and Shillingford, in Oxfordshire; from Goatacre and Lineham, in Wiltshire; from Weston Bampfylde, in Somerset; from the Forest, in Warwickshire; and from Birmingham, Bristol, Hampton Wick, and from Shoreditch. So, while Quakerism was being depressed in the nearby boroughs of Basingstoke, Kingsclere, Whitchurch (Hampshire), Andover, Alton, Thatcham, Newbury, and Reading, the woods abounding Baughurst were temporarily hiding from view the fact that here was growing a thriving centre for those newly-deprived adherents of the faith. While the doors of the urban meeting-houses were being closed on a more permanent basis, those in Baughurst were being opened to the swelling group of believers. The appearance of several strangers in the parish caused a great deal of alarm among the Anglican congregation, yet little was being done about it while Musgrave administered his flock.

By 1669 the Baughurst meeting had progressed sufficiently enough to be recognised as a monthly meeting as well as a local weekly affair.[2] This fact was mentioned in the episcopal returns for that year[3] which state that the meetings were held in "Baughurst Att the house of Richard Potter". The returns mention that the meetings comprised ten or twelve of the parish and as many from other places coming to their weekly meetings, but a considerable number, most of them on horseback, coming to their monthly meetings. Furthermore, some had considerable estates, while the mention of their heads and teachers were particularly recorded in typical Anglican fashion of the time, as one was being suspected of Jesuit leanings and most of the members at the meeting did not even know his name (they would certainly not have told if they did). By 1668, however, some Quakers had re-established their meetings in corporate boroughs once again, that is, if they had ever been closed in the first place, for the Alton Monthly Meeting had been organised that year in accordance with Fox's plans for the administration of the Quaker meetings on a regional level.

The Baughurst meeting had progressed significantly since its humble beginnings after James Potter had been released from prison in 1662. Of course, its success was due almost entirely to the non-persecution policy of the local Anglican priest, and the respite which it had earned during Musgrave's term of office would last only for the duration of that agreeable old minister's life. Therefore the respite was short-lived, for in 1666 George Musgrave was dying. As he lay expiring on his bed his conscience would disturb him, for he had unwittingly allowed the heretical beliefs to grow and expand within his ecclesiastical domain. He would, therefore, take the blame for the strength of Quakerism within that area — a strength which subsequent reprisals could not weaken and overcome. And when Musgrave had at last departed this world the Church authorities made certain that his policies towards the dissenters were never repeated. Parson Musgrave's successors were notable for their intolerance of nonconformity. An era had now passed away with the extinction of George Musgrave, and peace would not come again to the Baughurst Quakers until toleration had officially been granted.

III

"Richard Potter of Baghurst the 25th of the 1st Month 1668. Ralph Browne of Winton and two more with him, came to the said Richard Potter with two severall distresses out of Cheny Court, one for two yeares Tythes, to the vallue of foure pounds and a Mark for Elizabeth Musgrave Widdow late wife of George Musgrave deceased sometime priest of Baghurst, the other for priest Turner then priest of the said parish for one yeares Tythe to the vallue of about 2 lb 6 s. and drove away of the said Richards Cattell Six Cowes and one heifer worth 20 lb or upwards.

And upon the 27th day of the 2nd Month following came one Michael Butler of Winton, and one more with him, with an Execution for priest Turner and took away from the said Richard a Mare with a Bridle and Saddle, and

Cloth and all things belonging with one Cow and a heifer all worth about 8 lb being all the Cattle that they could finde of his at that time. And the 6th day of the same week following the said priest being rideing from his house, the horse he rode on threw him, and killed him dead in the place, and as the generall report was brake his neck, he was so wickedly intended, that he declared in the Court for ffourteen pounds Debt for the Tythe of one year, the other declared for 14 lb for two yeares, their Executions was for 17 lb and upwards apeice.

The 12th day of the 4th Month after came again the said Michael Butler, and two Men with him with an Execution for the said Widdow Musgrave, and went into Richd Potters house, and went out of one Room into another pretending to seize all his goods, but took onely ffoure Cowes — worth about 12lb and a brasse washing pan worth about 20s or upwards and went away threatning him they would come againe shortly and take all the rest, and not leave him so long as he should have any thing."

(Sufferings, Hants.)

IT WAS EARLY in the year of 1667 when the next incumbent took up residence in the parsonage next to the parish church of Baughurst. Parson Turner was as disagreeable as Musgrave had been agreeable, and immediately made it clear that he would not tolerate opinions differing from his while he held the benefice. He was made aware of the Quaker meeting within his parish and had declared that it was his intention to oppress these dissenters until their faith had been extinguished in that district. Yet he found it difficult at first to follow through his objective because he was now hampered by the law itself. He could not, as was his intention, persecute the Quakers on their own ground as the Conventicle Act had now expired. His attempts to coerce the justices into persecuting the Quakers failed as the magistrates were reluctant to act through lack of evidence that the Baughurst meeting was, in effect, seditious. Turner was forced to await his opportunity as the occasion arose.

Therefore, he turned to the ecclesiastical courts for support in his crusade, and, after waiting for a specified time, he was able to bring a suit against the Potters. This was on the grounds that the head of the family had refused to pay the tithes due to Turner, and, furthermore, the parish priest was able to find a confederate in the widow of his predecessor, Mrs Elizabeth Musgrave. Potter had not paid tithes to George Musgrave for the whole duration of the latter's term of office, therefore Turner had calculated that at least three years of arrears were now outstanding, equivalent to the sum of almost seven pounds.

In 1668 Turner obtained warrants from Cheney Court in Winchester to reclaim the outstanding arrears.[4] For eight or nine years now Richard Potter had not been persecuted for his tithe payments and now, all of a sudden, he was being pestered for not just the one year's tithes due to Turner, but also for a further two years' payment which had not been ordered by Musgrave. Even Benthall had been unsuccessful in his last attempt to claim back his dues from Potter. Times had changed and the Quakers of Baughurst now found that they were being confronted by a much more vengeful opponent than they had of late experienced. Turner had, in his enterprise, allied himself with the brooding widow of his late predecessor, and she had found strength in this calculating clergyman to pursue her claims against those whom she had for long despised despite her deceased husband's policy to leave matters alone. Elizabeth Musgrave may have been reduced to dire financial straits since her husband's death, and the promise of the redemption of the tithe debt would have greatly encouraged her to prosecute the Quaker yeoman. At the same time the country parson's stipend did not amount to much, and the tithe-collection greatly implemented the meagre salary. Therefore Turner was adamant that he should obtain that which was due to him. By refusing to pay the tithes, whether because of religious principles or for the reluctance to part with hard-earned money, the Quaker could cause considerable distress among the clergy, while, on the other hand, the clergyman's oppression for tithes would result in the abject misery of those assessed for the church tax. More often than not the oppressor gained rather more than he was entitled to, and many Anglican ministers saw the persecutions for the sake of tithes as the means of greatly enhancing their wealth. It was a cat-and-mouse game, and one in which the oppressor was normally successful. The end result was that the Anglican priest actually needed the dissenter within his parish, for the latter was a continuous source of extra revenue for him — a means of illegal exaction.

In 1668 Richard Potter's debt consisted of £4 12s. outstanding to Mrs Musgrave and £2 6s. to Parson Turner. Although his debt amounted to under seven pounds his refusal to pay was to cost him, in the event, his stock and goods worth in excess of forty pounds — a profit to Turner and Musgrave of over thirty-three pounds or nearly five hundred per cent over their legal dues.

On 25th March that year Ralph Brown and his two accomplices rode up from Winchester, armed with the warrants from Cheney Court, and presented them to Richard Potter at his home. The yeoman could ill afford the payments, and the three ecclesiastical officers immediately began to set about their business of depriving Potter of goods to the value of the debt. Despite Potter's verbal objections, the official tithe-gatherers had rounded up six cows and a heifer, which together were later valued at more than twenty pounds, and drove them out of Potter's farm. Naturally, the Quaker yeoman personally objected to the new parish priest when he went to visit him soon afterwards, but to no avail.

But the matter had not ended there. A month later, on 27th April, the Potter farm was visited by another two officials from Winchester. This time Michael Butler presented Richard Potter with a warrant on behalf of Turner alone. This visitation did not reap as much success as the former, for Potter's livestock had been much depleted by the first raid. However, Butler and his companion did find and seize a cow, a heifer, and a mare with its bridle, saddle, saddle-cloth and other accessories, totalling over eight pounds in value.

Turner, according to the Quakers,[5] was "so wickedly intended, that he declared in the Court for Fourteen pounds Debt for the Tythe of one year, the other for 14 lb for two yeares". Yet, no matter how much Parson Turner had exacted from his dissenting parishioners he did not live long enough to enjoy it.

The day after Butler's visit to the Potter copyhold farm, being a Saturday, Parson Turner was out riding in the fields around the parish in the company of a few of the local farmers and dignitaries, hunting a fox. Highly elated with his current spoils, he was vigorously whipping on his steed when the poor horse stumbled and threw its master. Fellow hunters and their servants quickly dismounted to see to the fallen clergyman, but he was already dead, having, it was believed, broken his neck. The news of Turner's untimely death spread rapidly throughout the parish and it was not only the Quakers who were somewhat joyed by the event, such was Turner's reputation.

But even Turner's sudden departure did not end the current oppressions. Elizabeth Musgrave, having been encouraged by the late ecclesiastic's persistent persecutions against Richard Potter, continued the process alone. On 12th June Michael Butler, in the company of two assistants, was authorised to enter Potter's farm with an execution on behalf of Mrs Musgrave. They entered the house itself this time, having some doubt whether Richard had any livestock left worth taking. They moved from room to room ransacking the place, despite Potter's objections, finding only a brass washing-pan worth the trouble. However, they proceeded outside once again and searched the farmyard, barn and fields, finding four cows which they immediately herded together. Butler was obviously surprised at the catch, expecting to find little more than nothing, and not realising that the Quakers had implemented a system of self-help whereby charitable donations formed the "stock" which would help the needy and those financially oppressed because of their religious principles. Therefore, as Potter's personal farming stock was being depleted through the tithe persecutions then the Quaker organisation would finance the replenishment of his seized goods. In the event this current raid cost Potter more than thirteen pounds in value of seized goods and livestock.

As the plunderers were leaving Butler turned to Richard and threatened him that he would return again shortly in order to take the rest of Potter's goods and would not leave until the Quaker had nothing left of value. The bailiff was obviously disappointed with the plunder.

Between 1657 and 1669 their adherence to Quakerism had already cost the Potters well over £63 in lost stock and goods, and over five and a half years of lost freedom. This latest visitation had almost impoverished the family once again and their future depended upon the charity of the members of the Baughurst meeting, some of whom had considerable estates. Before long Fox's highly organised society would found a "Public Stock" financed by all the Quaker meetings in the county in order to alleviate the distress caused by the religious persecutions ordered by Parliament and vigorously enforced by the Anglican squirearchy, and thus the Quaker charities could be amalgamated to cover a wider scope than that of which local meetings were capable. Therefore the Potters and others who had undergone similar trials were saved from utter ruin by the charity of their co-religionists.

IV

" At this Court of the said Manor the said Steward in full
court granted in reversion to James Potter by virtue of a
warrant from the Dean and Chapter signed and sealed in
their hands bearing date the seventeenth November 1664
to one messuage and a yardland (virgate) of land and the
toft of a messuage and half a yardland (virgate) of land
with their appurtenances in Baghurst now in the occupation of Richard Potter as tenant holding the said

messuage and all things pertaining to the above-mentioned premises with its appurtenances to the same James and to Ann Potter for and during their own lives and the lives of each other at the will of the Lords according to the Custom of the said Manor immediately after the death surrender or forfeiture of the customary tenant the said Richard and yielding first the accustomed burdens and services And the said James and Ann gave to the Lords for a fine 9d but their fealty was respited until and so forth. "

(Warrant (translated) of James and Ann Potter,
1667, Winchester Cathedral Library)

MEANWHILE, the domestic arrangements of the Potter family were being organised. In 1667 James Potter rode to Wootton St Lawrence to attend the Court Baron held annually at Manydown House. There he produced the confirmation from his brother nominating both James and his sister Ann as Richard's heirs in the copyhold tenure of their farm in Baughurst. The following year Joan Spencer nominated Richard Potter as heir in reversion to her copyhold estate after herself and James.[6] Thus legal arrangements regarding the inheritance of both farms had been made.

That same year, 1668, the Hampshire Quarterly Meeting was established when George Fox attended the meeting arranged at Captain Reeves' house,[7] where several Quaker deputations from all over the county met to deal with the affairs of the Hampshire Quakers in general.

On 13th December that year Richard Potter's house became the scene of the first Quaker marriage in Baughurst when Christopher Page of Sherfield-upon-Loddon accepted the hand of Joan Terry, formerly from Swallowfield, in the presence of several witnesses. The couple had been advised to seek the advice and approval of older Friends, and then to announce their intentions of marriage at the meetings which they normally attended. Then they were told to wait until enquiries had been completed relating to their fitness to marry. Once "liberated" by the local business meeting the marriage could take place, when a dated certificate had to be signed by all those present.[8] The certificate was the proof required by the magistrates that the marriage had taken place, and the system of certifying marriages dated from the Commonwealth and Protectorate period when civil registration of marriages was introduced. The Quakers continued the process even after the Anglican Church was restored and marriages were performed again by the clergy.

Richard Potter was one of the witnesses at the formal union of Page and Terry. The very next day he rode out from Baughurst with his brother to attend a special meeting at Froyle, about twenty-five miles away, near Alton. Here on the fourteenth day of December 1668 he married Mary Wheeler before witnesses, and then took her back to his copyhold farm as his wife. The couple had six children, all born at the Potter farmhouse in Baughurst: Mary on 25th October, 1669; Richard on 10th March, 1672; Elizabeth on 22nd November, 1674; Sarah on 3rd November, 1675; Matthew on 23rd October, 1678; and Ann on 10th January, 1682. As the farmhouse was to become a family home once more in which children would be reared, James Potter soon moved out to take up residence in his main copyhold inheritance — the home of Joan Spencer — where he had spent much of his time already helping to farm the estate.

The burial ground alongside Richard Potter's house was now being used more often. Within six weeks of each other a mother and her son were laid to rest in the plot of land set aside for interments. These burials took place quite openly, as there was little to hinder the Quakers as yet. Yet even as Mary and John Paice were being lowered into the earth, there were many present who knew that the scene would alter dramatically before too long, and that the Quakers would once again be pushed into defending their faith against one of their most vigorous oppressors. Already the latest in the long line of persecuting churchmen had arrived in Baughurst to set up his home.

Quaker Marriages and Burials at Baughurst 1662-1668

MARRIAGES

(1) CHRISTOPHER PAGE of Sherfield-upon-Loddon and JOAN TERRY formerly of Swallowfield, December 13, 1668

BURIALS

(1) ELIZABETH KENT of Tadley, April 23, 1663
(2) MARY PAICE of Sherfield, October 9, 1668
(3) JOHN PAICE, son of Mary Paice deceased, November 17, 1668

(The above entries are from the digests for Hampshire)

[1] This was the first recorded Quaker burial in Baughurst — the last was in 1791. The burial digest records no less than sixty-nine interments at Baughurst during that period, while the Baughurst parish registers (of which the earliest extant dates from 1678) confirms only twenty-nine of these, while, paradoxically, recording a further seven which were omitted from the Quaker sources. In the meantime, by 1791, four separate burial grounds

had been established within that parish. While fellow Quakers were being interred in the more recent cemeteries as the years passed, Richard Potter and his family and their descendants, the Browns, were being buried privately in a brick vault beneath the yew tree by the roadside in the garden of the original meeting-house. Florence Davidson, in her article on the Quaker burial grounds of Baughurst (Proceedings of the Hampshire Field Club, Vol. 7, Part 2, p. 42) published in 1915, mentions this as the only burial ground, at Brown's Farm, and assumed that it was open for all Quaker burials in the district at the time. (She states that this particular site was actually measured by Mr C. J. Stevens in 1893 to be fourteen yards by seven yards — it was he who had discovered the brick vault there.) However, Florence Davidson's account is full of errors and omissions and her sources were sparse. She makes no mention at all of James Potter, the most important member of that community, and puts too many assumptions into scanty records which could have been checked more thoroughly at the time. She did have access to the Quaker digests, but appears to have chosen to ignore the Book of Sufferings and the Alton Monthly and Hampshire Quarterly Minutes, which would have clarified the situation. She also leans strongly upon hearsay and tradition, and the whole article smacks of a hastily written essay on an important and little-known topic of historical value. With this in mind I must refute her assumption that the original Quaker burial ground in Baughurst was beneath the yew tree at Brown's Farm. In those days of religious persecution the Quakers would hardly have gone to the extreme of building a brick vault in which to rest their dead. The vault, plus the planting of the yew tree, may have been constructed around 1693 when the house itself was extended with the use of bricks made at the nearby kiln in Ramsdell. Until then the bodies of deceased Friends might have been buried in that plot alongside the road, but there is also a strong belief that the earliest site was in the meadow to the west of the house and near the old barn — referred to in the Court Rolls as the "toft" (or site of a house) — which is now the paddock. Yet this theory again relies heavily upon tradition, and one cannot be certain where the original burial ground was, except that it was within the confines of Brown's Farm, that is, the farm that was held by copyhold tenure by the Potter family.

[2] A monthly meeting was a business meeting at which representatives from the local meetings met to discuss administration.

[3] G. Lyon Turner: "Original Records of Early Nonconformity". Vol. I, 1911, p. 139.

[4] Sufferings, Hants.

[5] Sufferings, Hants.

[6] Cathedral Library, Winchester.

[7] Fox, p. 525.

[8] This was the first Quaker marriage which took place at Baughurst — the last was in 1785. In total twenty-one marriages took place in the three meeting-houses of that parish.

CHAPTER FOUR
1669-1671

I

"Richard Potter had taken from him in the 2nd Month 1670 by William Woodward priest of Baghurst and his Man a Lamb worth 5s. and the 5th Month following, as much hay as was worth 10 or 11s. And in the 6th Month following took away Wheat Sheaves. 6 and 6 together throughout the Fields as they were sett upp, and afterwards took 3 Sheaves together, pretending it because they had no Tythe wool, and also took away Pease, Oates, and Barley untithed and without consent. And another of the Priest Servants took away from James Potter severall Wheate sheaves untithed."

(Sufferings, Hants.)

WILLIAM WOODWARD arrived in Baughurst during the closing months of 1668 in order to take up residence at the parsonage. He was a devout man of the cloth who would not allow his Church to be undermined by the activities of the dissenting minorities, and was, therefore, an exceptionally hard man towards nonconformists in general. His appointment to the benefice at Baughurst followed the official policy of the Established Church, which encouraged the harrying of heretics whenever and wherever possible. Woodward was the natural successor to the oppressive Turner, and he would remain in office as the pastor over his flock in the parish of Baughurst for thirty-five years. For the majority of that period the Quaker grouping there would find little peace as Woodward continued to apply pressure upon the nonconformist element. He had already made a particular study of the inhabitants of his new parish, and knew exactly who his religious opponents were. Therefore persecution followed swiftly.

Oppression began early in the year of 1670 when the tithe payments were due. Woodward would not allow his dues to become arrears, for fear that the debts owed to him would temporarily be used against his beloved Church. In this respect he turned his attention towards the tenant of the Quaker meeting-house.[1] In the April of that year he and his servant entered into Richard Potter's farm and took out of it a lamb worth five shillings, being the only livestock of any particular value there at the time.

The Quakers had become so organised that they were able to make arrangements for the "disposal" of their goods prior to tithe incursions. Thus Richard Potter could easily arrange the removal of some of his livestock during the hours of darkness as the time for payment was approaching. When Woodward came at last to demand his dues he would find only an impoverished farm before him. Yet he would want some satisfaction, no matter how small, and would deprive Potter of the most valuable asset available.

Because Woodward's haul was so small on the first occasion, he would return later for richer pickings. The Quakers half-suspected this to be the case. In the following July Woodward's men entered into Potter's farm with the tithe-waggon, and loaded up the vehicle with hay valued around ten or eleven shillings.[2]

Then the following month, after harvest-time, the parson's men returned in the waggon and entered into Potter's fields, where they gathered up his wheat-sheaves, a dozen in all, as they were standing there in the fields, and filled up the tithe-waggon. Yet it was not all completed for that year. Later, these very same men returned to deprive Potter of another three wheat-sheaves, and other crops, including peas, oats and barley, and before they were finished they had crossed the Newbury road and entered into James Potter's field, where they took several more wheat-sheaves. James was not tenant of Joan Spencer's farm at the time, and Woodward's theft of his wheat was, in fact, illegal as the younger Potter was not due to pay tithes. Yet, at the time, it could have been said that it was Joan Spencer who should have made the payment, and it was her land in which James' wheat was standing. It did not really matter much, as Woodward was almost a law unto himself in his domain, and there was little that suffering Quakers could do while the law was being made and enforced by the Anglican majority of the kingdom. Tithe persecutions were of little consequence compared with another form of oppression legislated that year.

II

"For providing further and more speedy remedies against
the growing and dangerous practices of seditious sectaries

and other disloyal persons, who under the pretence of tender consciences have or may at their meetings contrive insurrections (as late experience hath shown), be it enacted . . . that if any person of the age of sixteen years or upwards, being a subject of this realm, at any time after the tenth day of May next, shall be present at any assembly, conventicle or meeting under colour or pretence of any exercise of religion in other manner than according to the liturgy and practice of the Church of England in any place within the kingdom of England, dominion of Wales or town of Berwick-on-Tweed, at which conventicle, meeting or assembly there shall be five persons or more assembled together over and besides those of the same household, if it be in a house where there is a family inhabiting, or if it be in a house, field or place where there is no family inhabiting then where any five persons or more are so assembled as aforesaid, it shall and may be lawful to and for any one or more justices of the peace of the county, limit, division, corporation or liberty wherein the offence aforesaid shall be committed, or for the chief magistrate of the place where such offence aforesaid shall be committed, and he and they are hereby required and enjoined upon proof to him or them respectively made of such offence, either by confession of the party or oath of two witnesses . . , or by notorious evidence and circumstance of the fact, to make a record of every such offence under his or their hands and seals respectively, which record so made as aforesaid shall to all intents and purposes be in law taken and adjudged to be a full and perfect conviction of every such offender for such offence. . . . ''

(An Act to prevent and suppress seditious conventicles –
"The Conventicle Act", 1670 (22 Chas II, cap 1)

ON 10TH MAY, 1670, the Second Conventicle Act came into force. It was deemed necessary for Parliament to revive the Act against seditious conventicles (which had expired in 1667) because the numbers of nonconformists were actually growing, despite former attempts at legislation to suppress their activities. The previous statutes of the so-called "Clarendon Code" had been particularly aimed at the dissenting ministers and teachers rather than at their congregations, in order to depress the activities of the leaders in the belief that their followers would subsequently fall away.

However, this had not been the case, and the Anglican Party now realised that the rank-and-file of nonconformity were just as ardent in their beliefs as were their instructors. It was now necessary to suppress the dissenting congregations at their hearts — at their meetings and conventicles where they assembled to worship. In order to do this the 1664 Act was not merely to be revived, but to be extended to cover all possibilities of failure.

Andrew Marvell, a member of Parliament, described the Conventicle Act of 1670 as "the quintessence of arbitrary malice", while more recently it has been judged that "probably no other single act caused as much suffering among nonconformist communities as the Conventicle Act of 1670".[3]

It struck at all dissenters — preacher and worshipper alike. A conventicle or meeting was determined as illegal if five or more persons over the age of fifteen, but excluding members of the household if merely holding a family service, were gathered together for religious worship other than that directed by the Established Church. Proof of such an illegal assembly would be obtained either by the confession of one of the party assembled, or on the oath of at least two witnesses to the act. Other means of proof could be made by "notorious evidence and circumstance of the fact". Each offender would be liable to a fine of five shillings for the first offence, and a record of his offence and fine was to be made by the justice. Subsequent offences for attendance would then be made punishable with a fine at the rate of ten shillings by distress of goods, or, in the case of poverty the fine would be levied upon the other persons present at the illegal meeting to the maximum limit of £10 per person.

The teacher or preacher would automatically be fined the sum of £20 for the first offence, and then £40 for each subsequent offence. If that person could not be traced then the fine would again be levied upon the others present at the meeting by distress of goods.

The householder where the meeting took place was also liable to a fine of £20, but in order that such prosecutions were possible certain precautions were included in the new Act. These conditions were quite novel even for the period under review, for they laid onus upon the enforcers of the law, thus making the persecution of innocent people more probable.

The overseers, constables, tithingmen, and other enforcement officers were strictly bound to bring all offenders to justice, and refusal to do so, or by obstructing the course of the law, made them liable to a fine of £5. Every type of help possible was to be made available in the prosecution of the members of an illegal conventicle, including the use of the local militia. Furthermore, any justice or magistrate neglecting the performance of his duty was liable to a fine of £100. However, the prosecutions of offenders were limited to a period within three months after the offences were committed.

In consequence, the poor nonconformist was now in danger of being ruined financially. Although the first offence was to be fined rather lightly, dissenters were rarely frightened off and subsequent fines could be crippling, especially if the person was the occupier of the meeting-house in an area where there was a considerable amount of paupers, and the actual preacher could not be found by the law officers (which was frequently the case as the dissenting congregation would not inform upon each other). Another grotesque fact was that the new law brought forth a great number of informers, for the dregs of the community were not only encouraged to ruin their neighbours, but were actively being enabled to compel the law officers to act as their accomplices.

Therefore the Conventicle Act received a tumultuous welcome from the hard-core Anglican brigade, but only a lukewarm reception from the moderates, for now they were being forced to persecute their neighbours against their own wishes. The plight of the dissenter increased a hundredfold as he now became the target of those who were to oppress him because of their natural fear of the authorities. There were many who would play upon this fear, and William Woodward was a master of the art.

III

"And the next morning I passed about fourteen miles into Hampshire: to a place called Baughurst (Thomas Briggs being with me) and when we came into the parish there were some sober people came to us and told us that the priest of the town was an envious man and did threaten us. But when our meeting, which was very large, was gathered, the priest had got a warrant, and sent the constables and officers; and they came into the house, but did not come into the meeting-room, and so they passed away again. And we knew not in the meeting that they were come and gone again. So after Thomas Briggs had done speaking, I was moved of the Lord to stand up, and I declared the word of Truth and life to the people, and a precious, fresh meeting we had. When I had done and stepped down, and ended the meeting, I heard a great clutter in the yard.

And after the meeting was ended we came forth, and the man of the house told us that the priest had sent the

constables again, and his own servant with them, in a
great rage; and they had been in the house, but came not
into the meeting-house, but went their ways. Thus the
Lord's power preserved us over the devilish design of the
priest, and out of his snare. And after we passed away,
many Friends passed by the priest's house, which set him
in a great rage."

(Fox, p. 568)

GEORGE FOX turned to James Potter and told him that he was pleased
with the way that the Baughurst Meeting had progressed and that his word
had been spread into the backwaters of the border districts from that
humble meeting-house. Once he had completed his business in Reading he
would make his way straight to Richard Potter's house and hold a meeting
there with the local Quakers.

So James rode back home to inform his brother that Fox had agreed to
come to Baughurst, and preparations were made to welcome the founder
into their meeting-house later that week. James himself visited the
neighbouring villages and towns to spread the news among the Quaker
communities there.

Early in the dew-laden summer morning of June, 1670, George Fox and
Thomas Briggs rode over the Kennet bridge and out of Reading towards
Whitley Wood and the southbound highway before turning on to the Bath
road. For fourteen miles they rode across the countryside from Reading to
Baughurst, passing through several villages on the way, including
Padworth and Aldermaston.

Finally they reached Inhurst after crossing the county boundary below
Brimpton and took a leisurely trot over the Causeway and past St
Stephen's Church on their left. Before long they were being escorted into
Pound Green by the Potter brothers and a few companions, who led them
directly to the meeting-house where a number of Quakers had already
gathered to pay their respects to their leader.

After preliminaries had been made, Richard Potter explained to Fox
that the present rector of Baughurst was a very vengeful person and that it
would be better to hold the meeting in the loft, which could easily be made
inaccessible. The Quaker leader smiled and replied that he had worshipped
in meaner places at other times, then bade the congregation to make haste
as there was little time left. Woodward would soon know of Fox's
presence in the parish if it had not been reported to him already.

By now James Potter and another Quaker had returned to the meeting-
house after stabling Fox's and Briggs' horses in Joan Spencer's barn, where

the mounts of the other equestrian visitors had been kept so that there was little evidence of a meeting taking place at Richard Potter's house. Now all was ready and Richard led the assembled congregation towards the stairs alongside the hearth, which could be negotiated only by one person at a time because of the width of the opening. There were about twenty-five people assembled there then, and progress to the meeting-room in the loft would be slow. Once on the first floor the Quakers had to climb up a crude ladder perched against the opening to the loft above. Slowly but surely the congregation filled the space below the thatched roof where the meeting would now take place. Fox was the last to ascend the ladder and he thanked Richard as he placed his foot on the lower rung. Potter was to remain below in the house in order to secure the hiding-place and to deal with trespassers. When Fox had entered into the loft above, the ladder was pulled upwards and into the meeting-room itself, and then the hatchway was closed. Richard then proceeded down the stairs and once there nervously busied himself with a few odd tasks while awaiting the expected onslaught. He had several duties to attend to outside in his fields but was rather reluctant to absent himself from the house at this critical time.

Woodward had been informed of Fox's arrival as well as the appearance of several strangers in his parish. He sent for Thomas Deane, the tithing-man, and ordered him to gather up a band of accomplices to enter Richard Potter's home. In the meantime one of Woodward's servants was sent to Kingsclere with a letter from the clergyman himself requesting a warrant to search Potter's premises as the offence now came under the jurisdiction of the civil authorities and not merely that of the purely ecclesiastical. While Woodward waited, his impatience grew stronger, and by the time that his servant had returned he was in a most foul rage. Therefore, as soon as he held the legal authorisation in his hand the group of "enforcement officers" were impelled into action.

The constable of Kingsclere led Deane and his accomplices into Potter's farm. The warrant was shown to Richard, who said nothing, and the small band of officers began their search of the house. They went from room to room finding nothing which would indicate the presence of a conventicle. Richard Potter accompanied the group on their tour, making sure that enough noise was being made so as to warn the occupants of the loft above. While on the first floor of the house standing with Deane and the constable, Richard Potter saw Deane briefly looking at the hatchway to the loft, but, catching Potter's eye, let his glance fall before the constable had noticed. However, the constable was not a stupid man, for he had also suspected the use of the loft and asked Richard for a ladder. Richard replied that the loft was not being used for they had no servants in the house. The constable was not satisfied with this and ordered those present to keep quiet while he listened for movement from above. For what seemed an eternity the party stood listening for noises, but nothing was heard. Richard was thankful that Quaker meetings were mainly conducted in silence. Then Deane persuaded the constable that there was no illegal meeting taking place in that house that day, and humourlessly the constable was forced to agree with him and thus ordered the band to depart the house.

When Woodward was told that the operation had been unsuccessful he went into a great fit of temper, threatening all the members of the law-keeping party. When his rage subsided a little he ordered his men to return to Potter's farm, but this time one of his servants would accompany them. When the group reached the farm they found Richard already outside, as if he were expecting their return. This time the priest's servant directed the operation and, on the advice of Woodward, had a search of the grounds made, including the barn. Yet again they were unsuccessful.

At this point the meeting was coming to a close. Thomas Briggs had already summed up his sermon and George Fox was now delivering his speech, full of the enthusiasm which the large gathering had installed in him. When Fox had ended his delivery the Quakers were made aware of a great disturbance in the yard below, and the meeting was reduced to silence once more.

When the enforcers had left the farm for the second time Richard Potter waited for a while before climbing the stairs to give notice that it was safe for the Quakers to come out of hiding. One by one the assembly descended into the house, and bade their farewells, for to stay too long would probably cause their undoing if the priest decided to send his men back there once again. Fox and Briggs took leave of the Potters, thanking the brothers for their hospitality and praising the members of the congregation who had made this " a precious, fresh meeting ",[4] before setting off in the direction of Kingsclere and the west.

Those Quakers who had travelled from Berkshire and from Tadley rode in procession northwards along the Newbury road, which meant that they would pass by Woodward's parsonage. As they approached his house, they could see the cleric waiting for them. He was livid, and began to threaten and abuse them as they silently passed him by. There and then he promised he would make them suffer for their success this time. And he made sure that he kept his promise.

IV

"Samuel Burges of the parish of Brimpton in the County of Berks having been a prisoner about a yeer and a halfe, it pleasing the Lord to take away his wife, who in the time of her sickness desired to have her body buryed at Baghurst in that place which Friends had sett apart for that purpose to bury their dead in. And on the 29th day of the 9th Month 1670 being in a Christian manner accompanied with severall Friends, and Neighbours to the burying place, where William Woodward priest of Baghurst with his man Richard Legate, and severall others to assist him, mett Friends, having gotten a Warrant from Nicholas Darrell called a Justice, and with his Assistants stood looking on, taking an account of Friends, untill a Woman spake a few words at the Grave, after the Corps was buryed, whom then threatned, and made a great Stirr, and would have had his Assistants have taken her as a Prisoner, but they being willing to avoid the trouble, lett the Woman passe away, for which the priest exceedingly threatned them. This priest William Woodward did there at that time acknowledge that he himself was the Informer, and some dayes after did with his man Richard Legate and others of his Assistants sweare against Friends before Richard Aylef and Nicholas Darrell called Justices, who having this priest their Informer, and another priest one Houldup stirring them upp, proceeded against our peaceable Christian like Buryall as an unlawful Convinticle, giving it that terme, and so proceeded, as they pretended according to the late Act of Parliament, and fined severall Friends first 20 lb for holding the unlawful Conventicle (as they termed it) which they divided into 3 parts, and layd one part upon Richard Potter, another part upon Sam: Burges, and the other part upon Thomas Buy, who was not at the place at that time. They fined also Richard Potter 10s. more for himselfe and his Wives being present, and Samuel 5s. more, for being present, and severall other Friends 5s. a piece, and seized and took away as followeth. . . ."

(Sufferings, Hants.)

98

SAMUEL BURGIS was the miller of Brimpton in Berkshire, and on a number of occasions he had allowed Brimpton Mill to be used as the alternative meeting-house to Richard Potter's farmhouse in Baughurst, especially when the danger of discovery was imminent. Thus Quaker records described the meeting in the early days as the "Baghurst and Brimpton Meeting", which extended over the civil boundary between the two counties, and therefore allowed the Quakers a limited refuge from the persecuting authorities whose jurisdiction only reached the county line.

On 20th August 1669 Burgis was at Reading, visiting fellow Quakers in the common prison there.[5] He was arrested and detained there until 19th January 1670, when he appeared before the magistrates under a writ of excommunication. Found guilty of the offence, he was sentenced to imprisonment. He had been in Reading Gaol for eighteen months when the news was brought to him that his wife was dying. Therefore the authorities released Burgis on compassionate grounds, under the strict promise that he was to return to prison after his wife's burial.

Mary Burgis died at Brimpton Mill in the November of 1670, just before her husband had arrived home. While on her deathbed she had already made known to the family servant, Andrew Pearson, that her desire was to be buried in Richard Potter's garden next to the meeting-house at Baughurst.

On 29th November the miller's cart brought Mary's crude wooden coffin into Potter's farm where it was unloaded and set down on the ground beside her grave. Already, as dusk was beginning to fall, there were several people gathered around the entrance to the farm. There was a curious mixture of spectators present. Some were fellow Quakers who had come to pay their last respects to the miller's wife and to witness the burial; others were her former friends and neighbours who, although not sharing her religious beliefs, loved and respected this woman; then there were the plain curious who had never witnessed a Quaker ceremony before, and were certain that their visit would be worthwhile, especially as they saw that the parish priest was also approaching with a fair-sized company.

As Mary Burgis' coffin was resting beside the freshly-dug grave, the tension all around was mounting. Woodward, in the company of Parson Holdip from the neighbouring parish of Wolverton, his own servant Richard Leggatt, who had led the second attack on Potter's house during Fox's visit, Thomas Deane the tithingman, and several others of their companions and servants, had walked into the grounds of the farm and had taken up positions at the edge of the burial ground. Since Woodward's failure to catch Fox and the Quakers while their meeting was in progress earlier that year, he had been refused warrants from Nicholas Darrell, the justice, for fear of bringing his office into disrepute. This time, however, he had had witnesses and other informers to testify that there was some Quaker activity about to occur in his parish. Reluctantly, Darrell issued Woodward with a warrant, advising him also of the course of action he should undertake.

This time Woodward would not fail. As the ecclesiastics and their companions stood by watching the scene developing, Woodward was asking his confederates for the names of as many as possible of those people gathered around the coffin, and it mattered little if they were Quakers or not. As each name was being related to him the rector of Baughurst scrawled them down on to a loose piece of parchment which he had been carrying for the occasion. This was to be used later as evidence against the members of the unlawful assembly.

The coffin was being lowered into its grave as Woodward and his men were taking account of those present. One by one the mourners filed past the shallow grave, carefully keeping their thoughts and prayers to themselves in the knowledge that the watching Anglican group would quickly interpret this last homage as a religious meeting. Silently the funeral continued under the watchful eyes of the opposing group. The tension was mounting more and more as the mourners silently worded their farewells and prayers, and as Woodward and his cronies listened intently for any murmur to come from the grieving friends, neighbours and relatives, while the light was fast failing. As more and more shadowy figures filed past the new grave the group at the edge of the cemetery grew more restless, yet afraid to speak lest they drowned words spoken in emotion from the graveside.

Then at last their opportunity came when a woman — one of Mary Burgis' neighbours — offered a short audible prayer to her deceased friend. Woodward could not contain himself any longer. He broke forth and raced to the graveside where he threatened the woman that he should have her taken before the justices for being present at an illegal conventicle. Woodward soon caused a great stir in the burial ground, and he was shouting to his companions, ordering them to arrest the woman who dared to speak. Yet his assistants would not move from their place at the edge of the cemetery, and again Woodward was screaming at them in a rage which made even the Quakers standing nearby tremble. He was now threatening Deane and Leggatt that they were obstructing the course of law and would pay for it. Even Parson Holdip was threatening his companions. And during the mêlée the unknown woman who had caused the disturbance had slipped away from the farm and out of sight.

At last Woodward had calmed down sufficiently enough to threaten the

Quaker group with legal action. He called out the names of several of the people whom he had noted down and told those remaining that he held a warrant issued by Justice Darrell and that he himself had informed the justice about the illegal conventicle which was operating there. With that he ordered the arrest of the recorded members of the assembly, and the company with him uncovered their arms and weapons and advanced upon the waiting Quakers. There was no attempt at all to flee the site nor to resist arrest. Woodward was well satisfied with the episode, and would soon bring those responsible to justice.

V

"Samuel Burges living in the county of Berks, which being out of the Liberty of the aforesaid Justices, they sent a Certificate to John Kingsmill called a Justice, and serves for both Countyes, who when he had sent forth his warrant for the levying of the said Fine on the goods of Samuel Burges; Thomas Worrall priest of the parish of Brimpton was very diligent to put forward the worke, for he sent his man with the Messenger that brought the warrant to see him deliver it to the Constable that it might be putt in Execution. And when one of the Officers pleaded with him (vizt) ye priest, That the Man was a prisoner, and his wife being dead, and said that, if wee take that little goods there is, the Children might come to the parish, for what we knew, and told him that he was the Minister of the parish, and should be a good example to them, after a scoffing and rageing manner, said he did not care for that, but threatned that he would make it cost them 5 lb a man (and much more to that effect) if they did not distrain. Observe the wickedness and unmercifulness of this priest, who first occasioned that Samuel Burges after a perpetuall manner to be imprisoned, and now with such eagerness to endeavour his utter ruine by stirring upp the Officers to such a worke, and they (vizt) Richard Blyth, Richard Mihill, and Edward Penbrook being doubtless willing to be drawne by him, as many appear by their excessive practices therein, for they took away all the Cowes that Samuel Burges had that gave milk, although they knew that he had a young Child that was motherless, and as it were Fatherless, and took away his Mare, as it was coming from Newberry Markett hard loaded, and would not lett his servants have her to draw the Load home, although they were within halfe a Mile of it, so that they were forct to borrow another horse in his stead; which was a griefe to some Neighbours to behold, and many of them do conclude, that they were glad with the worke that they might be spending it upon their lust."

(Sufferings, Hants.)

AT THE BEGINNING of December, 1670, Thomas Bye was arrested and brought before the justices Richard Ayliffe and Nicholas Darrell for attending the illegal conventicle at Baughurst on 29th November. Appearing with him before the local magistrates were Richard Potter, Samuel Burgis, Thomas May, and William Bye, with a few others. Each person was fined five shillings for attending the conventicle, while Potter, Burgis and Thomas Bye were also fined twenty pounds between them for holding the meeting. There was enough evidence laid against them as Woodward, Holdip and Leggatt were there with several others of the witnesses to testify that they had actually watched the illegal conventicle in progress, even though the accused would rather describe it as a peaceful Christian burial. After the proceedings had ended the prisoners were released, with the exception of Burgis who was at the time a convict serving his sentence at Reading Prison. While the miller of Brimpton was being escorted back to the Berkshire town, the others were returned to their homes. Some of the fines were paid promptly, but by the middle of December those of Potter, Burgis, May and William Bye were still outstanding, and attempts were then made by the authorities to retrieve them. At the same time Thomas Bye had paid his fine although the accused all swore that this man was not even attending the burial at the time.[6]

On 21st December 1670 Richard Potter's fine of £7 3s. 4d., which consisted of his part of the £20 fine and five shillings each levied upon himself and his wife, had not been paid, and that day he received a visit from Peter Hine and Robert Guest, the churchwardens of Baughurst, together with James Greene and Richard White, the overseers of the poor for that parish. The quartet entered into his farm and drove away from it sixteen sheep and a fat heifer, which were later sold for over £8 10s. Thus Potter's debt was redeemed.

On 17th January 1671 Thomas May of Ecchinswell received a visit from Robert Allen, the tithingman, William Walter, the chapel warden, and Nicholas Winkworth and Richard Benner, the overseers of the poor, who took from his house an iron weight of 28 lb, an iron pot, pothooks, a spit, and a warming-iron (to warm beer). These articles were taken in compensation of the five shillings for which he was fined, and they were then sold for over eight shillings.

About the same time William Bye of Tadley was visited by Thomas Faulkner, the tithingman, Thomas Simpson, the churchwarden, and Thomas Prior, the overseer. They took from his smallholding a hog which was later sold for about eight shillings, thus making a profit over and above the five shillings outstanding.

It was, however, Samuel Burgis the miller of Brimpton who was to suffer the most. Not only had he lost his wife and was deprived of his freedom, but he was to suffer the loss of most of his valuable possessions during his absence from his home. As he lived in Berkshire he was outside the jurisdiction of Ayliffe and Darrell, the justices who had dealt with his "crime". Therefore an application had to be sent to John Kingsmill, a magistrate who served for the border districts, and whose authority was thus extended into Berkshire. Kingsmill, whose seat was at Sidmonton Court, immediately issued a warrant and dispatched his messenger to the parsonage at Brimpton.

Thomas Worrell, the parish priest of Brimpton, was most enthusiastic to heap further misery upon the erring miller, for he had been instrumental in having Burgis imprisoned in the first instance. Therefore he eagerly sent his church-warden, Richard Myhill, with Kingsmill's messenger to the home of Richard Blythe, the constable for the parish, to make sure that the warrant was delivered.

Soon afterwards the parish officers were assembled at the parsonage. Worrell insisted upon the immediate action against Burgis and his surviving family, but was met with protests from Edward Pembroke, the overseer of the poor. Pembroke argued that as Burgis was already a prisoner, and his wife was dead, if what little goods that the man had left were taken then his children would become the responsibility of the parish. Furthermore, he stated that Worrell should set a good example to them all. Parson Worrell was infuriated by his overseer's last remark and turned on the officers, threatening that he would report them to Kingsmill for refusing to execute the warrant — for which they would surely be fined five pounds apiece.

On 9th January 1671 the three parish officers, under threat of being reported, entered Brimpton Mill and took away from the property three cows worth about eleven pounds.

Already the fine which Burgis owed had been paid and more besides. Yet on 16th February 1671 Worrell ordered his officers to return to Brimpton Mill for further booty. This time, however, Pembroke utterly refused, as the thought of the poor children was racking his conscience. For his humanity he was fined five pounds because he had refused to persecute offenders of the Conventicle Act.

Meanwhile Blythe and Myhill did not go to Brimpton Mill, as they had already found out that nobody was at home, and the servants were at Newbury market. They met Burgis' men on the road out of Newbury, as the servants were returning home with the miller's cart fully laden with produce being at the market. Despite the protests of Andrew Pearson, Burgis' oldest retainer, the parish officers there and then uncoupled the mare from the cart and led the animal away. The servants were left stranded in the middle of the road with a loaded cart but nothing to drive it, and their home was half a mile away. However, the younger servants were able to run into Brimpton and explain the situation to the miller's neighbours, who rallied around and loaned the stranded retainers a horse with which the cart and its contents could be pulled home.

Burgis' mare was sold for the price of five pounds. His cows, which had provided milk for his youngest child, who was merely a baby, were valued at eleven pounds. In monetary value Burgis had lost goods worth sixteen pounds when his fine had been set at no more than £6 18s. 4d., that is a third of the £20 fine levied for holding a conventicle, plus the five shillings. He was still a convict and now a widower, and after his release from prison he was to suffer more persecutions at the hands of Parson Worrell. Woodward and Worrell had been well satisfied with the proceedings. Conformity had won the day.

The situation for the Quakers in Baughurst was now extremely dangerous, for Woodward was now encouraged by his success to continue his crusade. The meetings were now being held regularly in secret in the loft of Richard Potter's house, but even then the Quakers could not be sure for how long these clandestine assemblies could continue before they were discovered. At the same time burials were kept to a minimum for fear of attracting unwanted spectators, and when the occasion arose the Quaker deceased was either buried in his own garden or, if he willed to be buried in the cemetery next to the meeting-house then the interment would have to take place during the late hours of darkness. The Quakers were thus being driven underground, even in the rural districts.

Quaker Burials at Baughurst 1669-1671

(4) MARY MAY, daughter of Thomas May of Ichingswell, at Baughurst, October 17, 1669

(5) SIBBALL PILGRUN, wife of Thomas Pilgrun of Midgeam, at Baughurst, January 11, 1670

(6)   SARAH APPLETON, daughter of William Appleton of Tadly, at
      Baghurst, January 19, 1670
(7)   MARY BURGIS, wife of Samuell Burgis of Brimpton Co. Berks,
      at Baghurst, November 29, 1670

(The above entries are from the digests for Hampshire)

[1] Sufferings, Hants.
[2] Sufferings, Hants.
[3] Cragg, p. 18.
[4] Fox, p. 568.
[5] Sufferings, Berks.
[6] Sufferings, Hants.

DISSENTERS BEING LED TO PRISON BY ARMED
CONSTABLES FOR ATTENDING A CONVENTICLE.

*'Met several poor creatures carried by, by Constables for being at a
Conventicle. They go like Lambs without resistance. I would to God they
would either conform or be more wise, and not be catched.' Pepys Diary.*

CHAPTER FIVE
1671-1675

I

"James Potter Ann Potter and Charles Whitacer were served wth a warrant from the Sheriffe by Richard Hood a Bayliffe, and at the Assises following being the 2 day of the 6 month 1671 were by him delivered into the hands of the keeper of the Common Goale at Winton to answere to certaine Riots Contempts Trespasses and such like before the kings Justices of the peace at that prsent Assises but being kept in prison all the time of the Assises and not had forth, and the Judg being Informed of it, who shewing dislike of their uniust keeping them privatly in Prison and reproveing som of them, they were the next day after the Assises set at liberty by the Goaler.

And the next Assises following James Potter Charles Whitacer and Thomas May being served againe wth a sheriffs warrant were likewise delivered prisoners to the said Jayler to answere to such things as afore written at ye prsent Assises it beginning the 29th of the 12th month 1671 and being not had forth, as other prisoners were, James Potter asked the Goaler when they should bee had forth, who said not at all, but that they might goe wth him to Mr Swanson (as he called him) and make agreemt wth him and they might have their liberty, and more to yt purpose; so by yt and other passages it appeared yt Swanson the Clarke of the Assises was the cause of their Imprisonmt to get money as was common wth him so to deale with Presbiters and other pfessors but his unrighteous way and practise being denyed and testifyed agst they were againe set at liberty by the Gaoler of the Assises."

(Sufferings, Hants.)

THERE WERE A few significant absentees from the incident surrounding Mary Burgis' burial. If James Potter or his sister had attended the funeral then Woodward would have surely seen that they, too, were brought to justice. As it was, James and Ann were not even in the district at the time.

Since Fox's visit in the summer of 1670 James and Ann had been employed in the business of spreading the founder's word throughout the more isolated regions of the county — the places where Fox himself could not go because of the pressures of his work. The younger Potters had had quite a long serious discussion with the Quaker leader over how they could best serve their faith, and Fox had convinced them of his need for "evangelists" to take his word into the hamlets and villages he was unable to visit personally through the extraordinary demands upon him.

Therefore the Potters, accompanied by Charles Whitacre, toured the Hampshire countryside, spreading their beloved faith wherever they could. In many districts they were met with severe hostility and confronted with open abuse, yet occasionally they gained new recruits to their ranks and were welcomed and feasted by those who had already succumbed to the "Inner Light" doctrine. More often than not, though, they were eventually run out of the district by the violent mobs which held sway over the people there, only to return defiantly when the general outcry had subsided. For almost a year they were occupied with their missionary expeditions — at times crossing the county borders into Surrey, Berkshire and Wiltshire — and it was only a matter of time before their reputations preceded them into the districts which they were due to visit.

The cry would be raised that the Quakers were coming, and the children would scatter to the safety of their homes. Vigilantes would bar their entry into the village, and the trio were forced to retreat until they could find a less obvious route into the settlement. Meanwhile the authorities had been warned of their presence and warrants were issued from the Sheriff's Court to detain them in prison. As the small band of missionaries proceeded along the overgrown lanes of the Hampshire interior, they were gradually riding further and further into trouble.

The way into the next village was not barred to them, and they reluctantly spurred their horses onward, sensing the trouble ahead. They dismounted at the village green where several inhabitants were busily engrossed in the gossip of the day, or the product of their hard labour in the fields. Immediately the Quakers began to preach to the disinterested crowd, but their words were drowned by the sudden clattering of horses' hooves along the flint-covered path to the church. They were completely surrounded by cavalrymen who barred their escape. Then a figure pushed his way through the dense throng and stood there while he unrolled a parchment bearing an official seal at its foot. Thus Richard Hood, the Bailiff of Winchester, read to the Quakers the warrant which had been issued by the Sheriff of Hampshire. They were arrested for "certain riots, contempts and trespasses" and escorted to Winchester where they were handed over to the Gaoler of the common prison in Jewry Street.[1]

It was the first day of the Assizes, 2nd August 1671, when the Quaker missionaries had been placed in prison, and less than ten years since James Potter had been released from the same establishment. He was rather reluctant to renew his acquaintance with the awesome building. But now, as he viewed his future with some trepidation, he had the added burden that his sister would not be able to bear the strain of a long imprisonment. Ann's health had been broken by the arduous journeys and the months spent in the open with damp clothing clinging to her skin; by the many sleepless nights as the raw wind whistled around their heads, and by the countless days when they received constant and violent abuse from the ignorant mobs. Yet she had continuously refused to give up, and doggedly forced herself onwards to sustain more abuse for her beliefs. At last they had shelter but the weeks and possibly months which lay ahead in that cold, dark and smelly prison might prove to be too much for the frail body of Ann Potter. She had already endured six months of confinement at Cheney Court back in the days of the Commonwealth, and she was much younger and fitter then. James' present priority was the release of his ailing sister. He began to complain to the gaoler but with little success.

It was the last day of the Assizes and James' complaints were still being ignored. By that time he had frequently pestered the gaoler's assistants with questions, and had become well-known to the other prisoners as a man who would never surrender. Therefore James found a general acquiescence with his fellow cellmates, who were equally concerned with Ann's worsening condition. It was easy to persuade those prisoners who were due to come to trial to pass on a message concerning the injustice which was currently occurring in Jewry Street Prison, for the Potters and Whitacre were not on the list for the Assizes, a fact which had become blatantly clear as the days had passed.

Yet prisoner after prisoner faced the assize judge and never spoke of the Potters' plight, generally out of fear rather than forgetfulness. It would appear that the Quakers would have remained in prison indefinitely without coming to trial if it had not been for one prisoner who had found the courage to speak up and complain in the presence of his judge about misdemeanours occurring in the city's common gaol. He passed Potter's letter to the honourable gentleman and the justice instigated an enquiry into the complaints as soon as the Assizes were over. Several of the court officials were brought to the judge's chambers and there reprimanded severely for omitting the prisoners from the list of those awaiting trial. The judge decided that it was a gross miscarriage of justice, and wrote a letter to the gaoler ordering the release of the Quakers the following morning. Thus the Potters had triumphed again, this time with the backing of one of the higher members of the legal profession. A cart was hired and the trio were driven home to Baughurst, with James nursing his weak sister throughout the journey.

For a short while James was content with managing the affairs of his copyhold tenant, Joan Spencer. But James soon lost interest in farming for a living and reverted back to the agreement that he had had with his brother prior to leaving Baughurst and setting out upon his missionary travels. Richard, the more practical member of the family, would farm the Spencer estate together with his own and, to all intents and purposes, both estates would be treated as one, and thus run more efficiently and economically. Meanwhile the cost of the rents and profits from the amalgamated business would be shared. This was beneficial to all the parties concerned, for Richard was able to expand his farming interests, and would be compensated in times of hardship or persecution. Joan Spencer was satisfied that her land was being farmed efficiently, and James was now free to concentrate on those things which interested him most — for example, the extension of his faith.

All too soon James Potter was feeling restless again. As the summer warmth gave way to the autumn chill he realised that he had to be on his way in order to spread the word of his leader throughout the countryside. He rode over to Ecchinswell to summon Charles Whitacre, who was more than ready to set out on their travels again. Ann Potter was not coming with them this time for, although she had recovered sufficiently from the ordeals of the first tour, she was not completely in good health. Despite her protests, her brother insisted that she remained at home.

Therefore, another had to be recruited to fill her place. Thomas May of Ecchinswell, who had been one of the unfortunates recognised by Woodward's cronies while he attended the funeral of Mary Burgis, did not need much persuasion to join Potter and Whitacre on their missions. The arrangements were speedily made, and directly the next meeting had finished James and his companions bade their farewells to their loved ones.

As the fearless trio proceeded along their way they encountered many adventures. They travelled into Berkshire, Surrey and even approached the capital. Yet again and again the violence and abuse which they had suffered earlier that year was repeated in differing settings. James made a point, however, of visiting the hamlet of Ashney in the parish of Bishop's Waltham near Southampton, where the Barefoot family made him and his fellow travellers particularly welcome. Potter was especially attracted to that home because of one of the younger Barefoot daughters, whose name was Margery. Time and time again he would visit their cottage until eventually he had summoned up the courage to ask for Margery's hand. However, for the time being the itinerant Quakers dared not linger there for too long. There was a great deal of work to do.

The appearance of missionary Quakers in the neighbourhood caused the alarm to spread through adjoining villages, which, in turn, alerted the authorities to the same menace that had disturbed the peace and tranquillity of the Hampshire countryside the previous year. In 1672 the writ against Potter and his friends was still in evidence. At all moments they were in danger. In that February history repeated itself, and the three Quaker evangelists were escorted to the common gaol at Winchester to await their trial at the forthcoming Assizes, as they believed. For Potter and Whitacre it was akin to reliving their experience of the previous Assize session. They had come to know what to expect, and were not the least surprised to find that nothing had radically altered in their treatment.

The Assizes began on 29th February 1672[2] and once again the Quaker prisoners were never summoned to face trial. But Potter would not let matters rest and continuously badgered the gaoler's assistants to allow him to see their master personally. Eventually, the Quaker spokesman was able to talk to the gaoler in private, where he asked the turnkey when he and his companions would appear in court. The gaoler laughed aloud in the prisoner's face and retorted that the three dissenters would not appear before the judge at all, and with that began to walk away. Potter grabbed the keeper by the arm and pulled him roughly towards him, demanding that he explain the meaning of his words. The gaoler laughed again and then told him, sneeringly, that Mr Swanson was the man to see. When James asked him who Mr Swanson was, the gaoler told him that he was the Clerk of the Assizes — the man who determined the fate of the prisoners in that locked establishment. He would willingly take Potter and his cronies to see Mr Swanson, and assured him that if the Quakers could make an agreement with the Clerk then they would likely be set free. With that Potter returned to his companions to discuss the new development.

Before long the gaoler was summoned to the prisoners' quarters where the Quakers requested that they should see Mr Swanson. The gaoler left the Jewry Street Prison soon afterwards, to return after nightfall with permission to grant Potter and his confederates an audience with the Clerk of the Assizes.

110

Mr Swanson sat at his desk next to the judges' chambers, attired in his court robes and long powdered wig. Pince-nez spectacles adorned his thin and sallow face and his eyes suspiciously glanced over the forms of the three chained men before him, flanked by the gaoler and one of his most trustworthy assistants. Swanson was reluctant to talk to the Quakers at first, but his egotism soon got the better of him and he began to threaten the prisoners with a long imprisonment unless they made an "agreement" with him. The so-called "agreement" was that their liberty could be purchased from the Clerk and no more would be said of their crime. The three nonconformists heard the official out without uttering a word, and as they made no criticism of his designs he began to boast that he had often made similar agreements with Presbyterians and other nonconformists.

When he had finally outlined his scheme, he sat back in his chair and surveyed the passive faces before him. Potter looked knowingly at his friends and then confronted Swanson with an emphatic negative to his proposal. Swanson was furious that such unfortunates could deny his help, for he had never experienced such behaviour until now. The gaoler and his accomplice made a grab for the Quakers but Potter had, by that time, forced the door open with much difficulty and was now shouting at the top of his voice for assistance. A group of court officials arrived on the scene almost immediately to see what all the commotion was about, but despite the insistence of the gaoler and Swanson that nothing was wrong they would not leave, owing to the attempt of the gaoler's assistant to gag Potter. Whitacre demanded that they should inform the judge that there was injustice being perpetrated in his presence, and eventually the justice was notified. He demanded that the Quakers were to be brought to his chambers, and once there they related to him the whole episode. Swanson was called to the chambers in order to relate his side of the story, but the judge was not convinced by the Clerk's tale. The whole situation appeared suspect, for there was no other plausible reason why prisoners who were not even listed at the Assizes (which in itself was unjust) would be escorted by prison officers to the Clerk's room, other than for an illegal exaction. Therefore the judge ordered the gaoler to free his Quaker prisoners.

As the party journeyed back towards Baughurst Potter promised his fearless companions that he would, if he could, fight for the cause of Quakerism in the courts of Hampshire, and would represent his unfortunate fellow-religionists whenever and wherever he could, for his experiences in Jewry Street Prison and the corruption of the law which caused so much distress there should not be repeated. From that moment James Potter began to take an interest in the law of the land as a means to defend his co-religionists against those corrupt individuals who

111

manipulated it for their own ends. He would become the Quakers' advocate and would speak for those who were unable to protect themselves from arbitrary practitioners. The study of the law now became his personal aim, along with the fulfilment of his faith.

James Potter's period as the missionary for his faith was now over. When he had finally returned home to Baughurst one of his first acts was to record his experiences of the last year or so. Ann was particularly interested in the most recent episodes. She persuaded him to give up missionary work and to involve himself in the business side of their faith, as the representative of the Baughurst meeting at monthly and quarterly meeting level. Ann was a great friend to her brother, and, on her advice, he began to pursue a more meaningful career.

II

"Our care and endeavours for the preservation of the rights and interests of the Church have been sufficiently manifested to the world by the whole course of our government since our happy restoration, and by the many and frequent ways of coercion that we have used for reducing all erring or dissenting persons, and for composing the unhappy differences in matters of religion which we found among our subjects upon our return. But it being evident by the sad experience of twelve years that there is very little fruit of all those forcible courses, we think ourself obliged to make use of that supreme power in ecclesiastical matters which is not only inherent in us but hath been declared and recognized to be by several statutes and Acts of Parliament. And therefore we do now accordingly issue this our declaration, as well for the quieting the minds of our good subjects in these points, for inviting strangers in this conjuncture to come and live under us, and for the better encouragement of all to a cheerful following of their trade and callings, from whence we hope by the blessing of God to have many good and happy advantages to our government, as also for preventing for the future the danger that might otherwise arise from private meetings and seditious conventicles. . . ."

(Declaration of Indulgence, 1672: 15. March 24 Chas II)

CHARLES II had prorogued Parliament in the February of 1671, after he had been granted the much-needed subsidy which he required at the time to govern his realm. Now he intended to rule without recourse to the troublesome assembly and his independence was maintained with the substantial pension which he received from his cousin, Louis XIV of France. The French pension was agreed upon with various other commitments at the so-called "Secret Treaty of Dover" in 1670. These unpublished conditions included the clauses that Charles was to give his military support to the French king, while at some unspecified time he was to bring his kingdom back into the Roman Catholic fold under the Papacy. In short, Charles was required to establish an autocratic monarchy on the lines already practised by Louis. In order to do this the constitutional assembly had to be suppressed, which was best enabled by putting it out of action, as Charles' father had done so for eleven years, over forty years beforehand.

In 1672 Willem III, hereditary Prince of Orange, gained the ascendancy in the United Provinces (Holland) and began to threaten the power of his Bourbon neighbour, Louis XIV. In March of that year Charles II declared war on the Dutch, in support of his cousin, and simultaneously on the fifteenth of that same month issued his second Declaration of Indulgence in favour of his dissenting subjects.

The Declaration of Indulgence has received more attention from historians than the actual declaration of war against the Calvinist Dutch. The reason for this is quite simple, as the religious declaration affected the common people of England more than the resumption of hostilities, and altered the stance of the Protestant nonconformists so acutely in their favour that the way was made easier for religious toleration to become a fact of the future.

Several theories have been applied to Charles' timing of his Indulgence. It may have been that such a grant of toleration was necessary while England was at war with Holland. The Dutch were Calvinists and so were the majority of the English Protestant dissenters, and the King did not need an attempted rising by those who felt more loyalty towards their co-religionists than to their fellow countrymen. Therefore it was politically astute to grant these possible rebels freedom to worship as they pleased.

At the same time it has been said that Charles did not intend to allow his Protestant subjects wholesale toleration but was forced to do so in order that the Catholics could similarly be liberated from the persecuting laws which confounded their activities. The next major step would have been the general Catholicisation of the realm. Yet some historians, in fact the majority of them, believe that Charles never intended to create a Catholic state at all, but as an astute diplomat and great statesman merely strung

Louis along in order to become financially solvent with the large French pension. Whatever reason Charles may have had for issuing his legal document, he surely needed the support of his dissenting subjects.

Charles' self-proclaimed reason was that, despite several attempts at persecution by statute, nonconformity was still as strong, if not more so than it had been. The opening sentences of the Declaration stated in the most cogent terms the futility of persecution. Charles had seen that, instead of uniting the people, the recent Acts of Parliament had divided them more, and the threat of civil unrest was always present. Charles, by his 1672 Declaration, was reiterating his declarations of 1660 and 1662, and it appears that he was most sincere in wishing for religious toleration, although his motives for such were never clear.

The Cavalier Parliament, being predominantly of High Church membership, would never allow complete religious toleration at the expense of the Anglican Church. Therefore that assembly had to be dismissed if Charles was to get his way. Immediately the King began to use the dispensing and suspending powers which he believed to have been inherent in the monarchy's prerogative, for in March 1672 he did not visualise that a resummoned Parliament would be as powerful a body as the one he had just prorogued.

With his ecclesiastical dispensing power intact and unopposed by constitutional argument, Charles announced to his subjects that all penal laws against nonconformists would be suspended upon certain conditions being followed. Roman Catholics were allowed to worship freely and unhindered in their own homes; Protestant dissenters were free to meet in public provided that they secured special licences both for their minister and for their place of worship. Now nonconformity was legal provided that a licence had been granted. Those who refused to apply for registration stood outside the law and would thus be persecuted as the penal laws were merely suspended for those who acquiesced to licensing.

Among the nonconformists the reaction to the Declaration was mixed. The concessions granted to the Catholics caused some concern, and there was considerable doubt about the validity of the King's use of his dispensing power, and therefore of the Declaration itself. Whatever the rights or wrongs of the constitutional position, the Commons would certainly dispute the King's claim, and when Parliament reassembled the beneficiaries of the King's Indulgence would probably suffer. But despite the question of legality tied up in the constitutional argument the offer of indulgence was an opportunity for the dissenters which it would seem foolish to decline, and there were many who were not the least concerned with the constitutional problem.

After years of enforced silence the dissenters now found that they were being given full liberty to preach and to worship, merely by applying for a licence to do so. Within ten months three and a half thousand licences were granted and many nonconformist groups date their existence from the time of Charles' grant of toleration in 1672. Only two groups refused to apply for these liberating pieces of paper — the Anabaptists and the Quakers. The Quakers ignored the Declaration, saying that the King had no more right to concede freedom of worship than he had to withhold it. Yet many of the Quaker written records started in 1672. That is because, although the Quakers refused to acknowledge such a remarkably benevolent act, they could not disguise the fact that the Indulgence did create a much more peaceful atmosphere, where nonconformists felt that they were safe and secure.

The Declaration of Indulgence was followed by a pardon being granted to those poor unfortunates who were in prison for religious "crimes". By George Whitehead's mediation the royal pardon was granted to 471 Quakers currently incarcerated. Others, including John Bunyan, who had been in prison for the last twelve years, were released on the advice of leading Quakers.

Therefore, Samuel Burgis of Brimpton Mill was released from Reading Gaol, where he had been residing since 1669, and with him Ann Greenaway. The couple were married at the meeting-house in Reading on 13th July that year,[3] less than two years after Burgis had lost his first wife, who was buried at Baughurst. Ann Burgis subsequently died in 1684 and was buried at Oarlfields in Reading.

So, even in Quaker circles the Declaration of Indulgence marked the dawn of a new era. At last, peace reigned over the kingdom for a while as the country itself was officially at war with the Dutch. The justices and local law enforcers were confused as to which policy to pursue, and, generally, decided to let matters rest until their doubts had subsided. Even the most hostile of the persecuting clergy found that it was probably more politic to ignore the presence of nonconformists in their parish, and were rather unsure whether or not they were legal or illegal worshippers. At last there was very little to disturb the apparent tranquillity which now covered the towns and villages of Restoration England since religion had been removed as a vital issue.

James Potter pursued his career in the administration of the Baughurst meeting, while representing his district at the higher levels. He also became more acquainted with the laws of the land, despite his lack of legal training. All in all, he was quickly gaining a reputation for himself which would become useful in later years.

Therefore, James would have been what could properly be described as an eligible bachelor. He had been accepted into the Barefoot home near Bishop's Waltham, and was now asking Margery's father for her hand in marriage. After the respectable period of "courting" under a chaperone, and Barefoot's assent to Potter's request, the couple sought the advice and permission of the members of the Alton Monthly Meeting. Their case was then discussed and queries were made over their "freedom" to marry. By late December they had been "liberated" by the monthly meeting and on the 26th of that month were united in marriage in the meeting-house at Alton. And, of course, James received a moderate dowry from Margery's father.

James Potter and his wife lived in Joan Spencer's cottage at Baughurst as James was the old woman's copyhold heir and would, one day, inherit the estate. In the meantime Ann Potter had already moved out and was living at Old Alresford. She married William Browne from Uffington the following year (1st March 1673), which was witnessed by her brothers among others, at the meeting-house in Alresford, but she did not live long. She was buried in the Quaker cemetery attached to the Alton meeting on 19th April 1677.[4]

James and Margery Potter had two children. Elizabeth, unfortunately, died young in 1675, and Mary, who was born on 3rd October 1676, was James' sole heir.

So, the Potters were married at a time when persecution had relaxed. The Indian summer of toleration, however, was brief. The respite was to end almost as suddenly as it had begun and toleration would again become a thing of the past — a memory of what could have been.

Charles II's Dutch War had been an expensive affair, despite the French subsidy, and had left the King in considerable debt. In the February of 1673 he was left with no alternative but to summon Parliament once again. As soon as the Commons had reassembled a constitutional battle ensued, as the honourable members began to attack the King's arbitrary use of his ecclesiastical powers to suspend and dispense with the statutes which had been passed through Parliament. The King was in no position to force the issue, for, despite his critical financial standing at the time, the issues involved could spark off civil war again since they were reminiscent of those of 1640, when his father was in the same position.

Charles, being the true diplomat that he was, conceded to his opponents and cancelled his Declaration of Indulgence. Overnight the dissenters had been pushed back into the position that they had held before the Declaration — that is, being persecuted. The licences which they had been granted under royal patronage were now useless. Yet even here the justices were divided and more confused than they had been in 1672. Were the licences legal or not? This issue prevented the union of a policy between the law judges all over the kingdom. While some were sympathetic to the dissenters' plight and, at the same time, were attempting to be impartial in their decisions, others were undoubtedly hostile to the poor nonconformists and had previously despaired of the King's promise of toleration to those who were deemed as seditious.

The nonconformists themselves had been affected by the change of plans. They had entered the situation of 1672 with suspicion, but had now grown accustomed to the peace which toleration had brought, and had grown secure enough to establish their underground activities as open and legal meetings. They had been granted toleration, but now were denied that which they had been given. They would become more forceful in their cry for more.

Then there were their neighbours who had been told that these people were the enemies of the State — seditious rebels, amongst other descriptions. They had found that in their own experiences these so-called "rebels" were no different from themselves. Some dissenting faiths actually bred upright and honest, hard-working people. The Quakers had earned this reputation already. These people presented no real threat to the community at large. In most cases they wanted to be left alone to worship as they pleased. Now they were illegal once more. With utter dismay many common folk shrugged their shoulders at the situation. It appeared to them that the sectarian was on a continuous see-saw. As toleration ended the Quakers found that they had more support from the people.

III

"Richard Wigg of Presson Candaver was complaned of for unsavoury walking and Freinds desire Robert Streater and Edward Coxhead to speak wth him and to admonish him and bring his answer next monthly meeting (13. Oct. 1673)

The Answer concerning Richard Wiggs unsavoury walking is her inserted he being accused of drunknes saied he was but merry and being further informed of his selling strongwater at his house on first dayes bringing disorder to his houshold and dishonour to god Freinds desires Robert Streater and Cocksheads of Alsford to speake wth him and bring his answer next meeting (10. Nov. 1673)

117

At this meeting none of Alsford came to give account of Richard Wigg at this meeting
(15. Dec. 1673)

Richard Wigg of presson Candavar hath been spoken to concerning his disorderly walking by Robert Streater and Edward Coxhead but seemeth to Justifie himselfe and deny ye accusations laied against him
(12. Jan. 1674)

Receved an account that Richard Wigg keeps disorder in his house and it is desired that John Wiggs wife do com next monthly meeting and give Freinds a further account
(9. Feb. 1674)

Richard Wiggs disorderly walking was laied before Freinds againe and it was desired that Anthony Parr and Robert Streater admonish him concerning it and bring his answer next monthly meeting
(13. July 1674)

Then Received an account from Robert Streater concerning Richard Wigg his disorderly walking and he hath promised it shall be so no more
(10 Aug. 1674)

A testimony given against Richard Wigg and his wife: Wee the people of God called quakers having often been made acquainted that Richard Wigg and his wife of Presson candavar have and do allow and suffer people to drinke strong waters in theire house till they be drunke and they have been often admonished and desired to leave it off and deny it but from time to time it is still continued to our greate greife wherefore wee do desire all people to take notice that wee doo utterly disallow of such doings and have no fellowship with them in so doing suscribed by us the day and yeare aforsaied
(14. Dec. 1674)

(Men's Minutes, Alton Monthly Meeting)

JAMES POTTER attended monthly meetings at Alton as often as he possibly could after his return from his missions in 1672. On rare occasions, as in 1674 and 1678, he was accompanied by his brother. James, as the representative for the Baughurst Meeting, kept that district clearly to the forefront of his dealings with the other representatives of local meetings who assembled at Alton every month.

The topics under discussion were various, although pertaining always to their common faith. Yet the most frequent problems which beset the Quakers in those days were to do with the members' human failings, and not so much to do with their sufferings. The two most notable problems were recorded in the Men's Minutes of the Alton Monthly Meeting.[5]

The problem of drunkenness raised itself in the account of Richard Wigg of Preston Candover. For over a year the Quakers discussed what to do with Wigg because of his love of alcohol. At the meeting of the 13th October 1673 attention was first drawn to Wigg's "unsavoury walking" which brought disorder to his house and dishonour to the Quakers themselves. Robert Streeter and Edward Coxhead of Alresford were sent to speak with Wigg and to admonish him. Yet, despite his promise to give up drinking, the boozy Quaker continued his supping while selling the liquid to others. In fact, he had turned his house into an alehouse which was attracting a host of unsavoury characters. Again and again Streeter and Coxhead were sent on account of the Alton Monthly Meeting to admonish poor Wigg. Yet again and again he would make promises, but would then be caught out when he was found wandering around in a drunken stupour. His sister-in-law was also sent to talk with him, and then Anthony Parr. Yet still Wigg persisted in his drinking bouts. Finally at the meeting of 14th December 1674 the members of the Alton Monthly Meeting framed a document whereby they denied fellowship with such persons as Richard Wigg, who persisted in drinking alcohol. They had issued their ultimatum, the final coup-de-grâce, and a wayward Quaker had to make a straight choice between alcohol, the root of evil, or the Quaker fellowship. Quakers had strict rules to abide by and these included abstinence, and for a Quaker who was weak in will or spirit these rules were particularly harsh. Wigg was such a Quaker. He had a problem with drink, and also a conscience, otherwise he would not have promised to give up the booze. He was now out in the cold, for the Quaker fellowship meant everything to these people.

The other major problem had to do with marriage. Quaker marriages took place in the meeting-house and were witnessed by the other members. After the declaration of marriage a certificate was issued for evidence if the authorities required it. Certification stemmed from the days of the Republic, when the Church was almost extinct. Quakers therefore frowned upon any association with the Anglican Church. Yet it was becoming more and more evident that in the 1670s there were Quakers who married their partners in a parish church, and this fairly frequent act was alarming the members of the society who were calling themselves "the people of God".

At the meeting of 15th December 1673 at Alton the members received a letter from John Paice:

> "freinds I doe write unto you to let you know how it is with mee I doe confess to you yt I have sinned against you which I do live under great condemnation for it but tis the desire of my heart to be restored out of it againe and freinds I desire to have the meeting next at our house as formerly it have beene if you have freedom and go I with my love to you"

Paice had shown some Quakers a certificate that he had been married by an Anglican priest, and having confessed his "sin", begged their forgiveness. At the meeting it was concluded that William Carter and John Brown of Basingstoke should investigate and see if the certificate was a true one or not. Brown appeared at the next meeting of 12th January 1674 and reported that he interviewed the parish priest concerned and that Paice had definitely been married by him about fifteen months beforehand.[6]

On 9th November 1674 William Knight of Basingstoke reported to the meeting that John Hunt, a basket-maker and formerly of Basingstoke, had married in the Anglican church without the consent of the Quakers "and contrary to ye way of trueth". The members then gave to Knight and Richard Potter the task of talking with Hunt about the accusation. At the next meeting, dated 14th December 1674, Knight and Potter reported that Hunt had been married by an Anglican priest in Berkshire ("beyond Headly") and had no certificate. It was then ordered that Nicholas Roberts and John Brown of Basingstoke should go and try to persuade Hunt to get a certificate (that is, to marry again at the Quaker meeting-house).

The next time Hunt's situation was under discussion was at the meeting which took place at North Warnborough, near Odiham, on 17th July 1675. Here it was acknowledged that no further news had been brought concerning the certificate that Hunt was supposed to have obtained. Therefore William Carter and John Brown were recruited to visit him. On 9th August Carter and Brown reported that Hunt had shown them a certificate that he was married by an Anglican priest. Then it was desired that James Potter and Nicholas Gates should go and speak with Hunt and another called John Cobberde concerning their marriages by Anglican clergymen. No more was reported after that meeting on the topic.

Yet despite the records of certain waywardness among the community the majority of the Quakers were very strong and disciplined in their faith.

Together they created a unit which gave them added strength in their later sufferings. Their strength bonded together their families, and from that central nucleus their strength and determination extended out into their community in general. They had known a short spate of tolerance when their problems focused on the more petty aspects of life. Now, they would know persecution again, and would accept it as a way of life, without complaint.

IV

"The 18th day of the 4th month 1675 came William Woodward preist of Baghurst wth his man Thomas Gosmore, and brought the tithingman and som assistants wth them to Richard Potters howse there being som freinds met togeather, and James Park being praying the preist endevoured to make the Tithingman pull him forth but he being more Civill did forbeare to answer his kinde sprit, soe in short after James had ended praying to ye lord, ye preist after ye maner of yt spirit used unsavory and lying words against freinds ordered ye tithingman to have James before ye Justice ye next morning but being gone forth of ye doore sent words to him he might take his time to goe within 3 or 4 dayes — so ye 5th day following being sett James wth some freinds went to ye tithing man to Justice Fauconers house from whom ye Prist obtained his warrant, where ye Prist and his man were ready to Informe and Ja; being upon his examination ye Prist was very forward to ye Justices office upon him, and to be ye examiner as well as ye Informer and at last gave in his Information in writeing against ye meeting upon his oath and his man also whom he made Informer with him, which as neare as can be remembered, it as followeth vizt.
That ye day above written were together at a Conventicle at Richard Potters house   Rich: and Mary his wife James Parke of ye Parish of Saint Touleys Street in Southwarke marter   John Bye of Reading mealeman, John Gidding of Brimpton Mill   Fardinando Tull of Midgeham   Tho: May of Itchingwell and Willm Apleton   these wth others are ye persons known   ye words spoken by Jas Parke was   keep us in ye holow of thy hand and in ye secret of thy pavilion   and it being

121

these spoken yt these words did manyfest yt they were
spoken in prayers and not in passing he said he did not
know our praying from our watching but if it were
praying it was watching for wh doe yu. pray but to
watch one another to pray — after he had taken his oath
aforesaid Ja: Parke told ye Justice that their was not
notice given according to the order of ye warrant ye Prist
haveing kept ye warrant in his hand more yn a quarter of
a yeare, but ye Prist severall times affirmed yt he had
given ym notice and at last afirmed upon his oath saying
yt upon ye same oath yt I have taken already laying his
hand upon ye booke I gave ym notice by Lawrence
Grantham and John Yeats

James Potter   This is ye very truth as farr as I Can
                                                    remember
Richard Potter   witnes my hand Willm Grene
                                                    tithingman

Now ye partyes Lawrence Grantham and John Yeates
doe deny yt they were Imployed in any such buesynes
nether did they heare of ye warrant till it was put in
execution as by a Certyficat under their hands doth
apeare This Informing Preist this yeare took out of Rich
Potters ground about Halfe a tun of hay together at one
time, 31 Wheatsheaves at another time 59 sheaves, 3
Cockes and part of another of oats and ten Cocks of
barley, beside pease to ye value of 3 lb 10 s or upwards. ''

(Sufferings, Hants.)

WHILE JAMES POTTER was becoming more and more involved in the
business of the Alton Monthly Meeting, events in Baughurst were
occurring with a regularity that made them appear rather commonplace.
Year after year Richard Potter had come to expect the usual invasions into
his farm by the tithe-gatherers on the command of their master, Parson
Woodward, who wished to relieve the yeoman of his hay and corn as
compensation for the dues dictated by law.

The vindictive cleric had to content himself with the plunders while
Charles II's Declaration of Indulgence was in force, for that unconstitu-
tional proclamation had, for a while, stayed any attempt on the part of the
persecuting authorities to hound the nonconformists for religious reasons.
The Quakers were included in the amnesty despite the fact that they had

not even applied for a licence for their meeting-houses. Men like Woodward were now out on a limb, for they would surely attempt to cause distress among their dissenting parishioners if only for the acknowledgement that the Church was supreme in the land. Yet they would receive no help from the justices and magistrates now. They had only their tithe persecutions to fall back upon, and these they pursued relentlessly. But even after the Declaration had been cancelled the justices were wary to prosecute dissenters for religious crimes, lest toleration would become fashionable again as suddenly as it had been rescinded.

Therefore the Quaker meetings in Baughurst continued without too much interference from the Anglicans. As time passed the meetings became more open as the members became more confident that they would not be pestered by informing agents of the parish priest. They were certainly lulled into a false sense of security while Woodward could do little to persuade the authorities that the Quakers were acting illegally.

While the meetings themselves were attracting more regular members, the Quaker burials in Baughurst were being kept down to a minimum in order not to repeat the incident of 1670, when Woodward last triumphed over his Quaker adversaries. On the occasion of death some families preferred that their late relatives to be buried in their own gardens, or transported to the monthly meeting burial-ground at Alton. Between 1673 and 1675 five burials took place at Baughurst, and of these three were private funerals of members of the Potter family. In 1674 Richard and Mary's daughter, Elizabeth, was buried in the plot next to their home; in 1675 Richard's mother-in-law, who had been living with them since her husband's death, was laid to rest in the same plot; and later that year James' first-born, Elizabeth, was placed in the soil there.

Woodward kept an eye on the affairs of Baughurst and noted these funerals with the other two. He had the sense not to pester the Quaker family over what were, in fact, private bereavements, yet his interest was keenly aroused by the activities in the burial-ground next to the meeting-house.

In the February of 1675 he was informed that a burial was about to take place at the Quaker cemetery which would be attended by a substantial number of this dissenting faith. One of the congregation would be none other than Samuel Burgis, the miller of Brimpton, who had already crossed Woodward's path and lived to regret it back in 1670. The corpse was Burgis' son, James, and Parson Woodward hurried off to the scene only to arrive too late to catch the Quakers in the act. He had been unprepared this time but vowed that he would be ready on the next occasion. With his servant, Thomas Gosmore, he rode over to Kingsclere to the house of Justice Faulkner and there explained the situation. Faulkner, being a staunch Anglican, readily issued the clergyman with a warrant against these conniving sectarians.

The months passed by with amazing inactivity as Woodward spied out the land but could find no trace of illegal operations at the Quaker meeting-house. They met at irregular intervals, and on occasions the Potters and their fellow religionists left the parish to worship further afield. Yet they had to meet at Baughurst with a large gathering at some time or another. Woodward was still as patient a man as he had been five years earlier, and he vowed he would catch the Quakers for sure this time.

Then on 18th June he was rewarded for his patience.[7] He had been told that a large meeting was about to take place in the Potters' farmhouse and that several dissenters had travelled there from places a considerable number of miles away. There was, in particular, a man from Southwark, near London.

Woodward sent Gosmore to fetch the tithingman, William Green, and to round up a group of men to assist them in their dealings with the Quakers. But, stressed Woodward, they were not to know the actual circumstances of the business for fear that they would refuse to accompany the expedition.

The Quakers had become careless in securing their meeting, for Woodward and his companions had no trouble at all in gaining access into the Potter home, and easily found that the meeting was already in progress in the hall of the house. As they entered they saw a strange man kneeling in the centre of the room, while the others were either just watching him or silently praying. The stranger, later identified as James Park, from Tooley Street in Southwark, was actually praying loudly, for the words he used sounded like:

" Keep us in the hollow of thy hand, and in the secret of thy pavilion. "

Woodward ordered Green to arrest the stranger, but the tithingman stood his ground and categorically refused the command. The company had now realised what Woodward's intentions had been and were reluctant to assist the clergyman further, for they had come to respect these quiet and friendly people during the last few years and would wish them no harm. Yet, at the same time, officers like the tithingman could not legally disobey men of authority such as their parish priest, and for them there was a constant struggle between their consciences and their onerous duties as the manorial police officer.

Woodward had the grace to allow the stranger the chance to finish his prayers, but once silence had returned to the mixed gathering of dissenters and conformists Woodward could no longer contain himself. He burst forth with loud and violent accusations against Park and the other Quakers assembled there, and then abruptly left the building, having ordered Green to haul Park before Justice Faulkner the next morning. Green and his assistants stood there in silence for a few minutes, their heads hung shamefully for fear of their eyes meeting with those of the Quaker neighbours. Then the tithingman began to apologise to Richard Potter and his guests, when his apology was interrupted by Gosmore, who told him that the parson had changed his mind and to leave the matter for the next three or four days.

On the fifth day after the incident, that is, on 23rd June, Green escorted James Park to Justice Faulkner's house, where they found that Woodward and Gosmore had already arrived and were now speaking with the magistrate. With Green and Park were Richard Potter and other Quakers who were in attendance at that fateful meeting, including Thomas May of Ecchinswell and William Appleton of Tadley. The proceedings against James Park began with Faulkner examining the offender, but before long it was Woodward who was controlling the interrogation. Not only was he the informer but he was also attempting to be the examining justice. The whole proceedings rapidly disintegrated into disorder and Faulkner was forced to call "enough" and to take control.

The justice then requested the written statement which Woodward had made prior to the examination, and after reading it aloud to all present he asked the priest to confirm the letter by the swearing of an oath. This Woodward did immediately and his oath was followed by that of his servant, Gosmore. The written statement was to the effect that the parish priest had named the following as attending the illegal conventicle with others not mentioned: Richard and Mary Potter, James Park, John Bye of Reading, John Gidding of Brimpton Mill, Ferdinand Tull of Midgham, Thomas May, and William Appleton. He had confirmed that Park was in the act of what could only be interpreted as prayer at the time, while the others were either in prayer or just watching Park, and that the meeting could only be deemed as an illegal conventicle as more than five persons over the age of sixteen were present and they were obviously in the state of worship.

After Woodward and Gosmore had sworn to the truth of the statement it was James Park's right to offer evidence against the prosecution. In his defence he brought up a technicality against the legality of the case. According to the conditions of the Conventicle Act of 1670 prosecutions were limited to a period within three months of the illegal act and that notice of a warrant had to be given by the intended prosecutors.

Woodward had given no such notice mainly because the warrant which he held had been authorised more than three months beforehand and was, therefore, cancelled by the conditions of its statutory use. Woodward countered this remark by affirming that he had given the Quakers notice of the warrant before the present incident. In fact Woodward did not affirm this was so just once but several times, eventually swearing an oath with his hand on the bible. Faulkner, knowing that Woodward had obtained the warrant from him several months ago, supported the cleric in his lies and ordered the arrest of Park, despite the protests from the Quakers there present.

James Potter returned home later that day after hearing the news of the disturbance in Baughurst. On hearing the latest development he took his brother with him to visit three important witnesses of the incident who were Anglican and, therefore, hardly regarded as sympathetic to the Quaker cause. Woodward had cited that Lawrence Grantham and John Yates had been the ones who had given previous notice to the Quakers of the warrant, while William Green was the tithingman who had led the company. James Potter obtained from each man a statement of the event. Green gave his account in full of the incident as well as Woodward's actual words. Grantham and Yates both denied any knowledge of Woodward's warrant until it was put into action on the 18th June. With such evidence the Potter brothers proceeded to Justice Faulkner's house and soon after-wards Green, Grantham and Yates were there in person swearing to the truth of the statements. James Potter also declared to Faulkner that he had retained a copy of the separate statements for future reference, and for added emphasis, he had Green's statement reproduced in the Sufferings Book of the Hampshire Quarterly Meeting.

Faulkner had no option but to order the release of James Park. Potter had outwitted the hostile authorities yet again and he continued to do so as long as Quakers were being unjustly oppressed. Meanwhile, Woodward did gain some satisfaction after his defeat by the Potter brothers. That year Richard Potter suffered a tithe persecution more extreme than it had been in recent years, when in total he lost nearly four pounds' worth of crops. The parish priest thus retained the upper hand in some spheres of the struggle against nonconformity. They gained considerable financial advantages from their position. In most other parishes they also won numerous victories over their opponents in all their battles. Baughurst was lucky in that it had James Potter, an extremely intelligent and active participant of the fight for justice. Woodward was a mighty assailant but could not quite match Potter's abilities. The struggle continued, for neither man would admit defeat.

Quaker Burials at Baughurst 1671-1675

(8) MARY KENT, of Tadly, Baghurst, 1673
(9) ELEZABETH POTTER, daughter of Richard and Mary Potter of Baghurst, at Baghurst, September 10, 1674
(10) JAMES BURGIS, son of Samuell Burgis of Brimpton Co. Berks, at Baghurst, February 6, 1675
(11) MARY WHEELER, widow of George Wheeler of Froyle, April 28, 1675
(12) ELEZABETH POTTER, daughter of James and Margery Potter of Baghurst, at Baghurst, July 16, 1675

---

[1] Sufferings, Hants.
[2] Sufferings, Hants.
[3] Digest, Berkshire and Oxfordshire General Meeting.
[4] Digests, Hants and Dorset General Meeting.
[5] Men's Minutes, Alton Monthly Meeting (H.R.O. Doc. No. 24M54/34)
[6] Men's Minutes, Alton Monthly Meeting.
[7] Sufferings, Hants.

ALTON FRIENDS MEETING HOUSE (1672).

Reproduced from The Friends Meeting House
by Hubert Lidbetter, FRIBA

127

CHAPTER SIX
1675-1683

I

"Kept in the hands of Moses Neave and James Potter keepers of the publick stock the som of seven pounds nineteene shillings —— 07 - 19 - 00 "

(Men's Minutes, Hampshire Quarterly Meeting,
7th March 1675)

"Then desired by ye meeting yt John Kilburn Moses Neave Nicholas Gates dospeake with ffreinds of Baghurst and Brimton meeting concerning ye setling of theire collections"

(Men's Minutes, Hampshire Quarterly Meeting,
7th October 1679)

"Then baghurst meeting sent twenty fower shillings being Collected for ffreinds of Cullumton distressed by fire by Willm Apelton"

(Men's Minutes, Alton Monthly Meeting,
11th September 1682)

Mth	Day	Year	Collected			Disbursed			to County Stock			Credit		
			£	s	d	£	s	d	£	s	d	£	s	d
4	1	1675	1	13	6	1	8	8	0	0	0	0	4	10
10	7	1675	2	11	3	2	10	6	0	0	0	0	0	9
4	6	1676	3	0	0	2	19	10	0	0	0	0	0	2
7	5	1676	1	12	2	1	11	11	0	0	0	0	0	3
10	5	1676	2	9	3	2	9	3	0	0	0	0	0	0
1	6	1677	2	9	6	2	9	6	0	0	0	0	0	0
3	29	1677	1	6	0	0	17	0	0	0	0	0	9	0
10	11	1677	2	0	0	1	12	0	0	5	0	0	3	0
1	5	1678	1	0	6	0	15	6	0	5	0	0	0	0
4	4	1678	1	10	0	1	5	0	0	5	0	0	0	0
7	3	1678	2	2	6	0	11	6	0	15	0	0	16	0

			£	s	d	£	s	d	£	s	d	£	s	d
10	3	1678	1	16	0	1	8	0	0	8	0	0	0	0
1	4	1678/9	1	15	6	1	10	6	0	5	0	0	0	0
4	3	1679	1	1	6	0	15	6	0	6	0	0	0	0
8	7	1679	0	0	0	— (James Potter gave 5s 0d to Collection)								
11	6	1679	2	0	3	1	10	3	0	10	0	0	0	0
2	6	1680	0	15	0	0	10	0	0	5	0	0	0	0
5	6	1680	0	18	0	0	10	0	0	8	0	0	0	0
8	5	1680	0	15	0	0	5	0	0	10	0	0	0	0
11	4	1680	0	16	0	0	12	0	0	4	0	0	0	0
2	5	1681	1	0	6	1	0	6	0	0	0	0	0	0
4	28	1681	0	5	6	0	5	6	0	0	0	0	0	0
8	4	1681	0	19	0	0	19	0	0	0	0	0	0	0
10	27	1681	0	14	0	0	9	0	0	5	0	0	0	0
1	28	1682	0	12	0	0	9	6	0	2	6	0	0	0
4	27	1682	0	19	6	0	9	0	0	5	6	0	3	6
11	2	1682	1	3	4	1	0	1	0	3	3	0	0	0
1	27	1683	0	12	0	0	12	0	0	0	0	0	0	0
4	26	1683	0	12	0	0	10	0	0	2	0	0	0	0
8	2	1683	0	12	0	0	2	6	0	9	6	0	0	0
10	18	1683	0	11	0	0	8	0	0	3	0	0	0	0

(Extracts from the Accounts concerning the Baughurst Meeting, Men's Minutes, Hampshire Quarterly Meeting, 1675-1683)

W HEN James Potter arrived in Baughurst to deal with the James Park incident he had been travelling some distance from Swanmore, where he had been attending the Quarterly Meeting for the county. James was now required to attend all the meetings concerning the administration of the faith in Hampshire, as he had, with Moses Neave, been appointed joint Keeper of the Public Stock on 7th March that year (1675). The Keeper of the Public Stock was the official Quaker term for the Treasurer of the fund which had been raised through collections among the several local weekly meetings of Hampshire. After the necessary disbursement of money for the relief of distresses among the local Quakers, the remainder was then calculated and if a certain minimum had been obtained, a donation was subsequently transferred to the Public Stock for the benefit of all the Quakers of that county. The Public Stock, which also contained legacies and voluntary donations, was therefore a trust fund set up and donated to by all the members of the Quaker community in Hampshire for their own benefit and that of their poorer associates. The fund was open to the membership upon certain conditions, such as the payment of interest on loans, while freely being used as a charity for the poor and needy and those who suffered from the regular tithe persecutions. Through the use of the Public Stock local meetings could purchase meeting-houses or greatly extend their existing ones, Quaker entrepreneurs were able to finance their business ventures or expand their markets considerably, livestock could be purchased thus replacing those lost in recent persecutions, and the poor would receive alms and perhaps lodgings, while the education of the Quaker children was greatly enhanced by the establishment of academies within the local meetings. In fact this form of self-help proved beneficial to the Society of Friends as a whole, and greatly aided the promotion of the faith as well as forming the nucleus of the saying that " Charity begins at home".

James Potter, in his capacity as Keeper of the Public Stock, was thus a vital member of that small administrative group which formed the Quarterly Meeting. At the same time he was the elected representative of the Baughurst and Brimpton Meeting at the Hampshire assembly. Normally there were two representatives of each local meeting at the Quarterly, and as James was the regular attendant he was often accompanied by a different person each successive session. James was accompanied by his brother, Richard, at meetings in the years 1678, 1679, 1680, and 1682.[1] At the same time James regularly represented Baughurst at the monthly meetings in Alton. Therefore he was an extremely busy man, and his service was required by the Quakers more and more as the years passed, for he was regarded as one of those few persons with several qualities — efficiency, skill in diplomacy, literacy and eloquence, and a true devotion to his faith.

Moreover, James Potter was the unofficial and unspoken " leader" of the Baughurst Meeting, and he certainly felt wholesale responsibilities towards his meeting. As joint Keeper of the Public Stock he had to make out the accounts of the collections handed in from the local meetings, as well as handling the accounts of the Baughurst Meeting itself. Between 1st June 1675 and 3rd June 1679 Baughurst collected a total of £26 7s. 8d., of which £22 4s. 8d. was disbursed towards its own financial needs, including the alleviation of poverty among the inhabitants of Baughurst, Tadley, Ecchinswell and other tithings in that district. Only £2 9s. of the money collected during that period went into the Public Stock. The highest single sum collected at Baughurst between 1675 and 1679 amounted to £3 on 6th June 1676, while the lowest was £1 0s. 6d. on 5th March 1678. Yet, although these sums seem trivial today they were fairly considerable at the time and it is essential to recognise the fact that the Baughurst Meeting collected among the highest totals within the county. On occasions the collections of the membership of the Baughurst Meeting amounted to the largest, while for the remainder of that period it was virtually on a par with the largest, from Ringwood. So it can be seen that

Baughurst was, during the 1670s, one of the biggest and wealthiest of the Hampshire Quaker meetings.

Its position in size and prosperity can best be illustrated by comparison with its neighbour and progenitor, Basingstoke. Baughurst was a rural meeting while Basingstoke was strictly urban and therefore more populated. Yet consideration must be granted in the latter's case as it was much affected by the Five Mile Act of 1665, which was still very much in force, although the account of collections show that the Quakers of that town still gathered together despite threatened persecution. Even so, the Baughurst Quakers were subjected to those same threats. The first account rendered for Basingstoke was on 5th September 1676, and between that date and 3rd June 1679 that meeting collected a total of £3 16s. 4d., of which £2. 16s. 9d. was disbursed for their own means, yet nothing was entered of the remainder into the Public Stock. Basingstoke was a poor place indeed in the eyes of the Quakers of Hampshire.

Although Basingstoke was the older of the two meetings, and, because of Fox's visit there in 1655, was the originator of the Baughurst meeting, the latter had for long surpassed its elder in size and importance. In fact, Baughurst had become the leading "light" in the Hampshire-Berkshire border area, and had already established its place in the hierarchy of the Quaker meetings in Hampshire because of the Potter connection. In 1669 two dozen people had been accounted for as members of the Baughurst Meeting. Now, in 1676,[2] there had been another survey which had recorded no less than nineteen nonconformists in the parish of Baughurst among a population which contained one hundred and fifty-four Anglicans. The nonconformists aforementioned were Quakers and their number reflected how strong the faith was there in a parish with such a small population. When Woodward broke up the meeting at Richard Potter's house in 1675 there were at least five members from parishes outside his jurisdiction. Therefore the Baughurst Meeting attracted attention from parishes well beyond its normal sphere of influence, and several of its regular membership came from over the border in Berkshire. These people encountered a particularly harsh experience from the persecutors in 1676.

On 26th May Samuel Burgis, the miller of Brimpton, was visited by Richard Smith, the bailiff, who demanded the tithe payment of £4. 18s. 4d. which was outstanding to Thomas Worrall, the parish priest, who had delighted in his victimisation of Burgis in 1670 and 1671. In the event Smith took away the miller's mare which was valued at around £10.[3]

Three days later the bailiffs William Merriman and Gabriel Buck entered the premises of Ferdinand Tull, who had already been involved in the James Park incident, at Midgham near Thatcham. They had been sent to collect goods to the value of the £4 tithe which Tull owed Bartholomew Springer, the priest of the chapelry of Midgham. The bailiffs eventually took away five cows from Tull's farm, together valued at £18.

Four years later, in 1680, Burgis was visited four times during the course of that year, on account of the tithes which he owed to William Geall, Worrall's successor. In the June he lost eleven cocks of hay, and on three separate occasions in July twelve cocks of hay, twenty cocks of grass, and two and a half cocks of barley were taken out of his property.

These sufferings affected Baughurst because Burgis and Tull regularly attended the meetings in that Hampshire parish. Therefore the collections made there were in part, if not all, disbursed to rectify the wrongs made by the tithe-gatherers, and lessened the contributions towards the Public Stock. In fact no contribution to the general fund was made by the Baughurst Meeting until December 1677, while in October 1679 enquiries were made at the Quarterly as to why there was no contribution towards the Public Stock.[4] An embarrassed meeting had to call forth an investigation into the matter and John Kilburn, Moses Neave and Nicholas Gates were conscripted to attend the next meeting at Baughurst and to enquire about the lack of funds. In the meantime James Potter himself, feeling responsible for his fellows, contributed five shillings to the fund in order to cover the loss to the fund. At the next local meeting James purposely made an appearance, despite his absences beforehand, and presented his case to the regulars assembled there. In consequence he was able to hand over ten shillings towards the county fund at the following Quarterly of 6th January 1680. However, the collections would never again reach the sums accounted in the 1670s. The highest total between 6th April 1680 and 31st March 1686 was £1 3s. 4d. on 2nd January 1683, of which only three shillings was paid into the Public Stock owing to the large expenditure which the Baughurst Meeting suffered at the time. At the other end of the scale only 5s. 6d. was collected for the quarter ending the 28th June 1681, which was duly disbursed for local needs.[5] The reasons for the decline in contributions were the increasing persecutions which the Quakers were suffering by that time, and, therefore, the natural fall in attendances; some members were even in prison at the time, while others were too poor to contribute or were now thinking of leaving the Quaker fold as the persecutions were growing more and more severe due to political influences. Yet while there was justifiably a decline in support in some spheres, the growing opposition encouraged greater adherence to the faith in others. Quakerism was not weakening through a certain percentage of desertion, for this was always apparent. It was, in fact, being strengthened by those who would always remain faithful, and as it was growing stronger in spirit the Public Stock which aided its growth also helped to bring prosperity to its most loyal adherents by providing them with the means of establishing and expanding their own businesses. More and more Quakers, denied of political ambition, concentrated their efforts into worthwhile business ventures and likewise helped their fellow religionists to achieve their goals in life. In 1678 James Potter's prosperity increased as he succeeded to his substantial copyhold estate.

II

"For the yeare 1679 in the 5th month the servants of William Woodward priest of Baghurst in the County of Southt wth his Cart and horses entred into James Potters Meadows and Grownds severall times and took away his Grass and hay to the value of 1 lb 4s or upwards

And in the harvest following in like manner took away his Wheat out of his Ground to ye value of 3 lb: 14 or thereabouts.

And also took away pease Barley and Oates to the Value of 2 lb 12s or up all taken without the Owners cosent somtime halfe a row of sheaves together and at one time 50 sheaves togeather prtending it to bee for a Mortuary tith Calfe Cheese Ester reckonings and such like, and the other as they could catch it severall parcells and cocks togeather in all to the value of 7 lb 10s or upwards

And in the same yeare the said preist took from Richard Potter (as hee hath don in yeares past sinse they gave off plundering, his hay wheat barly and pease and oates to the value of 3 lb 10 s."

(Sufferings, Hants.)

JOAN SPENCER, the Potters' most faithful friend, died at her copyhold cottage on 23rd October 1678, and was buried in Richard Potter's garden plot two days later.[6] The funeral was attended by the two Potter families and a few close friends, who were at pains not to allow the solemn occasion to be interpreted by their opponents as a conventicle and thus come into conflict with the law of the realm. As the rain fell incessantly upon the grave of the dearly departed, and as the sparse assembly of witnesses silently worded their prayers over her corpse, the air was heavily charged, for each Quaker there felt the presence of hostile spirits just beyond the bounds of the cemetery. Memories of the incident which took place in this very same garden back in 1670 were still fresh in the minds of the mourners. As the Quakers nervously watched the final arrangements, William Woodward and his henchmen were straining their ears to listen out for any indiscreet words being accidentally uttered by the assembled dissenting mourners. They were disappointed, for the burial was soon over. Prayers could be spoken over the grave at any time under the cover of darkness, when the interested Anglican party were safely out of earshot. Thus the burial was completed as quickly as possible and the visiting Quakers courteously bade Richard Potter and his wife their farewells and departed the farm, passing by Woodward and his men at the gate, graciously acknowledging them.

Seeing that nothing more would happen here this evening, Woodward walked into Potter's yard and approached Richard. The yeoman eyed the parson suspiciously for a moment and then decided to greet him as courteously as he could without showing his contempt. Woodward surprisingly returned Potter's greeting and then his next words astounded the Quaker. He offered Richard his condolences, saying that Joan was a good woman who offended nobody. With this the cleric turned and walked out of the farm. Richard was still in a state of mild shock as the sound of clattering hooves on the flintstones of the road melted away into the distance, and it was only the insistent voice of his wife that brought him out of his trance.

Later that evening William Woodward was sitting in his study and thinking over the consequences of Joan Spencer's death. More than once he had thought about returning to the burial-ground that evening in the hope of catching the Quakers at their conventicle, for he was acutely suspicious of the lack of activity among the Friends that day. Yet he now dismissed this idea from his mind, and concentrated upon the future. Spencer was dead but her copyhold heir, James Potter, was alive and well, and was becoming more powerful as the days passed. Now he had inherited a fair-sized estate which contained two yardlands,[7] and as he would shortly be admitted as full tenant of that estate he would also be responsible for his tithe debts. Woodward saw visions of Potter's impoverishment before his eyes and as he gloated upon this subject he set about the routine task of entering the necessary information of Joan Spencer's burial into the new parish register.[8] He was so engrossed in his thoughts while he was writing that he did not notice that he had written " James Spencer in Potter's yard".[9] Nor could he have ever checked that entry in years to come, for he would have realised then that he had entered James for Joan. The burial of a Quaker in the Anglican register was not uncommon, for the parish registers were normally the only means of recording such vital data, and Woodward was particular in his recording of dissenters in his parish.

James Potter appeared at the next session of the Court Baron at Manydown House on 20th November 1678,[10] to be formally admitted as tenant of the late Joan Spencer's estate. There was little need for copyholders to make out a will in those days as all transactions were deliberated and approved at the Court Baron, by inspection of the warrants of copyhold granted to the heirs after their nominations by an interested party in agreement with the other heirs. The system of copyhold tenure was virtually foolproof for it guaranteed rights for both the manor and its tenants. The manor, by guaranteeing its tenants the right to nominate their successors, was, in turn, guaranteed a system of proper and fruitful farming of its lands. So it was a perfect marriage which encouraged harmony between the lords and their servants. Such a system, however, enabled certain anomalies to enter into the dealings between the lords and their tenants. The manorial system was devoid of political and religious emphasis. While the kingdom as a whole was in the midst of political and religious upheavals the manor denied any suggestion of conflict in these areas. Here in Manydown this was no more apparent than in the admittance of James Potter to his copyhold tenure. The Manor of Manydown was a holding of the Dean and Chapter of Winchester Cathedral, and therefore an ecclesiastical estate, while the newly admitted copyholder was a radical Quaker, and vitally opposed to the Church system so represented by his lords. In manorial terms it mattered not in what one tenant believed so long as he farmed the lands to the best of his abilities and in a proper and organised fashion.

James Potter had to prove his title deed to the estate entitled ''a messuage and two yardlands with appurtenances in Baghurst'' upon production of his copyhold warrant granted on 26th October 1661,[11] which, in turn, was compared with the copy held by the Dean and Chapter, and with those of Joan Spencer dated 23rd September 1635, and of Richard Potter dated 25th November 1677.[12] When all the relevant documents had been inspected by the steward, a solicitor, and had been approved, then James Potter was admitted as tenant of the Spencer copyhold estate on the payment of a fine of £20. On the same occasion and before the jury assembled, which consisted of fellow tenants and copyhold heirs or their representatives, James nominated his own daughter, Mary, as the third life in the estate after himself and his brother, but with the proviso that if he and his brother should die, surrender or forfeit their

135

interests before she came of age then James Acton[12] of Basingstoke would take up the tenure for her as her trustee. A warrant was then made for Mary Potter, signed and sealed by James and his witnesses before the steward. The legal formalities now concluded, James had to serve as juror for the other businesses of the day.

Although James Potter was now the legally constituted tenant of his Baughurst estate, nothing had really altered. He was such a busy man that the burden of farming his own copyhold lands would have proved too much. Therefore the agreement with his brother continued, and life was much the same as before, with the exception that Joan was no longer around to help with the affairs of the estate and to offer guidance.

James was so often an absentee from the farm that his daughter hardly knew her father as she was growing up. All the discipline came from her mother, who was helped in her chores by her few servants. It was Margery who instilled the Quaker ideals into her daughter's mind. Daily prayers were a must in the household, along with regular attendances at the meetings which took place across the road. Quaker ideals were particularly laced with the rigidity of discipline and the respect for elders that frivolity and entertainment were pleasures that had to be avoided. Mary grew up endowed with the morality with which puritanism had since been labelled.

The cottage in which James Potter's family now lived was almost a copy of that in which he had grown up — only larger. Richard's and James' homes were built with almost identical bricks and were shaped almost the same as most yeomen's domiciles of the Tudor and early Stuart periods. However, whereas Richard's farmhouse supported two hearths, Joan Spencer's had four.[13]

Yet somehow the situation had changed, that is for one particular person. Woodward was swift to wreak havoc upon the domestic bliss of the Potter family. He had to wait though until the new year had begun on Lady Day 1679. Then he would justly sue the Quakers for the tithe dues which they had omitted to pay him. For James Potter there would be the added debt of mortuary tithes reserved for newly admitted tenants following the deaths of the previous copyholders.

By the end of 1679 James had been relieved of farming products valued in excess of £7 10s. 0d. by the tithe-gatherers.[14] In compensation for the mortuary dues, cheese, calf and easter tithes which Woodward expected from the new copyholder peas, barley, and oats worth over £2 12s. 0d. were taken from Potter's lands while he was absent.

In the July of that year the parish priest sent his servants with his cart and horses into the fields adjoining Potter's cottage, and on several occasions throughout that month grass and hay valued in excess of

£1 4s. 0d. were carted away. During the following harvest they returned to deprive James of wheat worth over £3 14s. 0d.

Now that James Potter had been admitted as one of Baughurst's manorial tenants he was naturally being assessed for tithes on a regular basis. Therefore the annual plunderings of his estate had only just begun. In 1680 grass, hay, wheat, barley, oats, and peas, all to the value of over £5 8s. 0d. were taken out of his fields; in 1681 the process continued and his loss amounted to more than £6 4s. 0d. when John Read and Edward Dicker performed the act of stealing seventy of the Quaker's wheatsheaves while he was absent; and in 1682 the loss was in excess of £6. That latter year William Woodward himself, accompanied by his brother-in-law and two others, entered James' property in the February and carted away two hundred faggots worth ten shillings. In his first five years as a customary tenant of the Manor of Manydown (1678-1682) James had suffered losses which amounted to well in excess of £25.

Meanwhile Richard Potter was suffering equal acts of repression as a matter of course. His experiences were so regular that the Quakers were not continuously recording his separate sufferings, stating that between 1676 and 1678 he merely suffered tithe persecutions. In 1675 he had been deprived of crops to the value of £3 10s. 0d. and above; in 1679 his loss equalled that of 1675; in 1680 it had spiralled to £6 1s. 0d.; in 1681 remained around £6; and in 1682 he suffered losses worth over £6 5s. 0d. Between 1672 and 1682 his total losses came to above £44, while since 1657 his adherence to Quakerism had meant that this yeoman had been persecuted to the tune of over £110!

III

" When Shaftesbury astutely turned the anti-popish frenzy to party purposes he carried with him the approbation of the nonconformists. When Charles dissolved the Long Parliament of the Restoration, the Whigs won three elections in rapid succession. The nonconformists were more than fascinated observers; so far as possible they were eager participants. They felt that they were sharing in the victory of a party which was certain to give them the largest possible measure of relief. When parliament began to consider ways of improving the lot of dissenters, they believed that they were on the point of reaping the benefits of cooperation. They did not see that though they might share the successes of their friends they were also committed to their follies. A wild irresponsibility had infused itself into English public life. The Whigs were apparently intent on using their advantage in ways that seemed destructive of national unity. A revulsion of public feeling took place. When the king dismissed his last parliament, he could strike at the Whigs with impunity because they had clearly alienated the goodwill of moderate men."

(Cragg, p. 24)

CHARLES II dissolved the so-called "Cavalier or Long Parliament of the Restoration" in 1679. Since 1673, when it had reassembled owing to financial need of the King for more subsidies because his resources had dwindled through the expensive operation of the war against the Dutch, Parliament had become more troublesome. Twice it legislated against nonconformist office-holders through the famous "Test Acts", and was being infiltrated by a neo-Republican faction which allied with the Country Party and opposed the royal policy with vehemence.

In 1678 the scandalous "Popish Plot" broke on to the political scene and heralded a period whereby hysteria against the Roman Catholics became the order of the day. Alarm found evidence of the treasonable intentions of the Papists on which to feed, and Titus Oates and Dr Israel Tonge found that evidence and fed the lies to a believing population. In their own words they had uncovered a Catholic conspiracy which involved the murder of the King and the invasion of England by the French to place Charles' brother, the Duke of York, on the throne. York himself was deeply implicated, while his wife's secretary had been made the scapegoat. The lies became more credible when the magistrate to whom Oates and Tonge had confided the details of the conspiracy was found dead. Almost immediately the discovery of the corpse triggered off national hysteria against the Catholics.

After years of persecution the Protestant nonconformists now found that attention had been deflected from them and they easily found a mutual alliance with the Anglicans as both sides shared the traditional English dread of popery.

The Country Party, with its element of neo-Republicans, discovered an able and ambitious leader in the Earl of Shaftesbury, and he, in turn, recognised the immense possibilities which lay in exploiting the situation. His battle-cry of "No Popery" gave the Protestant dissenters a new lease of life in the political arena. In the nonconformist groupings Shaftesbury could see the means of consolidating a political body which would be able

138

to challenge even the King and his supporters. He advocated parliamentary restraints on arbitrary government, religious toleration (but excluding the Catholics), and freedom from dependence on France. Above all, he represented the opposition to royal absolutism and a Catholic Church, and was regarded as a saviour by his supporters.

The divisions of the politicians now appeared more acute than ever before. Shaftesbury's supporters were being called "Whigs" by their opponents, while the Court Party received the name of "Tories" from Shaftesbury's Country Party. The political party system had been born out of the Exclusion Crisis. Shaftesbury now committed himself to the passage of the Exclusion Bill which was framed to deprive the Catholic Duke of York of his right of inheritance.

As the flames of civil unrest were still smouldering Charles II dissolved the "Cavalier Parliament" in its eighteenth year of sitting, when the members were attempting to impeach his chief minister, the Earl of Danby. He had hoped that the attempt to promote the Exclusion Bill through Parliament would now die, but he was so wrong. The new parliament which assembled was more radical than the old one. Elections had resulted in the watering down of the Royalist-Anglican grouping in the Commons. The Whig Party was in its ascendancy, and with it the hope of excluding James, the Catholic heir, from the throne. Shaftesbury's nominee, the popular and handsome Duke of Monmouth, became the country's favourite, despite his handicap of illegitimacy, and the scene was set for a constitutional revolution without the King's blessing.

Violence escalated in the streets of London and it appeared that civil war was only a short step away. Yet, despite the Whigs' success, Shaftesbury could not gain an easy passage for the Exclusion Bill. He met with opposition from all quarters within Parliament and government. As it appeared that the bill might pass into the statute book then the King would prorogue or dissolve Parliament. However, each new election and by-election produced the same results and the Whigs were able to retain their majority position. That was until 1681.

Fear of violence in the streets around Westminster as the mobs of London apprentices descended upon Parliament House caused the King to recall the assembly to Oxford. At that point Shaftesbury was nearing his objective, but the sight of the King dressed in full regalia caused the assembled House to reflect on their recent actions and attitudes. The appearance of their royal master in all his full splendour made the members realise how far along the road towards civil war they had travelled. The opposition began to melt away, until only Shaftesbury and his most ardent Republican supporters were left. At this juncture Charles dissolved the

Oxford Parliament and began the final years of his reign as an absolute monarch. His prerogative rule was devoid of parliamentary sessions.

Shaftesbury fled the country and the Whigs went into decline. With their defeat came a natural reaction against their Protestant dissenting supporters. As the Englishman was fast educating himself towards religious toleration during the preceding years, the situation had now changed through the meddling of the extreme anti-Papists.

In consequence the dissenting sects were to face the worst persecutions of a reign that was notorious for its persecutions of those who did not conform. They had supported the ill-fated new Country Party and had to suffer the consequences of that support. The King felt no desire, and still less any obligation, to defend the nonconformists against the recriminations of the Tories. The days of Indulgence had long since passed, and by their recent behaviour the dissenters had forfeited their monarch's goodwill. The time was now ripe for a new outbreak of activities against those who would not conform on religious grounds. Meanwhile, the succession of a Catholic king was made more fearful by the reality of the new wave of oppression. The future again merged with the memories of the past, and the prisons would again be full of religious criminals.

IV

" The 7th day of the 3d month 1682 ffriends of the towne of Andover being mett together to waite upon God at theire meeting place in Andover the preist of the sayed towne called Benjamin Culme came and looked on them and went and Informed the magistrates who with the officers and others came and tooke som names and hayled ffreinds into the street and lockt up their meeting house. The 14th day of ye 3d month 1682 Edward Walderne & Richard Mountaine of Andover Daniel Smith of Malborrough Thomas Downes of Titherly Robert Hopkins and John Browne of Whitchurch John ffaithfull of Wallop Nicholas Bull of Hunton George Lambden of bourne with som other ffreinds being peaceably mett together to waite upon God in theire meeting place in Andover were by the Bayliffe William Gammon and Walter Robison Towne Clerke & Robert Nois called a Justice with ye 2 constables George Kent & Valentine Tanner & William Brunsden serjant with many others came to the sayd meeting and asked ffriends to sweare and refusing to take the oath of allegiance and supremacy were all cast into the towne prison in Andover the day and yeare above written."

(Sufferings, Hants.)

"1682. Samuel Burgis for being att a meetting att 26. 10. was fined for himselfe & others £1 - 15s - 0d. for being att meetting againe 29. 10. & praying to ye lord was convicted by ye oath of ye sd informing officers (John Rogers constable and Ralph Lucas churchwarden) and fined £20. And Anthony Crawn and John Kingsmill sent their warrant to Richard Goddard and Ralph May officers of Brimpton who came and distrained 6 cows valued att £24."

(Sufferings, Berks.)

THE REACTION against the nonconformists was slow at first, but began to accelerate as the news of the Whig defeat filtered through the countryside. 1682 was the year when widespread persecutions began to be felt, as justices clamped down upon seditious dissenters.

In Berkshire recriminations were swift against those already well noted for their Quaker activities and familiar names were being recorded in the pages of the Berkshire sufferings,[15] including those with particular associations with the Baughurst Meeting.

For refusing to hear the common prayer Samuel Burgis of Brimpton and his wife, Ann, were deprived of a greatcoat, a waistcoat, two other coats, a gown, a petticoat, a kettle, and a skillet, worth together £2 8s. 0d., when their home was robbed. For the same offence their servant, Andrew Pearson, was dispossessed of a coat, a pair of breeches, an old waistcoat, trousers, two pairs of stockings, and a pair of shoes, all valued at 13s. 6d., on the same occasion.

Burgis was to suffer continuously for his adherence to Quakerism in that year. On 10th December he was caught in the act of speaking at a conventicle, and thus termed the minister, and was fined for this misdemeanour £40. In consequence the justice's men confiscated from his premises four horses and a waggon, together valued at £42.

Yet this did not deter the miller of Brimpton, who had known much trouble in the past from the "bully-boys" of English justice. He still frequented the Quaker meetings, and was, therefore, more at risk at every conventicle that he attended.

On 26th December he was holding a meeting in his own home when it was entered. He was fined £1 15s. 0d. for himself and others for this offence.

On 29th of that month he was caught again, this time in the act of praying, while holding a meeting and was convicted by the oath of the informing officers, John Rogers the constable and Ralph Lucas the church-warden. For this offence he was fined £20. The justices at the sessions were Anthony Crawn and John Kingsmill of Sidmonton in Hampshire. Crawn and Kingsmill sent their warrant to the parish officers of Brimpton, Richard Goddard and Ralph May, who immediately set about the task of distraining goods to the value of the warrant. Therefore they took away from Burgis' farm six cows valued at £24.

Burgis was not the only person to be hauled before the magistrates for holding Quaker meetings at their own homes. That year William Austell, John Sansome, William Spicer, and Martha Weston were convicted of such an offence in the Berkshire magistrates' courts. Meanwhile other, regular worshippers at Baughurst who resided in Berkshire suffered from the vindictiveness of the authorities. John Gidding was deprived of two kettles, a book, a warming-pan, and a platter, worth together £2 8s. 0d; John Haskins lost a pair of books, leather breeches, and a platter, worth together 15s. 0d.; and Ferdinand Tull saw the justice's men take away from his cottage a kettle, a skillet, a brass pot, and five platters which were worth £1 15s. 0d.

Then, at the petty sessions held at Speenhamland near Newbury on 16th April 1683 before the justices Anthony Crawn, John Kingsmill, and John Smith, four Quakers were offered the Oath of Allegiance and Supremacy by the magistrates, but they refused and Samuel Burgis, George White, John Sansome, and Edward Swaine were committed to prison for that offence.

In Hampshire the situation was no different, and, while Quakers all over the county were falling foul of the authorities, the sufferings book was mainly devoted to the events surrounding one meeting that year.[16] The Andover Meeting was very much in the news at that time.

On 7th May 1682 Benjamin Culme, the vicar of Andover, had been tipped off that the Quakers were gathering for a religious meeting in one of the houses in the town. He was then led to the house in question, where he peered through the window and saw for himself that such a conventicle was in progress. With haste he sought out Robert Noyce the justice and the other magistrates, and they rounded up their officers and other volunteers in order to descend on the illegal meeting. They arrived at the house in force and pushed their way into the room where the Quakers were congregating and, as troopers surrounded the house, began to question the

142

dissenting assembly. Names were taken and then the officers were summoned to eject the Quakers from the house. When the entire assembly had vacated the meeting-house Noyce ordered that it be locked up.

On 14th May the Quakers had returned to the house for a meeting. This time the authorities were ready. Noyce was accompanied on this occasion by William Gammon the bailiff, Walter Robinson the town clerk, William Brunsden the sergeant, the constables George Kent and Valentine Tanner, and many others. They entered the building and there and then the Quakers were offered the Oaths of Allegiance and Supremacy, which they characteristically refused. Noyce ordered his officers to cast them into the town prison, and that day Edward Walden and Richard Montaine, both of Andover, with Daniel Smith of Marlborough, Thomas Downs of Tytherley, Robert Hopkins and John Brown,[17] both of Whitchurch, John Faithful of Nether Wallop, Nicholas Bull of Hunton, George Lambden of St Mary Bourne, with many other Friends, were committed to Andover Prison.

On 24th May Richard Montaine's servant came to the prison to speak with his master concerning the latter's business. At the same time four Quakers were there on a mission of visiting prisoners. The jailer John Purdue was absent at the time and his wife took it upon herself to be responsible for her husband's charge that day. She resented the religious prisoners and their visitors, so in her rage she ordered the jailer's attendants to lock everybody inside the prison — the visitors included. This action caused something of a storm and that night William Gammon, the bailiff, had himself to go to the prison with a couple of officers and order the release of the visitors. However, only three of the five were set free.

Purdue ruled his jail with an iron hand. He denied his new prisoners beds with straw and would sell them only beer and water, the latter at 2d. per flagon. On the 18th June Purdue had five of his Quaker prisoners put into portable wooden cages, and had the two cages hauled through dirt and water.

On 25th June the Andover Meeting was broken into again, showing that the Quakers would continue to worship despite all attempts to stop them. There were only seven people at the meeting, but quite enough to constitute an illegal conventicle. Abraham Tarlton of Andover and four others were roughly hauled from the house and then dragged into the dirt of the street outside. A crowd soon gathered around the spectacle, and the audience was horrified to see Thomas Hooper's child being thrown by one of the constables into the dirt near where his father lay almost unconscious.

On 29th June Purdue the jailer laughingly revealed to his Quaker prisoners that he held no *mittimus* to detain them there, but they would not be released even after they had faced a trial. Then on 2nd July the Andover Meeting was broken up once again. This time Richard Elton, having been dragged into the street with the others, was kicked along the thoroughfare for a considerable distance by the officers.

It was on 13th July that the town sessions were held. The Quaker prisoners were brought to trial on an indictment for rioting. Openly the jury was being threatened by the justices to bring in a verdict of guilty against the dissenters. Yet the jury would not respond, and the Quakers' case was then adjourned for a week. The prisoners were returned to Andover Prison where, upon their arrival, they found that Purdue's wife had taken away all of their beds. At their next trial a week later they were offered the Oaths of Allegiance and Supremacy and their refusals convicted them.

On 26th July Edward Walden, Daniel Smith, and Richard Montaine were transported from Andover Prison to Winchester, where they were to be brought before the assize judges. The bill of indictment which was presented at the Andover sessions was read again at the assizes. After a while the jury returned a verdict of not guilty, but the three Quakers were not set free. Instead, the jury was advised by the judge to consider the charges again on an indictment of unlawful assembly, to which the verdict was unanimously returned as guilty.

The three Andover Quakers were then taken to Jewry Street Prison to begin their sentence, where they found several of their own kind already serving terms for similar offences. And it was there that they met James Potter, who had, by this time, gained quite a reputation for himself. Once again Potter was a prisoner, but it was for only a limited period, for even the authorities had realised by then that James was one of those men for whom imprisonment was merely a temporary inconvenience.

V

"1682. James Potter of Baghurst for refusing to sweare to serve the office of a Constable was sent to Winchester prison on the tenth day of the fifth month of 1682 by George Browne of wolverton called a Justice and at the next quarter sessions was called and offered the oath and because for conscience sake towards god he could not sweare though he proffered to serve the office he was committed to the common Goale for to lay twelve month or pay ten pounds

James Potter was Released by order of Judg Dolbin at the Assise held at Winchester the first and second dayes of the first month 1682/3 and on the 12th day following for refuseing to pay Roger War Goaler fees was by him put amongst fellows in the Common Prison, and Daniell Smith and Richard Mountaine with him; And the 22d day of the sd first month was let goe out of Prison haveing been a Prisoner 9 monthes and 3 dayes."

(Sufferings, Hants.)

"At Winchester Castle on the 11th July 1683 before John Norton barronet, Hugh Stewkeley barronet, Charles Windham knight, Roger Clavell, Henry Dawley armiger, William Harrison professor of Holy Theology, Richard Bishopp, Ralph Hastings, William Stephens armiger, Robert Sherrock Doctor of Laws, Thomas Brocas and Richard Norton armiger and other justices etc.

Whereas James Potter was at the last Quarter Sessions of ye peace held for this County no[m]i[n]ated and elected Constable for the Hundred of Evingar and the s[ai]d James Potter refuseing to take his corporall Oath for the due execuc[i]on of the s[ai]d office was com[m]itted to ye Com[m]on Goale of this County by Geo: Browne Esqr one of his Ma[jes]tyes Justices of ye Peace of this County and being brought before this Court was fined in p[ar]t for such his refusall and remanded back to the s[ai]d Goale there to remaine for the space of one whole yeare or untill he p[ai]d his s[ai]d Fine. . . ."

(Hampshire Quarter Sessions Order Book, 1682-1689, Doc No Q/0 6, Hampshire Record Office)

"27. 1. 1683. Then James Potters releasement was taken notice off and wee find James Potter was released by Judge Dolbin ye last assisses Then payd James Potter ten shillings yt he layd out about ffreinds busines Then James Potter & Nicholas Gates were desired to (?write) a letter of ye present sufferings to ye meetings of sufferings at London."

(Men's Minutes, Hampshire Quarterly Meeting)

145

AT THE Quarterly Meeting of 4th October 1681 James Potter was directed to attend the Assizes in order to find out which Quakers were being brought to trial there.[18] At the following meeting he reported that there were no Quakers listed for trial at the Assizes, but this did not quell the fears that a new bout of persecution was about to begin. Therefore it was directed that Potter should return to Winchester for the next assizes and take with him Mark Ford to act as his assistant. Record-searching at the Assizes was now James' specific assignment, and he would also speak in defence for those indicted Quakers with such astonishing eloquence that he would soon gain for himself the reputation of being the Quakers' advocate in Winchester.

At the beginning of March 1682 Potter and Ford travelled to Winchester in order to inspect the assize records for Quaker prisoners. They made their way to the Great Hall, where a great number of people were milling around, some engaged in conversation with the extravagantly bewigged barristers-at-law. The two Quaker agents made their way to the clerk's desk where the register was kept, and once there Potter discreetly engaged the clerk in conversation, gradually turning the small talk towards nonconformists awaiting trial. Upon asking to look at the register the clerk allowed Potter and Ford to make a search of the names listed for the current session. The listed indictments were various but none of the names were recognised by the agents for the Quarterly Meeting. When the session began the two Friends joined the spectators and noted the proceedings particularly when dissenters of all types were involved.

The following day the process was repeated, but this time the clerk called the attention of a court officer towards the two mysterious figures dressed simply in black. The officer instantly recognised Potter from the previous assize, and related his findings to another who remembered James as a prisoner some years beforehand. Enquiries were made concerning these men and before the assizes had been terminated Potter's reputation as a troublemaker who, on a number of occasions, had confounded the authorities here in the Hampshire capital had been firmly established. That reputation was further enhanced by the brief defence speech which Potter had made on behalf of a Quaker prisoner this current session. When the two Quakers left Winchester their suspected activities were relayed to interested parties throughout the county. The realisation that the Quakers had organised a legal defence system to counteract the national process of justice was met with a reaction to halt them in their tracks. Soon the justices and the Anglican priests in their home parishes would have to deal with these men severely in order to prevent a miscarriage of Anglican justice.

Potter and Ford were paid thirteen shillings our of the Public Stock as their expenses for attending the last assizes, and it was desired that James should attend the next. This he was not able to do.

The news of James' involvement in the business of the assize court had travelled to his home parish of Baughurst, and William Woodward was invited to Wolverton House to discuss with Sir George Browne, the justice for that district,[19] how to deal with Potter, who had by now become a thorough nuisance to the civil as well as to the ecclesiastical authorities.

On 10th July 1682 James Potter was brought to Wolverton House where he was to be sworn in as constable for the hundred of Evingar, an honour which nobody could really refuse for fear of being suspected of treason. Naturally, the Quaker refused to swear the oath and Browne had him arrested and taken to the common gaol in Winchester.

At the following quarter sessions Potter was again offered the Oaths of Allegiance and Supremacy, and again refused, protesting that although he could not swear an oath he was willing to serve the office of constable. However, his protests were ignored and he was committed to the common gaol once more to serve a sentence of one year or, alternatively, to pay a fine of £10. Potter was not willing to pay the fine, therefore he was handed over into the care of Roger Warr the gaoler.[20]

While James was in prison Woodward had a free rein to take out of the Quaker's fields as much as he wished as an excuse for tithe debts. In June and July he and his servants entered Potter's property and carted away hay to the value of £1 4s. 0d. and upwards.[21] During harvest-time they returned to take away wheat, peas, barley and oats worth together over £6. From Richard Potter's fields the same crops were taken at the same time, and together the two periods of incursion cost Richard in excess of £7 5s. 0d.

Meanwhile, the accounts of the Baughurst Meeting suffered, as in the September of that year no collection was made for the Public Stock, although twenty-four shillings had been raised to help the Quakers of Cullompton in Devon who had suffered from arson. William Appleton of Tadley had taken over James' office for this occasion.[22]

James was in good company at Jewry Street, for with him were the poor unfortunates who had attended the meeting at Andover: Edward Walden, Daniel Smith, and Richard Montaine. And because of the good company James was far from being inactive. He made use of the time by comforting other nonconformists and praying with his fellow Quakers. He was also busy writing letters to the authorities and to families of the illiterate convicts. He would also act as their agent in their dealings with Warr, and would make out briefs for defence in their court cases. Meanwhile he

147

would pay close attention to the calendar and as assize time approached he would bombard the jailer with protests and demands to fetch the court officials to hear his case of appeal. But the assizes came and went without James' appeal being heard, as if intended. This failure did not silence the Quakers' advocate and he made sure that by the next one his captors would be willing to allow him access to the judge.

The following assizes were held at Winchester on 1st and 2nd March 1683. Judge Dolbin was in attendance at this court and was renowned for his lenience towards religious offenders. James Potter was able, this time, to have a message smuggled out of the prison which found its way to Dolbin's chambers. Immediately the judge ordered enquiries into the cases of the Quakers incarcerated in Jewry Street Prison, and then had them released by the jailer.

James Potter and his friends returned home for a short while after being set at liberty, but their freedom was short-lived this time. On 12th March bailiffs were sent to the homes of Potter in Baughurst, Smith in Marlborough, and Montaine in Andover to arrest the Quakers for failure to pay Roger Warr the fees due to him while they were his prisoners: therefore they were sent back to Jewry Street Prison for ten days for this misdemeanour. Finally, on 22nd of that month, they were liberated. James Potter had spent nine months and three days in prison on this occasion. To date Potter had spent over six years and one month in prison for his Quaker activities, but this latest internment would not yet be his last.

Quaker Burials at Baughurst 1675-1683

(13)   JOHAN SPENCER of Baughurst, at Baghurst, died 23rd October 1678, buried 25th October 1678 (also recorded in the Parish Register as "James Spencer, in Potter's yard")

(14)   SARAH SWAINE, daughter of Thomas Swaine of Tadly, at Baghurst, 10th February 1681 (also recorded in the Parish Register as "Sarah Swaine, in Potter's garden")

---

1 Men's Minutes, Quarterly Meeting.
2 Bishop Compton's Census of Canterbury quoted by Davidson.
3 Sufferings, Berks.
4 Men's Minutes, Quarterly Meeting, Hants.
5 Men's Minutes, Hampshire Quarterly Meeting.
6 Burial Digest, Hampshire and Dorsetshire General Meeting.
7 A yardland or virgate was roughly equivalent to thirty acres. Joan Spencer's estate was measured to contain about 47¼ acres in 1650, while Richard Potter's was slightly under 40 acres and recorded as a yardland and a half.

[8] This is the earliest surviving register for Baughurst and was begun in 1678. In an account about fencing the churchyard, dated 1723, there is reference to an earlier account in the old register. The date of the earlier account was given as 1622.

[9] Baughurst parish register, H.R.O.

[10] Cathedral Library, Winchester

[11] Cathedral Library, Winchester

[12] Cathedral Library, Winchester. (See note 23.)

[13] Hearth Tax Returns, 1663, P.R.O. Doc. E179/176/565.

[14] Sufferings, Hants.

[15] Sufferings, Berks.

[16] Sufferings, Hants.

[17] John Brown was born at Basingstoke in 1646, the son of John Brown. He became a personal friend of James Potter and is much recorded in this book in later chapters. He was one of the founder-members of the new Basingstoke Meeting in 1696, and his son married Richard Potter's daughter and thus his son in turn inherited the farm in 1747 and gave it its present name of Brown's Farm.

[18] Men's Minutes, Hampshire Quarterly Meeting.

[19] Browne inherited the Manor of Wolverton on the death of his father, George Browne of Spelmonden in Kent. The elder George had purchased the manor after 1660 from the executors of Lord Newburgh of Fife (who had died in 1644). By the end of the 18th century the manor was in the hands of the Pole family and was subsequently purchased from them in 1828 by the Duke of Wellington.

[20] Sufferings, Hants.

[21] Sufferings, Hants.

[22] Men's Minutes, Alton Monthly Meeting.

[23] "James Acton died in 1690, testate, seised of the Manor of Inhurst. He also held the Advowson of Bentworth, and lands in Binley and Basingstoke, and until April 1690 the brick-kiln at Basing, which he had recently sold. By his will he established four almshouses in Flexpoole Lane in Basingstoke. His brother, Michael Acton, inherited the Manor of Inhurst and the copyhold estate in Baughurst, under the Dean and Chapter of Winchester, which today includes Digweed's Farm and the "George and Dragon" public house. Michael Acton was a cleric, probably curate for St Michael's in Basingstoke. He died testate in 1697, by which time he had disposed of the Manor of Inhurst, but held the Advowson of Collingbourne Ducis, in Wiltshire. One of his legatees was William Woodward of Baughurst, who received a "guinea ring"."

CHAPTER SEVEN
1683-1689

I

" In ye yeare aforsayd 1683 James Potter of Baghurst had taken from him by William Woodward preist and his servants wheat and barly and oates to the value of fower pound five shillings and on the 11th day of ye 7th *m* 1683 the preists bayliffe Richard Hood of Kingscleare by an order out of ye Chayney Court at winchester tooke away six cowes worth about eighteen pounds for tithe pease and hay and aples and calves and eggs and cheese and such like for two yeares value worth 4 pound ten shillings In ye yeare aforesayd Richard Potter of baghurst had taken from him by ye aforesayd preist wheate oates barlye aples and one pigg to the value of five pound thirteen shillings

In the 5th and 6th monthes 1684 James Potter of Baghurst had taken from him by William Woodward Preist of ye same and his servants wheate barly and oates to the value of Three pounds And on the sixth day of ye *8th m* 1684 Mary buy servant to the sayd priest came with two Winchester Bayliffes and by a Chayney Court Distresse tooke away three cowes to the value of seven pound from ye aforesayd James Potter "

(Sufferings, Hants.)

" Wee p'sent James Potter to be rent reave for the tithing of Baghurst for the yeare ensewing "

" I nominate my son Matthew Potter to take ye Benefitt of this warrant — Richard Potter "

(Warrants and presentments of the estates of the Dean and Chapter of Winchester Cathedral, the Cathedral Library, Winchester)

A FTER HIS release from prison James wasted little time getting back into the routine of Quaker business. At the Quarterly Meeting of 27th March 1683 notice was taken of his release in the minutes, along with his receipt of ten shillings which he had spent out on Quaker business while he himself was in prison.[1] At the same meeting he and Nicholas Gates were directed to write an account of the current sufferings of the Hampshire Quakers and to deliver it to the General Meeting in London.

Thus Gates and Potter journeyed to the city at a time when it was becoming increasingly dangerous for nonconformists to travel there. By the time the year had completed its natural course the lot of the dissenting communities had become extremely critical. The Rye House Plot, although probably as fictitious a conspiracy as the Popish Plot of 1678, did for the Protestant nonconformists and the Whig Party what the hysteria of 1678 had done for the Catholics. After it had burst upon the scene in the June of that year the recriminations against the sects grew much more severe as they were being accused of supporting the ill-fated conspiracy which was intended to rid the country of the King and his Catholic brother, and to replace them with the Protestant "darling", Monmouth. Failure had cost William Russell and Algernon Sidney their heads, the City of London its charter, the Whig Party much of its support, and Monmouth his birthright as he was forced to flee abroad before the prevailing storm.

By the time that the consequences of the Rye House Plot had been fully disclosed Potter and Gates had returned from their expedition to the capital. In Hampshire, recriminations had been lessened by the fact that over the recent years the activities of the nonconforming groups had been found to be no more than apparently peaceful intentions aimed at the continuation of their worship without involving others. Now they could count on the general support of their neighbours, who were unwilling to bear witness against them, and the authorities themselves were discovering that their attempts to prosecute the dissenters were becoming increasingly more difficult. In order to persecute the sects upon purely political or religious grounds, the magistrates now required some substantial evidence. In the case of the Quakers only tithe persecutions were allowed without formal legal backing.

The tithes were specifically legal exactions imposed upon all and sundry and were assessed by rate on the personal profits or incomes of each parishioner. Only the poor were officially exempted from these Church taxes. At the same time an incumbent whose parishioners included Quakers could greatly profit from the refusal of these people to pay towards the maintenance of the Church, for he was legally entitled to claim the dues outstanding by distress of goods, which would be in excess of the value of the tithes because the incumbent could claim that he would not obtain the full price of the items if he sold them.

In 1683 Woodward's servants extracted from James Potter's fields wheat, barley, and oats to the value of £4 5s. 0d., and from Richard Potter the same crops, with apples, and a pig, together worth £5 13s. 0d.[2] Then on 11th September Richard Hood the bailiff from Kingsclere, armed with a warrant from Cheney Court in Winchester, seized from James Potter's lands six cows, worth about £18, and peas, hay, apples, calves, eggs, and cheese, etc., worth £4 10s. 0d.

In 1684 crops valued at £3 were taken from James' farmlands. Then on the 6th October Mary Bye, Woodward's servant, brought to James Potter's farm two bailiffs from Winchester, who held warrants issued out of Cheyney Court, and, after a fracas, led away three cows valued at £7. In all, the tithe persecutions of 1683 and 1684 had cost James £36 15s. 0d. — a vast amount of money which reflected his wealth at the time.

That same year (1684) James had to attend the Court Baron at Manydown where he was presented to act as the rent-reeve of Baughurst for the ensuing year.[3] This meant that he had to collect the rents due to the Manor, and would be given this post again in 1699.[4]

On the 5th August that year he officially surrendered his title to his brother's copyhold estate.[5] The surrender was made legal at the Court Baron held on the 15th October that same year, and in his place his brother nominated his own son, Matthew, as the third life. Matthias Potter, Richard and James' father, had been nominated as heir to the property in 1582. He died before 1660, when Richard, whose warrant was dated 1628, was admitted as tenant for his life. Richard nominated his brother and sister James and Ann to succeed him on the 17th November 1664, but Ann, then married, died in 1678, and Richard's son, Richard Potter the younger, was thus nominated to replace his aunt on 1st July 1678. Now, in 1684, the brothers had come to the conclusion that each had his own inheritance to bestow to his own family, and that there were no practical reasons in leaving the determination of succession as it was. Richard had a large family and James was little interested in inheriting the family's copy-hold estate. Therefore he surrendered his interest in Richard's farm to allow his brother to devise the estate to his sons. James had an only child — a daughter — and was willing to allow his personal lands to descend to his brother's family if it happened that both he and his daughter died without heirs. Therefore, the future of the brothers' properties were settled in full that year.

II

"There was an acct that Robert South of Pamber John Turner of Medsted was brought to prison for theire not going to heare the preists"

(Men's Minutes, Hampshire Quarterly Meeting)

"The accession of James II promised no substantial improvement in the lot of the nonconformists. Neither their conviction nor their past associations were such as to commend them to the new king. As a fanatical Catholic he would have little sympathy with the Puritan aspirations, and he was not likely to have forgotten their share in the Exclusion agitation. At first there seemed no reason to expect that James would alter in any significant respect the pattern which had been established in the last years of his brother's reign. . . ."

(Cragg, p. 26)

CHARLES II DIED, aged fifty-four, of euremia and mercurial poisoning at Whitehall Palace on 10th February 1685, and was buried amid pomp and pageantry in the crypt below the small chapel dedicated to his ancestress, Lady Margaret Beaufort, in Westminster Abbey. He had been on the throne for twenty-five of the most critical years in English history, although he officially counted his reign from the murder of his father in the January of 1649, eleven years beforehand.

His successor was one of the most unpopular princes to ascend the English throne. As Duke of York he had gained a reputation for being extremely bigoted and unbending — completely opposite in character to his late royal brother. Yet, above all, he openly confessed to his fanatical attachment to the Holy Church of Rome, and this more than any of his other traits brought him the immediate dislike of his subjects. Although he courted the Anglican Church this policy was viewed with the utmost suspicion by the faithful adherents of the Establishment. Naturally, he would continue the policy which was in use against the Protestant nonconformists during the closing years of Charles' reign, for the dissenters, more than any other group, had earned his hatred. They had allied themselves with the Whigs and had openly attempted to exclude him from his birthright — the throne of England, Scotland and Ireland.

153

Therefore, the Protestant dissenter was isolated under James II and could not expect any quarter from this vindictive king. Retribution upon the former Exclusionists and their allies was swift, and that retribution was even more intensified when the ill-fated Monmouth's Rebellion was put down and the rebels dealt with severely. In fact, although the non-conforming minority suffered extreme persecutions during the last years of Charles II's reign, they were to suffer worse deprivations in the early stages of James' rule.

On 3rd June 1685 there were no fewer than eleven Quakers being held in the Common Prison at Winchester.[6] Of these, one was a member of the Baughurst Meeting. Robert South[7] of Pamber was committed with John Turner of Medstead on account that both had not attended services in their respective parish churches.[8] This was in March 1685, and South was not released until the general pardon was issued on 13th April 1686. In the meantime James Potter had been advocating his release, and had attended the assizes on 31st March that year in order to " take off member's name by sessions ".[9]

However, as the months progressed persecution against the dissenters was beginning to relax substantially, both by popular demand and by royal decree — although the motives were basically different.

III

" In the yeare 1686 in the harvest time William Woodward Preist of the saied Baghurst caused to be taken from James Potter wheate barly oates and pease to the value of 5 lb 2s.
In the 9th month following ye aforsayd preist of Baghurst with Richard Hood a bayliffe under pretence of a county court warrant tooke away a timber peice and planks to the value of 3 lb for tithe ye yeare past from James Potter"

(Sufferings, Hants.)

" It having pleased Almighty God not only to bring us to the imperial crown of these kingdoms through the greatest difficulties, but to preserve us by a more than ordinary providence upon the throne of our royal ancestors, there is nothing now that we so earnestly desire as to establish our government on such a foundation as may make our subjects happy, and unite them to us by inclination as well as duty; which we think can be done by no means so effectually as by granting to them the free exercise of their religion for the time to come, and add that to the perfect enjoyment of their property, which has never been in any case invaded by us since our coming to the crown; which, being the two things men value most, shall ever be preserved in these kingdoms during our reign over them as the truest methods of their peace and glory."

(James II's First Declaration of Indulgence,
Whitehall Palace, 4th April 1687)

PROTESTANT DISSENTERS had known varying degrees of oppression throughout the course of the two and a half decades since the Restoration. At times they faced full scale parliamentary suppression, bolstered up by the local parish priest and magistrates. At other times they faced merely local resistance to their beliefs, and found that this type of persecution was the more severe and critical, as the oppressors were always on hand to deal out punishment.

Yet, as the years passed, local resistance became more subdued as the nonconformist's neighbours realised that he was a peaceful individual who merely wished to worship in private as he pleased, without attempting to press his beliefs upon others. This realisation appeared early in some districts, such as on the occasion when Parson Worrell faced opposition from his overseer of the poor in Brimpton because of the incumbent's treatment of the Burgis family. Nevertheless, the Anglican Church upheld the letter of the law in this matter and continued the policy of suppression and oppression despite local sympathy towards the victims of that policy. Therefore, persecution continued unabated by the application of the law by the authorities, but was hindered to a great degree through a lack of response from a number of those officers conscripted to help with its enforcement. On the other hand, there were always the few who were willing to do anything for monetary or other gain.

Anglican supremacy had to be maintained, and this could only be done through the strict process of law. In practice, the High Church policy was bound to fail through lack of popular support. Therefore, wholesale persecution against dissent was a policy doomed to failure in the long run. Here, the English dissenters were particularly lucky, for their continental counterparts suffered fates far worse than those inflicted upon the sectaries of this country.

As the sectaries had survived, partly through their own beliefs and through the inspiration which those beliefs provided them, then it was also deemed by their neighbours that they had earned at least partial toleration. David Ogg, the historian,[10] suggests that the average Englishman regarded the Church of England as an institution designed for the maintenance of public order. He further suggests that Mr Average considered that the non-conformists had committed a crime by standing aside from their fellow men, for they rejected the authority of the bishops, and refused to attend the services in the parish church. In so doing, quotes Ogg, the dissenter was withdrawing himself from a system of discipline and control.

Yet, there never was, and never will be, such a person as the average Englishman, and if there was, it is certain that his views would not have been made so clearly. When one speaks of the average person, one usually means the majority view. Unfortunately, in seventeenth-century England the majority view was never heard. The Anglican-dominated parliaments of Charles II's reign were the mouthpiece of the country, but were, in fact, only the representatives of the few — albeit the powerful few. Although the nonconformists were a minority group, then equally were the High Anglicans, represented by the aristocracy and the higher gentry, upon whose benevolence the Church depended for its survival. The majority, including the labouring classes, were undoubtedly Anglican in the main, but moderate Anglicans who were not particularly interested in persecuting nonconformist views out of existence. There were radicals in every sector of society, but even these were minorities. One would expect that the so-called average Englishman had had enough of violence and suppression and merely wished to live in peace, to tend to his own affairs, and to let others get away with things as long as nobody else was affected, and these would include tithe payments.

When the Quakers came into conflict with the Church over tithe dues they often paid dearly for their actions. Their refusals to pay the tithes would generally result in their paying many times more the original amount in distressed goods. In this way they were not necessarily dangerous to the Church system, for, in most cases, they provided the incumbent with a greater income, and became a source of wealth which could easily be tapped when times were hard. In the long run the Quaker objectors could easily have been helping to maintain the Church system. As the Quakers were being accused of acting illegally by refusing the tithe payments, then the ecclesiastics must stand equally guilty for the crime of exacting in excess of their dues, for the tithes were assessed at a fixed rate.

The so-called average Englishmen may have objected to Quakerism on the grounds of tithes, but it must be said that often the Anglican moaned about the Church tax yet continued to pay his dues. The Quaker had principles to which he adhered, despite the opposition, and had no fear of the law. The moderate Anglican, on the other hand, feared the law and the consequences of his own actions. In time, although the Quaker could be deemed irresponsible in this sphere, his attitudes were reflected in legislation and such Quaker principles as the refusal to swear on oath (which was based on the principle that his word alone was his bond) made their way into the statute book via the Act of 1696 which allowed a person to make a declaration instead of swearing an oath. The only difference between the so-called average Anglican Englishman and the Quaker was their particular observation of the laws of the land, which were legislated by those who were far from average, and in the interest of the upper classes.

But the laws of the land could have been suspended from time to time by royal decree, although this power had often led to constitutional arguments between the King and his Parliament, with the King acknowledging the supremacy of Parliament in the sphere of legislation. In 1687 James II's courtship with the Anglican Church was almost at an end. He had lost much of his support from the Anglican Tories because of their well-founded suspicions that he would attempt to establish a Catholic despotism of the type already in use in the France of his cousin, Louis XIV. He had alienated all the goodwill from this sector by his recent activities. Therefore, the King had no other alternative but to attempt to win over support from those who had formerly attempted to exclude him from the throne — the Whigs and the dissenters.

On 4th April 1687 James issued his Declaration of Indulgence from his palace at Whitehall. Through it he granted unrestricted toleration towards his nonconformist subjects, and it would appear that freedom of worship had been granted for the minorities at last. He received addresses of thanks from several individuals, while the majority of the dissenters accepted toleration as their due but remained silent in their gratitude. The Earl of Halifax pleaded with the dissenting community to treat the promise of toleration with suspicion. He need not have worried, for the nonconformists by and large refused to support the King, although a few individuals, such as William Penn the Quaker, were personal friends of James Stuart. But Penn did not represent the Quakers as a whole. Their attitude had not changed since 1672. They could not recognise toleration, for they refused to recognise persecution in the first place.

Therefore, for the Quakers at least, life continued in much the same vein as it was before the Declaration of Indulgence in 1687.

In 1686 James Potter suffered tithe incursions on the order of William Woodward to the value of £8 2s. 0d.[11] In the first raid of that year he lost wheat, barley, oats and peas worth £5 2s. 0d., and then in September

Richard Hood the bailiff entered the farm with a warrant from the county court and carted away timber and planks worth £3. In 1687 Potter had been assessed for £6 in tithes, but Woodward had a load of bark, a load and a quarter of timber and wood, a load of hay, and wheat, barley, oats, peas, and thatches taken from the Quaker's premises. In all this last incursion was valued at £11 12s. 0d. In July and August of 1688 the tithe-gatherers visited James several times, and carted away loads of hay worth £1 3s. 0d. During harvest-time wheat, oats, and peas worth £2 17s. 0d. were stolen from James' fields. On the same occasion Richard Potter had barley, oats, peas, and thatches worth more than £4 taken from his fields.

IV

" And whereas there are certain other persons, dissenters from the Church of England, who scruple the taking of any oath, be it enacted . . . that every such person shall make and subscribe the aforesaid declaration and also this declaration of fidelity following, viz.,
I, A.B., do sincerely promise and solemnly declare before God and the world that I will be true and faithful to King William and Queen Mary, and I do solemnly profess and declare that I do from my heart abhor, detest and renounce as impious and heretical that damnable doctrine and position that princes excommunicated or deprived by the Pope or any authority of the see of Rome may be deposed or murthered by their subjects or any other whatsoever, and I do declare that no foreign prince, person, prelate, state or potentate hath or ought to have any power, jurisdiction, superiority, pre-eminence or authority, ecclesiastical or spiritual, within this realm. And shall subscribe a profession of their Christian belief in these words, I, A.B., profess faith in God the Father, and in Jesus Christ his Eternal Son, the true God, and in the Holy Spirit, one God blessed for evermore, and do acknowledge the Holy Scriptures of the Old and New Testament to be given by divine inspiration.

And every such person that shall make and subscribe the two declarations and profession aforesaid, being there-unto required, shall be exempted from all the pains and penalties of all and every the aforementioned statutes made against popish recusants or Protestant nonconformists, and also from the penalties of an Act made in the fifth yeare of the reign of the late Queen Elizabeth entitled, An Act for the assurance of the queen's royal power over all estates and subjects within her dominions, for or by reason of such persons not taking or refusing to take the oath mentioned in the said Act, and also from the penalties of an Act made in the thirteenth and fourteenth years of the reign of King Charles the Second entitled, An Act for preventing mischiefs that may arise by certain persons called Quakers refusing to take lawful oaths, and enjoy all other the benefits, privileges and advantages under the like limitations, provisos and conditions which any other dissenters shall or ought to enjoy by virtue of this Act. . . ."

(Toleration Act: "An Act for exempting their Majesties' Protestant subjects dissenting from the Church of England from the penalties of certain laws", 1689, 1 Gul. & Mar., cap. 18, X)

ALTHOUGH THE Quakers on the whole would not recognise James II's promise of toleration, they did appear to take advantage of the situation which offered some respite from the persecutions which they had been suffering.

Nothing could suggest their confidence in lasting peace more than the spate of marriages which took place in 1687. On 29th March 1685 the second Quaker marriage of the Baughurst Meeting took place in Richard Potter's house, after a space of sixteen years. This would probably have been an isolated incident had it not been for the Declaration of Indulgence in 1687, for that year no less than three marriages were performed in James Potter's house.[12]

Yet, despite the confidence which his Declaration had bestowed in dissenting circles, the King was utterly disappointed with the reception it had received. It was intended as a vehicle to win over the full support of this important and prosperous minority group, for they were crucial to the implementation of his programme of Catholicisation. With or without the support of the dissenters he was committed to this programme, although their unrestricted support would gain him a greater advantage over his opponents.

He was already systematically removing Anglicans from positions of trust and replacing them with either Catholics or those Protestant nonconformists who had rendered him the support he needed. But that support from the Protestant sects figured as only a very small percentage of the whole, as the vast majority stood aside or even opposed the royal scheme. They had learned from experience that toleration often meant that they had to give more than they were willing to offer, and that the only successful means of gaining full religious freedom of worship was through the enactment of Parliament. James held no such approval, and his grant of liberty for tender consciences was thus doomed to failure.

In 1688 the King's programme of Catholicisation was in progress, but he still needed the support of the dissenting minority to make it fully successful and permanent. Therefore he issued his second Declaration of Indulgence, as an attempt to win over the support of those who were wavering the first time around. This royal edict was more radical in its terms than the first. It had the effect of causing the nonconformist support to detach itself further from the royal policy than before. Furthermore, it was the instrument which completely broke up the traditional Anglican support for the Crown, and heralded the period of anxiety for the Tories whereby they had to choose between the King and the Church.

James II's proclamation was to be read in every parish church in the kingdom, but its terms were so abhorrent to conscientious Anglicans that trouble was bound to follow before too long. The clergy was irate, and when seven bishops presented the King with a petition defending their position he had them sent to the Tower and committed for trial. Before long Anglicans and Protestant dissenters were united in their opposition to the Catholic king. Matters came to a head with the birth of a son to James' queen in the autumn of 1688, and this event persuaded a deputation of Whigs to invite the King's son-in-law, the Calvinist William III of Orange, to "invade" England.

The Prince of Orange landed on 5th November, a day with notorious associations, and as he proceeded towards Westminster the opposition began to dwindle. James fled before the ensuing storm and the so-called "Glorious Revolution" was staged without human fatalities, enabling it to be also labelled the "Bloodless Revolution".

In February 1689 James II was formally deposed by Parliament and William and his wife, Mary, were crowned in his stead. This time Parliament was particular that the conditions which had brought about James II's attempted autocratic rule would not prevail, and that the grievances which were never redressed at the Restoration of 1660 should now be righted. The monarchy was limited by the terms of the Bill of Rights, and Parliament was made into the supreme institution in the realm. Further constitutional changes were effected through the Revolutionary Settlement of 1689, and finally the religious question was also resolved with the Toleration Act.

Parliamentary toleration was granted in 1689 because, as the official statement reports, the Protestant dissenters had refused to support the former King in his programme of Catholicisation, or had stood aside from the argument, thus not lending him the much-needed support. The nonconformists had been promised religious freedom on several occasions in the past, but had never achieved it yet because of the fear of the authorities and the Anglican Church that such toleration would have been abused. Charles II had promised liberty to "tender consciences" at Breda in 1660, and at Whitehall in 1662 and 1672; his Parliament had attempted it with the abortive Toleration Act of 1680; and James II had dabbled with it in 1687 and 1688, for his own particular motives. Now, in 1689 Parliament had successfully granted it, because of the non-activity of the sects during the moment of the Church's gravest danger. Yet, even here the motives were rather suspect.

The incidents of 1688-9 were as revolutionary as those of 1649 and any other constitutional change in the past. It was unique in the case that a king had been deposed after an almost bloodless coup and that he had been replaced by another whose powers had been curtailed by a superior assembly made up of the so-called representatives of the people. This had, of course, happened in 1649 to an extent, but at that time the king had been "legally" murdered. If James II had been caught in 1688 then perhaps the outcome would have been the same. But he was not, and the fact remained that he could return to claim the throne which he was said to have forfeited through his act of disposing with the Great Seal in his flight from the country.

So, the "Glorious Revolution" was in danger of being overthrown by a counter-revolution in favour of the former king. This fact was uppermost in the minds of the members of Parliament who had consciously or unconsciously masterminded the operation. Toleration was no longer a strategy to be promised to the dissenters, in order to be taken away at will. Toleration for the dissenting minorities was now a fundamental necessity, for these were the very people to whom James II could appeal successfully if their lot was made worse by the change in government. In the event they could make or break the Revolution. Therefore their wishes had to be adhered to as they were now one of the most important factions in the country.

Thus the Toleration Act included every aspect of the nonconforming sects in its framework, and particularly outlined the various exemptions from the main conditions of the Act for such denominations as the Baptists and Quakers. All consciences, except for the Catholics and Unitarians, had to be considered in its all-embracing terms and conditions. Therefore the Quaker was allowed to make a declaration instead of the required Oath of

Allegiance. Yet they were not exempt from tithes, as these dues were still legal requisites from everybody, no matter their beliefs. All in all, there was nothing to which the Quaker could hold objection in the Toleration Act, and although he could not acknowledge the Act on the principle that he should not be persecuted for his religious beliefs in the first place, he did accept with gratitude the peace that such an enactment would bring. After almost half a century of prejudice and oppression the Quaker was now allowed to walk among Anglicans and to be treated as a brother, and was accepted as a respected member of the community. That is, until such a time as he was being persecuted for not paying tithes. This element of resistance continued unabated, for such resistance to order and authority was an essential part of the Quaker's character. He was a religiously proud man and would not surrender anything in the face of adversity. The law had to bow down to him, not him to the law. And so it did eventually — as in 1689. Finally, he changed the laws of the land in certain ways to his own beliefs, as with the Emancipation of Slaves, Prison Reform, Education, and the Welfare State. Few of these were Quaker enactments, but they were achieved by much Quaker propaganda and through Quaker influence, and were integral to the system already being operated by the Society of Friends. They believed in Man's equality and would not allow slavery to continue; their experiences in prison encouraged the reform of these places, of which Elizabeth Fry was one of the instigators; it was a Quaker, W. E. Forster, who introduced the Education Act of 1870, based on the system already in use in Quaker circles, which provided elementary education to all children; while the Welfare State itself owes much of its origins to that very same system in operation in many Quaker factories, such as those owned by the Cadbury and Rowntree families. The Act of 1689 did not allow the Quakers to involve themselves in these schemes, as they were already involved to a smaller degree in similar schemes, owing to the funding of the Public Stock. What it did do was to free them from the burdens of persecution on religious grounds and to allow them to involve others in their schemes of benevolence to mankind. They would, as the years passed, find a voice that would be heard instead of one that was constantly being suppressed. Thus the Toleration Act, for all the motives behind it and for its exaggerated significance in the history of the country, did prove beneficial to the growth of the spirit of humanity in the world.

Quaker Marriages at Baughurst 1683-1689

(2)   EDWARD BARNES, of the Psh of Baughurst, and MARY ABERY, of the Psh of Baughurst, at Richard Potter's house, in Baughurst, 29th March 1685.

(3) ROBERT SOUTH, of Pamber, and MARGARET ALDER, of Midgeam, Co, Berks, at James Potter's house, in Baghurst, 26th August 1687.

(4) WILLIAM SMITH, of Midgeam, Co. Berks, and JANE GILL, of Midgeam, Co. Berks, at James Potter's house, in Baghurst, 23rd September 1687.

(5) JOHN HASKINS, of Midgeam, Co. Berks, and ALICE HASLETT, of Brimpton, Co. Berks, at James Potter's house, in Baghurst, 22nd November 1687.

Quaker Burials at Baughurst 1683-1689

(15) WILLIAM BUG or Buy, of Tadly, in Potter's garden, 21st December 1683 (this entry was only recorded in the Parish Register, and thus omitted by the Quakers themselves).

(16) JOSEPH GODDIN, son of Jeremiah & Ann Goddin, of the Psh of Kingscleare, who died 15th March 1683/4, and was buried at Baughurst, 16th March 1683/4 (also recorded in the Parish Register as "Joseph Greene or Godwin, in Potter's garden, the 6th March 1683" — Greene was his mother's maiden name).

(17) DANIELL GODDIN, of Kingsclere, in Potter's garden, 25th July 1684 (only recorded in the Parish Register).

(18) JOHN HOSKINS, of Thatcham, in Potter's garden, 24th September 1684 (only recorded in the Parish Register).

(19) ANN GODDIN, wife of Jeremiah Goddin, of Kingsclere, who died 1st July 1685, and was buried at Baughurst 2nd July 1685 (only recorded by the Quakers).

(20) JOHAN HASKINS, wife of John Haskins, of Midgeam, Co. Berks, who died 23rd July 1685, and was buried at Baughurst 24th July 1685 (also recorded in the Parish Register as "Joane Hoskins, of Thatcham, in Potter's garden").

(21) MARY BURGIS, of Brimpton, Co. Berks, who died 19th September 1685, and was buried at Baughurst 20th September 1685 (also recorded in the Parish Register as "Mary Burges, in Potter's garden").

(22) ANDREW PERSON, of Brimpton, Co. Berks, who died 19th September 1685, and was buried at Baughurst 20th September 1685 (also recorded in the Parish Register as "Andrew Deane, in Potter's garden").

(23) MARY SOUTH, wife of Robert South, of Pamber, at Baughurst 22nd December 1685 (also recorded in the Parish Register as "Mary South, in Potter's garden, 23rd December 1685).

(24) NICHOLAS RABBETS, of Basingstoke, who died 6th January

1685 and was buried at Baughurst 8th January 1685 (also recorded in the Parish Register as "Nicholas Roberts, in Potter's garden, 8th January 1683").

(25) JOSEPH GODDIN, in Potter's garden, 26th August 1686 (only recorded in the Parish Register).

(26) JOHN GLOVER, of Itchingswell, in Potter's garden, 19th January 1686 (only recorded in the Parish Register).

(27) MARGARETT SPENCER, of Baghurst, who died 14th June 1688, and was buried at Baghurst 16th June (also recorded in the Parish Register as "Margaret Spenser, in Potter's garden, the 17th June 1688).

[1] Men's Minutes, Hampshire Quarterly Meeting.

[2] Sufferings, Hants.

[3] Presentments, Cathedral Library, Winchester.

[4] Court Books, Cathedral Library, Winchester.

[5] Warrants and Court Books, Cathedral Library, Winchester.

[6] Sufferings, Hants.

[7] He married Margaret Alder in James Potter's house in 1687 (his second wife), and was buried in Richard Potter's garden-plot in 1691.

[8] The law required that people attended church services at least once a month.

[9] Men's Minutes, Quarterly Meeting.

[10] "England in the Reigns of James II and William III", O.U.P., 1955, p. 95.

[11] Sufferings, Hants.

[12] Marriage Digest, Hampshire and Dorsetshire General Meeting.

CHAPTER EIGHT
1689-1695

I

"James Potter is now desired to look after the Clerks returne of freinds, into the Exchequer, and give us an account next Quarterly meeting."

(Men's Minutes, Hampshire Quarterly Meeting,
dated 29th December 1687)

"Then John Browne of Basingstoke proposed concerning two Ancient maidens who are helped by Freinds yt they might live together and it is the advice of Freinds to them that they should live together in love and be helpful to one another."

(Men's Minutes, Alton Monthly Meeting,
dated 13th April 1691)

"Then Robert Aplgate acquainted Freinds that George Browne of basingstoake insist and speake wanting reliefe this meeting desires him to take care that the man be supplied and bring the charge to the next quarterly meeting."

(Men's Minutes, Alton Monthly Meeting,
dated 15th April 1695)

FOR THE QUAKERS in 1689 there was little need to harken back to the past, for the way was clear ahead for a bright and peaceful future. James Potter had, thankfully, been deprived of one office, yet had gained another. In 1687 he had been elected the Clerk, or Secretary, for the Quarterly Meeting of Hampshire, for life, and among his responsibilities was the entering of the Sufferings. In order to provide an efficient history of the past persecutions experienced by Quakers in that county, he transcribed the old book, grouping each account under a particular heading, and then entering the new sufferings after those taken from the original. In so doing he was able to make a brief summary of the costs of the persecutions to the Hampshire Quakers, in money, wasted time through imprisonment, and in lives.

At the same time his role as the advocate for the Quakers appearing at the Assizes in Winchester had ended. At the meeting of 29th December 1687 he and John Burroughs were paid £6 for "taking out prisoners last sessions", of which the advocates retained £5 for the relief of those who had suffered through imprisonment.[1] This was James' last visit to the Assizes as the spokesman for erring Friends.

He still attended both the monthly and quarterly meetings as the representative for the Baughurst Meeting, and in his function as a member of the administration. The business meetings at Alton were mainly concerned with the relief of those Quakers in acute distress. In 1691 John Brown brought up the matter of two old women who were in dire need of each other's company, for, as Quakers, they still faced an alien world. Although they had received help from local Friends, they were constantly being disagreeable. The advice from the Monthly Meeting was that they should learn to love each other and to use the Quaker code literally by helping, instead of hindering, each other.

Then, in 1695, Robert Applegarth brought to the attention of the Monthly Meeting the plight of George Brown of Basingstoke, who was severely distressed. Applegarth was ordered to provide for the man and his family, and his expenses and costs would be repaid to him at the next quarterly meeting.

In so many ways the Quakers helped their fellows to overcome their problems, with the aid of the County Stock and local contributions, which were being supplemented with purely physical help from their charitable friends and neighbours. The Quaker community was expanding rapidly, now that most of the legal barriers had been officially demolished. Yet, within a couple of decades the faith would lose much of its appeal because it had become too respectable and its adherents were too "quiet". It is ironic that during its most dangerous years it had appealed to a number of people because of its associated rebelliousness, although, at the same time, many had fallen by the wayside because it was regarded as too dangerous to support, and many had found it extremely difficult to adhere to its strict moral code and disciplinary ways. By the time that it had lost its appeal for its "quietness", the majority of the old school, who had maintained the religion throughout its most persecuted period, were dead. This would then suggest the theory that it was the people rather than the faith itself which gave the right impetus to such beliefs. It is questionable whether

Quakerism would have gained such a strong hold on certain communities if it had not been for people such as James Potter. If he had not lived would Baughurst have been practically a Quaker bastion within the wilderness of High Anglicanism?

As the persecution had generally died down, especially since the passing of the Toleration Act, James found that he had more time on his hands, and would spend it at home, from where he had been absent for most of the time. He was well-known in Baughurst, and was regarded more as a celebrity by his neighbours and friends. His status in life was now definitely that of a gentleman. His brother farmed his land efficiently, although in the 1690s Richard himself was living in semi-retirement while his son was actually doing the hard work associated with husbandry. In all, the two estates amounted to a grand total of eighty-seven acres, a large amount of land to farm on one's own.[2]

II

"Item we present Jeams Potor to find a Tything bagust for the yeare insuing 1691."

(Presentments, Court Rolls of the Manor of Manydown, Cathedral Library, Winchester)

"On the 18th day of the 7th month 1692 James Potter had taken by William Woodward and Jeremiah Overton bayliffe by distresse out of ye Chayney Court For tithes one brasse pot and three pieces of pewter to the value of fourteen shillings, And on the 28th day of the 8th month came againe the aforsayd bayliffe and bryant woodward the Preists brother and tooke by execution out of ye aforsayd Court for tythes a horse and sadle and halter and seven milch Cowes a pennell and a Cushen and a cloth being worth twenty foure pounds for three yeares Tithe valued thirteen pounds."

(Sufferings, Hants.)

GREGORY KING'S estimate of the population of England and Wales in 1688[3] accounted for 5,500,520 persons. Of these 40,000 families, numbering about 280,000 persons, were classed as freeholders of the better sort with an annual income of around £91; 120,000 families, numbering about 660,000 persons with an income of £55, were classed as freeholders of the lesser sort. In 1687 James Potter's tithe dues were valued at £6, and, as tithes were meant to represent about one tenth of a person's income or profit, then he would have earned an annual income of £60 or more. Thus he would, even then, have been classed as a freeholder of the better sort, or the equivalent. That is, James was among the gentry of England, and the profits from his forty-seven-acre farmlands, along with other properties that he had accumulated in the area, made him a fairly wealthy person.

In 1691 he attended the Court Leet at Manydown where he was elected as the tithingman for Baughurst for the following year.[4] This office, although in some ways similar to that of constable, was a manorial service which extended over the good behaviour of the customary tenants and their families and heirs. The tithingman also had to collect the head-pence or chevage, a manorial form of poll-tax, from all the inhabitants of his tithing. This sum regularly amounted to 6s 8d for the residents of Baughurst. Normally, this unpopular task was farmed out to others.

In 1692, after two years of inactivity, William Woodward decided to prosecute Potter for non-payment of tithes.[5] Woodward had been in a quandary since the Toleration Act came into force. Although tithes had been stipulated as legal exactions by the conditions of the Act, and such refusals to pay would be treated as felonies, clerics were still rather unsure how they stood in respect of prosecution without the formal support of the Exchequer and its courts.

Woodward, therefore, had not attempted to deprive James Potter of goods, crops or livestock since 1689, while Richard Potter had not received a visit from the parish priest's marauding servants since the year before that. Now, in 1692, Woodward had travelled to Winchester again in order to have a warrant issued from Cheyney Court for the distress of James' goods because of his nonpayment of tithes for three years. The action was probably instigated by the Quaker's election as the manorial tithingman, and Parson Woodward may have wished to make an example of him before the tenants for whom he was supposed to have been responsible, as their police officer.

On 18th September Parson Woodward accompanied the bailiff, Jeremiah Overton, to James' farm, where they forced an entry into the house, despite Potter's initial objections. The bailiff showed the Quaker his warrant for distress and then proceeded about his business. He was rather perturbed about his work, and when the officials left the premises all they had taken from the house was one brass pot and three pieces of pewter, which were later valued at fourteen shillings. However, the bailiff returned on 28th October, this time with the priest's brother, Bryant Woodward, and proceeded about his business in the yard instead of in the house. This time James was deprived of valuable stock, comprising a horse, with its saddle and halter, seven milk-cows, a pannel, a cushion, and a cloth, worth together £24. James' tithe debt for the three years had amounted to £13, while his losses totalled £24 14s. 0d. He had been deprived of almost double his outstanding dues. But, even then, he could afford such outrages into his personal property. Consequently, he could well afford to pay his tithe bill in the first place. It was only his Quaker principles which deterred him from making contributions to an alien church, which he deemed that he should not support despite the approval of toleration granted by that Church.

III

"Mr. Potter greatly enlarged and added to the farm house from a still older one on the same site, and it stands to-day practically the same now as then. On the central gable is the date 1693, and the initials R.P.M. for Richard and Mary Potter, his wife; while A.N. for Ann Potter is on the south chimney."

(Florence Davidson: "The Quaker Burial Grounds at Baughurst" (P.H.F.C.J.) 1911)

HAMPSHIRE QUAKERS had a particularly active year in 1693. On 27th June that year the Quarterly Meeting gave its assent to the establishment of a monthly meeting at Basingstoke "adjacent every 4th first day in the month".[6] This meant that Basingstoke became the site of the Monthly Meeting in the northern part of Hampshire, holding meetings there every fourth month, while for the other months of the year Alton was retained as the venue. This would then allow those representatives living remote from the eastern edge of central Hampshire to gain easier access to the Monthly Meeting at least three times a year, and was the direct consequence of the occurrence in 1691 when the Whitchurch and Andover meetings detached themselves from the Alton Monthly Meeting to form their own monthly at Andover. There had already been undercurrents since that year, whereby other meetings were threatening to leave the union centred on Alton and to set up on their own, or to attach themselves to Andover. Suddenly, there appeared to be a certain amount of disharmony among the people who had remained united throughout the severest of persecutions.

The constant years of hard work and investment in the future were now yielding a ripe harvest for Quakerism. The coffers of the County Stock

169

were full, despite the continuing tithe oppressions which depleted the average Quaker's hard-earned income. Over the years many of the meeting houses had been allowed to fall into disrepair because of the plight of many of the poorer families whose breadwinner was facing heavy fines or suffering imprisonment for his adherence to his faith, and their need for financial support from the County Stock or the local funds. The majority of the contributions went to the relief of those who were suffering for their beliefs, or to aid members of other meetings who had been distressed by fire or other accidents, physical or otherwise. There was never anything much left to repair buildings which had suffered from the ravages of time or inclement weather. And there was certainly nothing left with which the Quakers could purchase additional properties for the use of worship.

Now that religious persecution had ended, there were only those people who were suffering from the normal conditions of poverty, or were being threatened with heavy tithe debts, who were now burdens on the Quaker funds. Even they were being sufficiently aided by their neighbours. Thus the County Stock grew, and could be put to better use as a finance house or bank. Loans for building repairs or purchasing new buildings were now made available to the several meetings in Hampshire, and in 1694 purchases of meeting houses were made by the members of the meetings of Fordingbridge and Ringwood with the aid of the County Stock. Before too long Basingstoke would be having a new meeting house, while in Baughurst plans had already been made for the improvement of the existing one.

The rebuilding and extension of Richard Potter's farmhouse was completed by the end of 1693 with capital supplied by James Potter and the regular members of the Baughurst Meeting, and subsidised by a loan from the County Stock. The old house had not been demolished, but was encased in new brickwork and plaster to match the larger extension which was attached to its southern wall. The farmhouse was now a much grander affair, measuring three times its original size, and adapted to the current style of architecture. Even the roof was altered, and thatch was replaced by slate. The old newel by the hearth disappeared to make way for a door leading from the old house to the new extension, while the northern and eastern entrances were closed up and filled in, and access into the house was made via the gabled western wall and the single-storey servants' entrance on the eastern side.

There were now three reception rooms instead of the single all-purpose hall of the husbandman's cottage. Each room had its individual hearth, the central room favouring the out-dated inglenook, while the southern room had a fashionable curved fireplace. The beams in the extension were appropriate for that period, a single king-beam running the length of the extension from north to south, with chamfered edges denoting its period. The house now boasted a wide stairway which was situated in the eastern part of the house, with its carved balustrade, leading up to a fairly wide and open landing which led into four adequate bedrooms. Long pegs were even added to the walls of the bedrooms for the male occupants to hang their wigs at night, or to delouse them. The famous attic which served its purpose well during the twilight days of the clandestine meetings was now made accessible by stairs leading from the landing, instead of the old portable ladder. Now the house had two lofts, the original wattled wall separating them.

It was no longer the humble yeoman's cottage which had witnessed so many historical scenes, but rather the comfortable house of the new middle class. The old house was retained for sentimental reasons,[7] and because it was associated with so many events and people that it was of historical necessity.

The structure itself was a major achievement by the skilled artisans of the time, for it blended the old and new to such a degree that one cannot tell the difference between the two types of building without entering the premises. To signify his work for all posterity the builder carved over the second-storey window, which was situated on the gabled protuberance over the main entrance, the year "1693", under which was a "P" surmounting "R M", which initials stood for Richard and Mary Potter. On the southern wall he placed the initials "A N" for himself. He built the house from bricks made at the Ramsdell Kiln, which was a leasehold estate of the Manor of Manydown.

IV

"Then James Potter acquainted Friends that hee Intends to settle the meeting howse he Built wth a Parcell of Ground for a Burying place in trust on Henry Streater of Brampshot yeoman Robert messer of Ringwood Cloathier Moses Neave of Alton Jun Cloathier Nicholas Gates Jun Alton Cloathier & John buy of Reading Mealman.

Then James Potter & John Browne pposed to Friends the haveing a publike meeting at Basingstoke monthly for Busyness, & it is refered to consideration till next Quarterly meeting."

(Men's Minutes, Hampshire Quarterly Meeting, dated 25th December 1694)

171

"Whereas James Potter of Baghurst in the County of Southton Yeoman hath by Deede beareing date the fift of the month called June 1695 setled a messuage or tennemt with the Outhouses & Buildings wth the Garden Orchard & little Pittle of Ground with the Appurtenances thereunto belonging within the said Parrish upon us whose names are hereunder written our heires And assignes to the use & behoofe of the said James Potter for & dureing the Terme of his Naturall life. And after his decease to the use & behoofe of Marjery his wife dureing the Terme of her Naturall life. And after their decease to the use of us our heires & Assignes foreaver Provided that the said James Potter do not make another settlement of it in his life time as by the said Deede may more at large appeare. Now wee do hereby declare that the said Messuage with the Appurtenances so made & setled as aforesaid is only in Trust for the use & Benefit of the People of God called Quakers And that it is the Intent & agreement betwixt the said James his heires and assignes : And us our heires & assignes that they the said People shall have the use & benefit of all the said Premises with free liberty to meet in the said Howse to do & performe any such duty or service as may tend to the honour & Glory of God; And to the good of his People called Quakers; Or to Performe any other service in it which they shall see meete. And that the true end & intent hereof may bee truly Performed wee do promise for our selves our Heires & Assignes that if the said messuage or Tenemt shall descend & com into our Power by the death of the said James Potter & Marjery his wife that wee shall order & dispose of the said messuage or Tennemt with the Appurtenances as our Friends of the monthly meeting now setled at Alton (or that may or shall bee setled at any other place for the service of God & of his People aforesaid thereabouts on that side of the County) shall from time to time, And at all times hereafter direct & Appoint. And if it shall so com to pass (as wee hope the Contrary) That any difference shall arise by or betweene the friends of the monthly meeting concerning the Premises aforesaid that then such difference shall bee referred to the Friends of the Quarterly meeting of the said People in the County aforesaid to bee determined by

172

them, Or by such as they in the Wisdom of God shall see meet to commit it unto to put an end to it. And wee do each of us Promise for for our selves our heires & Assignes truly & faithfully to Performe the trust therein comited to us. In witness whereof wee have hereunto set our hands the 24th of the month called July 1696.

Whereas in the Deed of Trust to Robert Messer Nicholas Gates Jun Moses Neave Jun Henry Streater & John Buy the Tenemt is setled on us for the Terme of our Naturall Lives. Wee do hereby Promise that wee shall not hinder our Friends to have the use & Benefit Of the said Howse to meete togeather in to Performe that Duty which they ow unto God; And one to another But rather endeavour to Propagate the same. And also that they shall have liberty to Bury their Dead in that Parcell of Grownd already Planted & set forth for that use & service with free Ingress Egress & Regress to pass & repass to the said Howse & Parcell of Grownd as often as they shall have Occasion, or see a service in it witness our hands the 24th of the month called July 1696.

James Potter

And whereas there is a Power reserved to mee in the said Deed that In my lifetime by Will or otherwise may alter the settlemt of the said Tenemt. I do hereby Promise not so to alter it as that it may bee Converted to any other use then is Intended or is herein after Expressed. And whereas one motive was at the first Indureing mee thus to settle the said Tenemt so as that it might bee a place for gods People to serve & worship him In them them Parts. And that they might not bee to seeke for a Conveanient Burying place. And also that it might bee a place if need require to Accomodate Publike Freinds that shall bee drawne forth in their spirits to visit that meeting or other meetings thereabouts. So its my desire of the monthly & Quarterly meetings wth the Power is committed to which shall or may succeed when it shall please god to remove us out of this Troublesom world to Emdeavour to keepe an honist friend of truth in it. And let him have the use & Benefit of it so far as hee shall assist & Entertaine such Publike friends as aforesd If it should so

173

please God (which its hoped otherwise) there should not
bee any other friend in that Place thats able & so given up
in his spirit to assist & entertaine such publike friends as
aforesaid. But if there shall bee any Friend or Friends
thereabouts Conveanient that is able & freely given up in
that service Then the Benefit or Rent that shall bee made
of it may goe into the Publike Stock for friends of that
County to bee Imployed in the service of Truth among
the despised people called Quakers witness my hand the
24th of the month called July 1696.

James Potter "

*(Deed conveying the Title of James Potter's house to the
Trustees of the Baughurst Meeting, dated 24th July 1696
(Hampshire Record Office))*

WITH THE COMPLETION of the rebuilding of Richard Potter's farmhouse,
work began immediately on James Potter's house. For some time now the
brothers had shared the responsibility of hosting the meeting, and, more
often than not, the marriages were performed in James' home. While the
rebuilding programme was underway at the official Potter residence, all
weekly meetings were being held in James' house.

The rebuilding of James Potter's copyhold tenement was more or less
completed by the autumn of 1694, as the insignia at the upper section of
the gabled entrance states " 1695 P. J. M. " (James and Margery Potter),[8]
but the record of the Quarterly Meeting for 25th December 1694 shows
categorically that the house was built by that date.[9]

The house itself resembled his brother's new building, although little of
the late seventeenth-century development is noticeable today, owing to
major renovations and additions during the early part of the nineteenth
century, when it was rebuilt to the design of a typical grand mansion
house, complete with extra wings. At the same time it was given the
grander name of Baughurst House, in line with its appearance and the
status in the community of its owners. Yet even before such aggrandisement had begun, the interior of the house had been through several phases
of transition from the simple decor which had met with James Potter's
approval, to the more elaborate furnishings associated with the upper
gentry of the eighteenth century. Plastered walls made way for oak
panelling, and simple white-washed ceilings were replaced by ornamented
plaster. It all gave the house an illusion of grandeur which betrayed its
former glory as the house occupied by Quakers.[10] Yet the total alteration

of James Potter's house was well into the future. His rebuilding scheme, although it had enlarged his copyhold messuage on a wide scale, was devoid of the trappings of the upper gentry who were allied with the Anglican Church. His extension programme had a real purpose behind it.

Richard was nearing his seventieth year and was looking forward to retiring from the arduous business of farming, and was disinclined to keep his house open for weekly meetings. It is true that his son now farmed his copyhold estate, but this the younger Richard felt it adequate to farm his father's lands, which now contained almost forty acres, and felt that the extra acreage of his uncle's estate was an additional burden, now that some of his brothers and sisters had moved away and the family was somewhat smaller. Even so, he continued to farm a little of James' lands for the combined benefit of both families and the Baughurst Meeting in general. But this was only a fraction of James' fairly large inheritance. Therefore, the Quaker gentleman had to find another farmer to till his soil, and he approached Richard Baghurst, who had his farm near the parish church,[11] and the two came to an agreement whereby Baghurst would lease the lands from Potter for a period of ten years. James then had to apply for a licence from the Dean and Chapter to allow for such a lease. Permission was granted, and the application was duly enrolled in the Court Rolls of the Manor of Manydown in 1695.[12]

At the same time James had approached several members of the Alton Monthly Meeting over his future proposals. He was intending to make his newly-extended house into the meeting house for Baughurst, thus allowing his brother the freedom which he now desired, and, in order that Richard's retirement would be complete, the current burial ground in the elder Potter's garden would be terminated as a public cemetery. In its place James would offer over to the Quakers the meadow which he had recently purchased at Town's End.[13]

At the following Quarterly Meeting, on 25th December 1694,[14] James and his friend, John Brown, put forward a proposal to have a business meeting at Basingstoke on the occasions when it was the venue for the Alton Monthly Meeting. This motion was entered on to the minutes for discussion at the next Quarterly, but then it was deferred at the March meeting.

Meanwhile, James also made it public that he intended to hold future meetings in Baughurst at his newly-built home, and that he planned to open up his meadow at Town's End as the burial ground attached to that meeting. In so doing he presented to the Meeting a list of the Quakers who were willing to perform the duties as Trustees of the Baughurst Meeting. The members of the Quarterly Meeting duly acknowledged Potter's intention and the process of drawing up a draft deed began.

On 5th June 1695 James Potter's house officially became the meeting house for Baughurst,[15] and on that day Henry Streeter, yeoman of Bramshott; Robert Messer, clothier of Ringwood; Moses Neave the younger, clothier of Alton; Nicholas Gates the younger, clothier of Alton; and John Bye, mealman of Reading, took up their duties as trustees of the meeting house and burial ground. An era had ended as Richard Potter's house no longer functioned as the centre for Quakerism in that district. It had been the bastion of Fox's ideals now for thirty-three years, through the most critical period that the Friends had ever known. It had faced assault from the unflinching Anglican oppressors, yet had never yielded to their constant attacks upon its privacy. It had witnessed the most historical scenes that Baughurst had ever known, and had housed at least one of England's more notorious personalities, George Fox, creating for him an adequate refuge at a time when his freedom was threatened, as it had been on most occasions. Now Potter's farmhouse would sink once more into oblivion, yet even as it retired from its public task as the venue for the Quaker meetings, as its doors opened to fewer visitors, the regular members would often look across at it from James' house and reminisce of those days of yore. It was loved and respected in more ways than its successors could be, for it was the key to that faith in this isolated and rural domain, and even today it is honoured as a historical building of some renown, whereas the functions of the others had been forgotten long since.

Quaker Marriages at Baughurst 1689-1695

(6)   JOSEPH GILPIN, of Dorchester, Co. Oxford, and HANNAH GLOVER, of Ichingswell, at Baughurst, 23rd February 1692.

(7)   WILLIAM BLUNDEN, of Brimton, Co. Berks, and ELIZABETH APLETON, of Tadley, at Baughurst, 23rd May 1693.

Quaker Burials at Baughurst 1689-1695

(28)   SAMUELL BURGIS, aged 22, of Brimpton, Co. Berks, who died 4th October 1689, and was buried at Baughurst 7th October 1689 (also recorded in the Parish Register as "Samuell Burges, in Potter's garden, 7th October 1689").

(29)   HANNAH WHITAKER, wife of Benjamin Whitaker, of Ichingswell, who died 11th December 1689, and was buried at Baughurst 14th December 1689 (sleo recorded in the Parish Register as "Hannah Whitaker, in Potter's garden, 14th December 1689").

176

(30) LYDIA WHITAKER, daughter of Benjamin Whitaker of Ichingswell who died 12th March 1690, and was buried at Baghurst the 15th March 1690 (also recorded in the Parish Register as "Lydia Whitaker, in Potter's garden, 17th March 1690").

(31) JEREMIAH GODWIN, son of Jeremiah Godwin, of Kingscleare, who died 5th February 1692, and was buried at Baughurst 7th February 1692 (also recorded in the Parish Register as "Jeremiah Godwyn, in Potter's garden, 11th February 1692").

(32) ROBERT SOUTH, of Pamber, who died 7th February 1692, and was buried at Baughurst 9th February 1692 (also recorded in the Parish Register as "Robert South, in Potter's garden, 19th February 1692").

[1] Men's Minutes, Hampshire Quarterly Meeting.
[2] Parliamentary Survey of the Manor of Manydown, 1649, Cathedral Library, Winchester.
[3] Quoted by G. M. Trevelyan: "English Social History", Penguin, 1967, p. 293.
[4] Court Rolls, Manor of Manydown, Cathedral Library, Winchester.
[5] Sufferings, Hants.
[6] Men's Minutes, Hampshire Quarterly Meeting.
[7] The original part of Brown's Farm is a treasure for the architectural historian, with its low, beamed ceiling and exposed crucks, while in this part of the loft the observer can see the wooden pegs which joined each beam, with their carpenter's mark carved into them.
[8] The inscription is rather illegible, owing to what could be cracks appearing in the surface around it. The date has been suggested as either 1693, 1695, and 1698 (Davidson states the latter, but she had been consistently incorrect). The Quarterly Meeting Minutes state that it had been built before December 1694.
[9] Men's Minutes, Hampshire Quarterly Meeting: see p. 171.
[10] Only one of the walls of the original sixteenth-century house survives as an interior wall, and as a reminder of the simple yeoman's cottage that used to stand on the site.
[11] Now Violet Farm.
[12] Court Rolls, Cathedral Library, Winchester.
[13] Now Forge Fields.
[14] Men's Minutes, Hampshire Quarterly Meeting.
[15] See the Deed of Conveyance, dated 24th July 1696, p. 173.

CHAPTER NINE
1695-1703

I

"On the 25th of the 9th month James Potter of
Baghurst was served with a subpena by one Searle a
lawyer in winchester and another man with him to
appeare the last day of the terme in the Exchequer at the
suite of William Woodward preist in a case of Tithes
And the 12th of the 12th month a proclamation being
put against him he went to one Crop of Winchester the
Sheriff's Deputy and delivered himselfe to him who the
same day delivered him prisoner to the Jaylor."

(Sufferings, Hants.)

R EGULAR WEEKLY meetings now took place at James Potter's
house, and people still travelled a distance to worship there among the
regular congregation. Although the trustees had been constituted by the
deed of 5th June 1695, a further legal document had to be framed and
witnessed in order to regulate the descent of the meeting house. On 24th
July 1696[1], James, in his capacity as a lawyer for the Quakers, had had a
deed of conveyance, with a copy of the same, formally sanctioned and
made lawful as the last instrument determining the future of his house, but
with the express right that he could alter such an agreement through his
last will and testament.

The deed itself stated that James and Margery had the full use of the
house during their respective lifetimes, allowing Quakers to worship there
and to bury their dead in the little meadow set aside as their cemetery. On
their death, however, the meeting house and burial ground would then
come into the full possession of the trustees constituted by the deed of
1695, and they would place a nominee of their choice as their tenant and
occupier in that house. The Trustees themselves were responsible to the
members of the Alton Monthly Meeting, and if any dispute arose then it
would be resolved by the Quarterly Meeting. The terms of the deed were

met with the condition that at all times there would be free access for the Quakers to both the meeting house and burial ground.

In the meantime, before the second deed had been made, all such things were understood. James and Margery lived in the house with their unmarried daughter, welcoming visitors at odd times and holding the weekly meeting there. The Quaker gentleman was now at home and at peace, and had little desire to leave his estate, except for the monthly visits to Alton or Basingstoke, and the quarterly visits on Quaker business. Occasionally he would have some duties to perform elsewhere in the country, but these were now kept to a minimum, for he was aging and had wished to retire from public life. Pressing business in Quaker circles would never allow him to do so, unfortunately. James Potter would never stop working while he had breath in his body, for, although the persecutions had died down and in many places had ceased altogether, he still bore the many responsibilities of his community as the representative of his faith in that district.

He had last suffered from tithe incursions back in 1692, and had been waiting anxiously since that time for the next bout in the continuing process. It was now the third year of non-payment again and he considered that Woodward would have made his way to Cheyney Court once more for a warrant against him. He was not unduly surprised when two men appeared at his door on 25th November that year.[2]

Mr Searle was a solicitor from Winchester. With his clerk, he had made his way from that city to the rural backwater of Baughurst in search of Parson Woodward's adversary. Once he had located his target then the rest was rather easy. He had expected some trouble and was surprised to receive none. At the same time the Quaker was in the same frame of mind, for he had expected these two men to invade his property to steal his best goods and stock. He would have offered no resistance, for he was a Quaker, yet such invasions and the thefts which went with them were, nevertheless, distressing to say the least. Therefore, Potter was remarkably surprised that this portly gentleman and his skinny assistant did not attempt to force their way into his property, but had politely made their way to his door and knocked.

Instead of ordering their intentions to deprive Potter of his possessions the solicitor, in a rather pompous voice, enquired the Quaker's name, and then, without waiting for an answer, offered him a piece of paper, telling him emphatically that it was a subpoena ordering his attendance at the Court of the Exchequer on the last day of the term at the suit of one William Woodward, parson of the parish of Baughurst, for the non-payment of tithes.

But James did not attend, and a summons was made out for his arrest. On 12th February 1696 he travelled to Winchester voluntarily, and there handed himself up to Mr Crop, the Sheriff's deputy, who on that day had him delivered to the Debtor's Prison at the West Gate.

The Debtor's Prison was reserved for those of gentle stock,[3] and conditions were much more comfortable here than James had known in the common gaol in Jewry Street. He was treated quite respectfully, had fairly decent food, and was less restricted in his movements, although the prison itself was much smaller, being a single room over the gateway to the city.

James' last term of imprisonment was short, for he was released a month later. In all, his time in the prisons of Winchester had amounted to well over six years of his life. He was extremely grateful this time to be set at liberty, for he had indeed grown weary of the life of a martyr, and was now much too old to spend his remaining years enclosed by rough prison walls. He had too many things to do in the free world before he expired. And priority at that time, in the March of 1696, was to witness the marriage of his only child.

II

> "Then came John Harris of Goataker in the parish of hillmarton in the County of Wilts and Mary Potter of baghurst and proposed theire intentions of coming together in marriage and a young man being present that had shewed love to her and so sayed would not hinder her this meeting takes notice of it as a proposall the first time."
>
> *(Men's Minutes, Alton Monthly Meeting)*

JOHN HARRIS married James' daughter, Mary, at the new meeting house in Baughurst on 25th March 1696.[4] They had proposed their intentions at the Monthly Meeting in Alton on 10th February that year,[5] two days before Mary's father handed himself over to Deputy Crop for imprisonment. Harris was not Mary's sole suitor at the time, for there was an anonymous young man who had already approached James for his daughter's hand well before Harris arrived on the scene. This had been a love-match, but, unfortunately, against James' wishes, for he expected more for his only child than the young gallant could offer. Harris had been James Potter's personal nominee in the marriage stake for his daughter, as Harris was wealthy and had several lands to his name, and would, therefore, provide a better inheritance for his grandchildren. So, the anonymous young man gave way to Potter's wishes, and the unhappy girl went through the acts of proposal on 10th February, formal betrothal when the certificate had been granted at the Monthly Meeting of 9th March, and, finally, the marriage on 25th of that month.

John Harris was born on 25th March 1674, the only son of John and Joan Harris of Goatacre, in Wiltshire. His father, a clothier, was a prominent Quaker in the parish of Hillmarten,[6] and, as a resident of Charlcott, had married Joan Richmond of Christian Malford in 1666. The couple had five children — four daughters and one son — and had moved to Goatacre, which appeared to have been a strong centre for Quakerism in that part of Wiltshire.

John Harris, senior, was consistently persecuted for his Quaker beliefs during the latter period of the oppressions against nonconformists. His greatest adversary here was Daniel Salloway, the parson of Hillmarten. In 1682 Harris was prosecuted in the Court of Exchequer as a Popish recusant for two-thirds of his estate to the King, and, in the event, was dispossessed of goods to the value of £29.[7]

He spent several months in prison, at the instigation of Salloway, and therefore had occasion to reflect upon his treatment at the hands of his tormentor. In 1684 he wrote:

> "The envie of my adversary, the Priest is now more manifasted than before, for his endeavour with the keeper is to have me so close confined as that I may not have the benefit of the air and not only so but he wants the laws to be more severe, that is that I might be kept with an half-peny loaf a day and also wants to have the Laws to be in force as they were in Queen Mary's days, that I might be burned with fire and faggot, so that in those things he hath laid open the cruelty of his heart to his hearers and as far as I understand and they are set much in their minds against him."[8]

On another occasion he wrote to Charles Marshall of Tetherton, a renowned Quaker of that time:

> "That through the mercy of the Lord and his goodness towards me and my fellow prisoners we have no cause to complaine in our sufferings, for the Lord is pleased to afford us his powerfull presence to attend us, which refresheth our souls and gladeth our hearts, who makes things easy and heavy burdens light."[8]

John Harris, senior, died in 1693 and was buried in the Quaker burial ground at Goatacre on 14th April. However, Harris' death did not mean the end of the persecutions his family was to suffer under Salloway. His widow died in 1704, and between 1693 and the latter date Joan Harris was distrained of goods to the value of almost £150, which included farm produce and fine yarn (worth £51), and three packing cloths worth nine shillings.[9] She was buried at Goatacre on 4th February 1704. With her death her son inherited the lands at Goatacre, and other properties belonging to his father. So, John Harris, junior, came from a good stock of Quaker martyrs, who had gained properties in and around their native homeland through their sheer industrious efforts. No wonder James Potter deemed that his daughter should marry such an illustrious person.

John and Mary Harris went to live at Goatacre for a while, where the husband tended to his late father's business, and gradually extended the Harris estate through purchases. The couple would often return to Baughurst during that period, to their second home. One day, when both the Potters and Joan Harris had died, the couple would inherit a fair-sized estate between them. Although James Potter's deed would devise his house and the little meadow at Town's End to the trustees of that deed, there was the greatest possibility that those trustees would give to John and Mary Harris the use of the house. In the meantime, James was still firmly in control of the situation, and, like the Harrises of Goatacre, was still paying the price for his Quaker sympathies.

III

"On the 19th day of the 9th month 1702 James Potter had taken from him by Ralph Harmsworth the tithingman by a warrant of John Fawkener and Thomas Deane at the complaint of William Woodward preist one Fat bull worth 55 shillings, and on the 1st day of the 10th month by the same warrant one Fatt hogg worth 48 shillings and six pence, and on the 20th day of the 11th month by the same warrant sixteen bushells of wheate worth 45 shillings, all for tithes which were worth six pounds, and afterwards Ralph Harmsworth took away from James' land two bushells of wheate to the vallue of six shillings towards the repair of the steple house."

(Sufferings, Hants.)

ENCOURAGED BY Potter's recent temporary imprisonment, Woodward lost no opportunity in returning to his former style of persecution. In 1696 he ordered the tithingman, Samuel Smith, on to James' property after obtaining a warrant from the justice, John Faulkner, for two years' non-payment of tithes worth about £8 10s. 0d.[10] Smith entered Potter's farm on 26th August, and departed from it with three heifers, which were valued at £9 15s. 0d.

182

Then on 7th October that year the new tithingman, Henry Hasker, armed with a warrant issued this time by the justice, Edward Chute, and for tithes worth £5 10s. 0d., took from James' farm two beasts valued at £5 16s. 0d. The latest incursions this year had cost him in excess of the amount he would have had to pay in tithes, the princely sum of £2 1s. 0d. Even that was preferable to prison. So, in a way, both oppressor and oppressed favoured the annual and biennial invasions of property — James, because he had kept his freedom, and could really afford the extra cost which keeping to his Quaker principles had meant to him; and Woodward, because imprisonment of the Quaker meant no financial reward to him personally. At least, by distraining the offender's goods the parish priest earned extra income.

Yet the oppressors did not return in 1697 and 1698. In 1699 Woodward had obtained another warrant, this time from the justices, John Faulkner and Thomas Deane, in respect of tithes outstanding amounting to £3. 6s. 0d. Edward Harmsworth, the tithingman, was summoned to show the warrant to Potter and to relieve the Quaker of as much livestock as was estimated to cover the value of the outstanding tithes. He took away with him one heifer and a calf later valued at £4. This event took place on 10th May 1699.[11] It is significant to note that in 1698, when there were no tithe incursions into James' lands, his brother, Richard, was serving as the rent-reeve of Baughurst, and after his term of office had expired James himself was elected to that manorial position for the year 1699.[12] Yet, throughout that period covering the two separate terms of office there was only one encroachment recorded into the Potter estate for the sake of tithes.

On 11th April 1700 Robert Batt, the current tithingman, with a warrant in his hand, had three quarters of oats loaded on to the tithe-waggon which had been taken from James Potter's barn, while on 2nd May he extricated a further three quarters and four bushels. The tithe debt this year stood at £6 12s. 0d.; the value of the crops confiscated in this manner came to about £7.

Now the process continued regularly once again. Francis Grantham was the tithingman for Baughurst in the year 1700 to 1701. In June he had nine quarters of oats and four bushels of wheat taken out of James Potter's lands, worth in all £7 for the sake of £6 tithes outstanding. Then he proceeded with his accomplices to Richard Potter's farm across the road, as Richard owed £7 10s. 0d. for tithes for that year. From Richard's fields the persecuting host led away two cows and two calves, and loaded up the waggon with four bushels of wheat, all of which were together valued at £8. Richard had been lucky during recent years, as he had not witnessed such distraints since 1688, and had been left comparatively at peace for twelve years by the vindictive Woodward. Yet, even now, the parson and his assistants in crime had mellowed, for the profits from their ventures were nowhere near as high as they had been. Public opinion had played an essential part in the tithe oppressions, while the law itself veered towards the oppressed, as he was now legally tolerated.

Yet, once again, in 1701, the brothers had to bear the brunt of the parson's tithe exactions. This time it was Richard Baghurst who was the offending tithingman, the very same farmer who had leased James Potter's lands for the term of ten years. James' tithe bill was for £14 0s. 0d. that year, and £8 0s. 0d. was still outstanding at the time of Baghurst's visitation later in 1701. Therefore, Richard Baghurst, reluctantly, ordered the distraint of one cow, one heifer, three quarters of oats, and one quarter of wheat from James Potter's property, and nine quarters of oats from that of Richard Potter. Richard had owed £5 0s. 0d., but had been deprived of crops worth £6 6s. 0d. So, in all had lost £14 6s. 0d. that year for the sake of £12. 10s. 0d. tithes. Meanwhile James had been deprived of livestock and crops to the value of £14 12s. 0d. thus losing by aggregate only 12s. 0d. Obviously, Baghurst had to display some sympathy towards James who was, after all, his landlord, and the tithingman did not wish to offend his lessor too much. Privilege paid even if one was a felon in those days.

In 1702 James suffered no fewer than three such invasions. Each one was performed by the same tithingman, Ralph Harmsworth of Little Ham, and made legal by the same warrant, issued by Faulkner and Deane on the complaint of Woodward. On 19th November a fat bull worth £2 15s. 0d. was driven out of the farm; on 1st December the Quaker lost a fat hog worth £2 8s. 6d.; while on another occasion the deprived goods were two bushels of wheat worth six shillings, which were for payment towards repairs to the parish church.[13]

On 20th January 1703 Harmsworth had sixteen bushels of James' wheat, worth £2 5s. 0d., loaded on to the tithe-waggon and placed into Woodward's barn. The bill outstanding for 1702-3 was for £6 0s. 0d. in tithes, the losses amounted to £7 14s. 6d. including the wheat for church repairs.

This was to be James Potter's last persecution by the Church, for he was not to live much longer. He had been paying for his rebellion dearly since its beginning in 1657. Now, almost half a century later, the total bill can be calculated. In actual financial terms he had lost almost £175 0s. 0d., while in the loss of his liberty, which could not be assessed in monetary terms, he had lost about six years or more of his life. This was a heavy sum, which could not be recouped. At the same time, Richard Potter had also experienced his last oppression by the Church's servants. His total was in excess of £120 0s. 0d., with no loss of freedom. Despite the heavy losses, the Quakers remained unperturbed, and with such persecutions their zeal actually increased. Quakerism was definitely not bankrupted through the oppressive activities of the Church, and more and more the members of that dissenting faith found the time, the energy, and the money to expand. In real terms their heavy financial losses could be exaggerated through the inflation of the past fifty years, while, at the same time, their real estate properties had increased in value. They were, at the turn of the seventeenth and eighteenth centuries, better equipped financially to face the future with optimism, as more and more meetings had been established or re-established.

IV

"Then John Browne desired the advice of this meeting concerning a burieng place in basingstoke which Freinds may buy with a house adjoyning to it & it is ye advise of this meeting that Freinds purchase the sayd house and lands if ye title be good referring him to the quarterly mmeting."

(Men's Minutes, Alton Monthly Meeting,
dated 11th May 1696)

"Then James Potter Brought a Lease made from william knight to him & John Browne sen with an assignment of the sayed lease from him & John Browne to James Hawkins henery Warner and Thomas warner and Richard Bull of Sherfeild ye sayd wrighting is in the hands of James Hawkins of Alton."

(Men's Minutes, Alton Monthly Meeting,
dated 15th December 1701)

THE YEARS IMMEDIATELY following the Toleration Act had seen several important changes in the constitutions of the Quaker meetings throughout England. Now that dissent was legally accepted, there could be no hindrance to the new establishments of meeting houses in the towns. The Five Mile Act had not been repealed but had been made almost invalid by the conditions of the Toleration Act, in respect of freedom of worship, and the Conventicle Act was, in itself, totally obscured by the same statute.

Thus, the importance of such rural refuges as the Baughurst Meeting began to decline now that its important task of nurturing the faith during its darkest hours was over. Its regular attendants still included people from just over the Berkshire border, but these were there more for loyalty towards their foster-meeting than for the need of a place to worship. The Newbury and Oare Meeting had now absorbed many of the Berkshire Quakers who had formerly attended the Baughurst Meeting, while Brimpton Mill was being used more as a regular meeting house by its inhabitants and neighbours since the change in policy towards nonconformity.

Another constituent district served by the Baughurst Meeting had been the borough of Basingstoke and its surrounding area. The Basingstoke Meeting had been extinguished during the oppressions of the 1660s and 1670s, and its members forced to travel to Baughurst for the assemblies. With the coming of toleration the time had been ripe to re-establish the meeting in that town.

At the Quarterly Meeting of 5th April 1681[14] John Brown had applied for, and received, a loan of £10 from Richard Sanders' Charity, which was held in trust for the Quakers by Moses Neave. The loan was on behalf of himself and James Potter, that they might buy some property in Basingstoke for the use as a meeting house. The interest rate on such a loan was 2s. 6d. by quarterly instalments, which the borrowers had agreed to pay half each. However, they were unsuccessful in obtaining and purchasing the property on that occasion, as soon afterwards events had made it absolutely dangerous to open a meeting house in that town at that time. Therefore the loan remained in hand until an opportune moment had arisen.

The Basingstoke Meeting was re-established soon after toleration had been legally granted, and members of that meeting were obliged to hold it in their own homes for the time being. At intervals James Potter attended it as its patron. By 1693 William Knight's old meeting house was once more being used as the regular weekly venue, and, at the Alton Monthly Meeting of 27th June that year permission was granted for its use as a monthly meeting in every fourth month.[15] In the following year James Potter and John Brown applied for permission to hold a business meeting there, but such assent was withheld at that time.[16]

By 1696 the meeting house was no longer considered appropriate for the larger meetings taking place there, while the need for a public communal cemetery had now made the purchase of additional land of the utmost priority. William Knight offered the meeting his meadow at Norn Hill, with a house adjacent, and the transaction was under way by the time that John Brown had approached the Alton Monthly Meeting on 11th May to inform its members of the need for expansion.[17] The Monthly Meeting advised caution, allowing for such a purchase to take place only when and if the title to the land could be proved sound. The matter was then referred to the next Quarterly Meeting, which supported the opinion of the Monthly Meeting.

On 15th June Robert Applegarth, representing Basingstoke, informed the Monthly Meeting that the title was good, and, without further ado the purchase went ahead.

The lease of the house and land was purchased that year by James Potter and John Brown from William Knight for the term of one thousand and five hundred years.[18] That year the new Basingstoke Meeting at Norn Hill was established.[19] The collections from that meeting which went into the Public Stock showed that for a period until December 1697 the Basingstoke Meeting was spending all its financial resources on the improvement of its new meeting house and land, as nothing was being contributed to the central fund.[20] However, this was rectified by the collection preceding the Quarterly Meeting of December 1697 when that urban assembly deposited no less than £2 11s. 8d. into the Public Stock, and thereafter contributions averaged between seventeen and twenty shillings.

At the Alton Monthly Meeting of 15th December 1701,[21] five years after the purchase of the lease, James Potter, on behalf of himself and John Brown, assigned the lease of the property over to the newly-constituted trustees of the Basingstoke Meeting, namely James Hawkins of Alton, Henry Warner, Thomas Warner, and Richard Bull of Sherfield-on-Loddon. Potter and Brown retained interest in the meeting as the other trustees.[22]

By 1775 all the previous trustees had died, and a new conveyance had been made during the interim period. The surviving trustees of this the second conveyance were Henry Portsmouth, William Heydon, and William Dawes junior, who, on 9th July 1775, made over the meeting house and burial ground to the new trustees, namely Thomas Benwell, Richard Gilks, James Wallis,[23] William Heath, Charles Heath of Eastrop, William Jeffrey, Daniel Richins, and William Hack.[24] Richins and Hack were dead by 1788, and Jeffrey by 1795. Benwell and Gilks had been removed by that latter year, along with Wallis, who, nevertheless, appears to have been reconstituted.

On 4th May 1802, Charles Heath of Eastrop, with his trustee, James Wallis, purchased the lease of " a messuage and a garden " in Oat Street,[25] in Basingstoke, from John Carpenter for the sum of £100 6s. 2d.[26] Then on 21st June that year Carpenter leased a parcel of land attached to the above-mentioned house to James Wallis, Charles Heath of Eastrop, Thomas Heath, John Merryweather junior, Samuel May, William Curtis, William Heath, William Pritchett, and William Jeffrey for the term of two thousand years, at the cost of £29 13s. 0d.[27] The house was known as Warren House, and was situated near the "Angel Inn", while the land attached was reserved as a burial ground for the Basingstoke Meeting. The former meeting house and burial ground at Norn Hill ceased to function from that year, and the new establishment remained in the hands of the trustees of the Basingstoke Meeting until the 1960s when the redevelopment of Basingstoke brought the property under compulsory purchase. The burial ground had, at that time, ceased to function for the corporation cemetery had replaced it for some years past. The demise of Warren House meant the re-establishment of the Basingstoke Meeting elsewhere in the town. Its present meeting house is in Cromwell Road.

V

"Then came John Browne Jn: of Basingstoke & Mary Potter Daughter of Richard Potter of Baughurst to declare there intentions of Marriage with each other & hath Left it to Freinds Consideration tell the next meeting Tho Astine & Robt: Applegarth is desired to inquire into John Browne clearness & bring the answer the next meeting."

(Men's Minutes, Alton Monthly Meeting,
dated 14th December 1696)

"Then came John Browne Jun of basingstoake and Mary Potter of baghurst to receive ye approbation of this meeting concerning theire coming together in mariage and Freinds finding upon enquiry that they are cleare from all others do leave them in the wisdome of God to waite a convenient time to accomplish it they now having a certificate from this meeting of theire approbation concerning it."

(Men's Minutes, Alton Monthly Meeting,
dated 11th January 1697)

"Then came John Browne the elder of basingstoke & proposed his intention of taking Elizabeth Park of hampton weeke nigh kingstone in Midlesex to be his wife desiring the advise of the friends of this meeting."

(Men's Minutes, Alton Monthly Meeting,
dated 14th August 1699)

POTTER'S DEAREST friend was John Brown of Basingstoke, and their friendship had extended over almost thirty years when they surrendered their joint tenures of the lease on the Basingstoke meeting house and burial ground to its trustees. They had met at the monthly meetings during the early 1670s, and had cemented their friendship with their intense common interest in the furtherance of their faith. Potter had enjoyed his discussions with Brown, and, although the latter was a mere labourer, he displayed an unusual intelligence for that class by being able to comment upon any topic with which Potter was acquainted. Such was their compatibility that they were able to form a fairly successful business partnership.

John Brown was born in Basingstoke in 1646,[28] the son of John Brown. By the mid-1660s he had become a fully-fledged adherent to Quakerism. As persecution intensified he was forced to flee his native town and to settle in Whitchurch. He married Mary Burret, a Whitchurch girl,[29] and the couple had, in all, seven children, of whom two were born in Basingstoke, and the rest at Whitchurch.[30] The period was so full of hostilities for such urban Quakers that they often had to commute from town to town. In the case of the Browns, their normal escape-route was from Basingstoke to Whitchurch, and vice versa.

John was a prominent member of the Whitchurch Meeting, especially after the demise of that at Basingstoke, and as the representative of the former, he would regularly attend the Quarterly Meeting after 1678, as well as the Alton Monthly Meeting. On occasions he was to fall foul of the authorities, and was one of the members of the Andover Meeting thrown into the town prison in 1682.[31] He also served the Quaker community well as a regular visitor to the prisons of Hampshire, where he gave comfort to the religious felons and help to their suffering families during their incapacities.

After 1680 he and his family were allowed to return to Basingstoke on a permanent basis and to set up home once more, and he became prominent in the re-establishment of the meeting there, as one of the founder-members with amongst others, Robert Applegarth and Nicholas Gates.

John's wife, Mary, died in Basingstoke in 1695 and was buried in a small plot of land which John had reserved for his family on 16th May.[32] For four years he remained a widower, consoling himself in that time by concentrating his attention upon the affairs of the new Basingstoke Meeting. In due course he married again, this time Elizabeth Park of Hampton Wick.[33]

Brown was seventy-six when he died on 4th October 1722,[34] and he was buried in the Quaker cemetery at Norn Hill, in the very same ground he and James Potter had purchased over a quarter of a century before. John Brown had very little to bequeath on the day that he died. Even his home was not his own: for some years now he had been widowed for the second time, and had chosen to live with his son, John, and his wife Mary, in their little house in Basingstoke. The old man loved his daughter-in-law for she was a constant source of help to him, and the couple would often discuss topics which interested them both. She was a typical Potter, full of the characteristics both of her father, Richard, and of her uncle, James, old John's dearly departed friend.

John Brown junior[35] had married Mary Potter in James Potter's meeting house on 21st January 1697,[36] after their eligibility to marry had been discussed at the Alton Monthly Meeting of 14th December 1696, and approved by the investigations of Thomas Austin and Robert Applegarth on 11th January 1697.[37] The couple went to live in Basingstoke, where John worked as a labourer, and regularly attended the meeting there, although, on occasions, they would join in worship with the regulars at the Baughurst Meeting. Unfortunately, they had only one surviving child, Richard,[38] yet it was this child who later inherited his grandfather's farm to give it its present name — Brown's Farm.

So, in 1697, the pattern had been set for the future. Already the inheritance of James Potter's estate had fallen irrevocably into the hands of the Harris family. Richard's farm, however, was still open to question at that stage for there were enough Potter sons to make certain that there would be no change of name in the forseeable future. Richard Potter, junior, was the next in line after his father, followed by Matthew, his brother, and on 12th September 1702, Matthew had approached the Alton Monthly Meeting[39] for permission to marry Catherine Austin, daughter of Thomas Austin. A certificate was granted after the investigations made by John Harris and Robert Applegarth at the Monthly Meeting of 12th October.

The marriage of John and Mary Brown had been the outcome of a strong friendship between the two families, with no real thoughts of material gain for the descendants of old John as its motive. Fate, however, proved otherwise. Eventually the simple labouring family would have a substantial stake in the future of the history of that rural parish. Until that time they would have to be content to remain in the background of events as the Baughurst Meeting evolved into a different creature from its former self.

VI

"Then was signed a testimony against disorderly proceedings of Susanna Cole of baghurst shee coming

190

into a meeting at James Potters house in baghurst with a man not a Freind & theire they declared they took each other in marriage freinds then testifieng against them in so doing they not appearing in any monthly meeting. . . . "

(Men's Minutes, Alton Monthly Meeting,
dated 15th October 1697)

" then was signified by James Potter yt in barksheere care is taken against sleeping in meetings and it is desired it may be charged against in other meetings and care may be taken in all meetings. "

(Men's Minutes, Alton Monthly Meeting,
dated 12th August 1700)

" William Blunden of Tadlye wheelwright, on the complaint of John Westwood priest for the demand of twentyeight shillings, of whch 10 shillings was for mortuary the warrant granted for twelve yeares past the said William living in a small house standing on the Common which was never knowne to pay any tithe or any demanded before the warrant was executed by Thomas Pryor tithingman. . . . "

(Sufferings, Hants.)

AT THE QUARTERLY Meeting of 30th June 1697, James Potter placed 14s. 0d. into the Public Stock from the collection contributed by the Baughurst Meeting. At the same time the amounts collected at other Quaker meetings throughout the county were: Southampton 18s. 0d., Alton £1 8s. 3d., Fordingbridge 18s. 0d., Ringwood £1 7s. 6d., Portchester 7s. 0d., Andover £1 13s. 1d., Whitchurch 18s. 6d., Romsey 7s. 6d., Isle of Wight 15s. 0d., and Winchester 5s. 3d. There were no contributions at all from Basingstoke, Odiham, Portsmouth, Alresford, Bramshott, and Wallop.[40] On 5th October Baughurst's collection amounted to 11s. 0d., and Potter handed over to Moses Neave his own personal contribution of 5s. 0d., which then brought the Public stock to the total sum of £15 8s. 3d. The last collection of that year (28th December) included 12s. 0d. from Baughurst. In 1698 that meeting's total contributions to the Public Stock amounted to £1 14s. 6d., while on 4th October Baughurst collected £3 14s. 0d. towards the relief of Quakers in distress in Scotland, Dunkirk, and Emden.

A couple of lesser events occurred during the closing years of the seventeenth century. In 1697 there was a disturbance at James Potter's house when Susana Cole brought into that meeting house a man whom she declared she had married. The Quakers were horrified as this man was not even one of them, and Susanna and her husband were told that they had to report to the Monthly Meeting in order to have that marriage sanctified by the members' approval. They did not bother to appear, and soon afterwards the girl left the Quaker fold.[41]

On 12th August 1700, James lectured the Alton Monthly Meeting[42] over the dangers of allowing members to use the religious meetings of silence as an excuse to catch up on their sleeping. Apparently, the misuse of the time for religious observance had been discovered in meetings in Berkshire, and ardent members had become alerted to such misdemeanours and were now forever watchful of the dozing worshippers. Potter advocated that such methods should be installed at the meetings throughout the jurisdiction of the Alton Monthly Meeting so as to discourage people using meetings for worship as extensions of their bedtime habits. In the eyes of the Quakers this was not a matter to be treated lightly. It was probably almost as serious as the tithe persecutions which were still taking place and, indeed, increasing against the poorer classes of Quakers.

William Appleton, who lived in a cottage on Tadley Common, died in 1699, and was buried at the cemetery at Baughurst Town's End. His daughter had married William Blunden from Brimpton, and, with Appleton's death, Blunden, who was a wheelwright, took over the occupation of the cottage. Now, in 1702 John Westwood, the rector of Tadley, issued the tithingman, Thomas Prior, with a warrant to claim goods from Blunden to the value of tithes and mortuary dues outstanding on the cottage — 28s. 0d. in total — despite the fact that Appleton had never paid tithes on that cottage during his occupation of it, nor had been any demanded from him.

The warrant itself was dated 1689, and was, therefore, several years old, and now legally extinct. Prior entered into Blunden's property and bundled together 300 spokes which the wheelwright had carved, worth altogether about £3 10s. 0d., and removed them from the premises in payment of the so-called tithes and mortuary debts.[43]

Before that year was out John Brown of Basingstoke had also received a visit from the agents of the oppressive authorities. He, being a mere labourer, was untithed as his income was inadequate and his profits were nil. Yet he was obliged to pay certain other duties to the Church. That year he had refused to pay towards the repairs of St Michael's Church in Basingstoke, and, consequently, a warrant was issued against him by

Councillor Tutt and Thomas Jervoise, and served upon him by the officers of the parish, George Prinne, Charles May, and Andrew Butler. They took out of his house seven pounds of flax worth 4s. 8d.[44]

These events James Potter recorded in the Sufferings Book before he appeared at the Quarterly Meeting of the 31st March 1703.[45] At that meeting he was instructed to take the Sufferings Book for Hampshire to the Annual Meeting in London, where it would be transcribed as a copy of the record of the persecutions which the Quakers had suffered.

VII

" I James Potter of the Parish of Baghurst in the County of Southton Yeoman being weak of body but of perfect memory Doe ordaine and make this my last Will and Testament as followeth First I commit my Soul to God who gave it And my body to be buryed according to the discrecon of my Executrixes hereunder named And as for the Worldly Goods and Estate which God amongst other of his mercyes hath graciously been pleased to endow me with In the first place I give my house Barne and Land called Colliers lying in the Parish of West Sherborne and alsoe my Land called Alderland in the Parish of Baghurst both in the County aforesaid to my wife Marjory Potter and to my Daughter Mary Harris wife of John Harris for and dureing the terme of their naturall lives   And after their Decease to the Heires and Assignes of my daughter Mary Harris aforesaid. And farther my will is that my daughter Mary Harris shall have power to make a farther Settlement of the said Estate to one or more of her Children if she shall see meete or as she shall be advised thereunto that it may be for the good of her Children and safety of the said Estate with full power to cutt sell and carry off any Trees or Timber Trees now growing or which may then be growing on the said premisses without Impeachment of wast   It. I give to the poor of the Parish of Baghurst three pounds   And to the poor of West Shirborne and Tadley twenty shillings apiece Alsoe I give forty shillings to such poor people as my Executrixes hereunder named shall judge meete to distribute it unto   It. I give to my brother Richard Potters four Children vizt Richard Potter   Matthew Potter   Mary Browne wife of John Browne the younger

193

and Anne Potter five pounds to be equally divided amongst them   And if it shall soe come to passe that any or either of them shall dye before the said money be due and payable then his her or their parts soe dying shall be due and payable to the Survivor or Survivors of them   It. I give to my Nephew James Silver twenty shillings And to my Kinswoman Sarah Silver daughter of John Silver late of the Citty of London Deced Plaisterer forty Shillings   All which above menconed Sumes of money to be paid within one yeare after my Decease   It. I give to my two Grand daughters Mary Harris and Hannah Harris twenty pounds apiece to be paid to them when they shall accomplish the age of one and twenty yeares vitz their particular parts as they one after the other shall accomplish the said age   All the rest of my Goods and Chattells of what nature or kind soever it be I give and bequeath to my loveing wife Marjory Potter and my loveing Daughter Mary Harris aforesaid whom I make full Executrixes of this my last Will and Testament
    And I desire my loveing brother Richard Potter of Baghurst and my loveing Cousen Henry Streater of Brampshott both of this County aforesaid Yeoman to be Overseers of this my Will and my Executrixes to pay them forty shillings apiece   In Witness hereof I have hereunto put my hand and Seale the Seaveteenth day of the Moneth called June one thousand Seaven hundred and one.   James Potter Signed sealed and declared to be his last Will and Testament in the presence of Richard Greene James Silver The marke of Sarah Cooke."

*(The Last Will and Testament of James Potter,
Public Record Office, London
(P.R.O. Doc. No. PROB 11/475))*

"Memoriae Sacrum Revdi Gul. Woodward hujus Ecclesiae 35 annos Rectoris, viri antiqua fide, summa Gravitate et Sapientia praediti; cujus vitae innocentia non minus quam doctinae Sanctitas quam plurimis Saluti fuit; qui pauperibus quibus beneficum, amicis quibus fidelem se praestitit, propinquis affinbusq: de quibus optime meritus est, liberis praesertim et conjugi

quos eximie dilexit, dinturnum et Gravisium sin
desiderium reliquit ob: Anno Dom 1703 Aetat 64,"

*(Monumental Inscription to William Woodward
in Baughurst Church)*

" Then it was agreed that ye book kept by James Potter of
ye Quarterly busieness be desired from John Harris &
kept in Alton Monthly meeting to be registred ye
quarterly business once in a Quarter of a yeare by whome
the Monthly meeting shall think fitt."

*(Men's Minutes, Hampshire Quarterly Meeting,
dated 28th December 1703)*

JAMES POTTER returned home from the business which had kept him a
while in the capital, an extremely exhausted man. He was now heading
towards his seventieth year and had recently discovered that he was
extremely handicapped by the limitations his age had placed upon his
willing mind. Ill health was a constant companion these days, and he could
never forget the time two years beforehand when he thought that he would
not survive another night. It was then that he had made his will. Now, as
he rested from his tiresome journey, he wondered for how much longer his
God would allow him to continue in his service in this mortal frame.

But James had a strong will and that will had brought him through his
greatest trials, some of which had already killed lesser men than he. Now
times were different and the world seemed peaceful enough, but there was
still work to be done and little time to sit back and take stock of the
situation. Even though ill health might accompany him, he simply did not
have the time to lie down and die.

He had lived a long time, for which he constantly thanked his Maker,
and had survived the reigns of six monarchs and a republic. He had, in that
time, experienced the varying tempers and attitudes of those in power
towards the dissenting communities, and had noted that for the greater
part of that time the Quakers had been regarded as one of the more
dangerous sects, akin to the Jesuits. This he could never understand, as he
believed that the Friends were just that — friends to all mankind. He did
not contemplate the fact that the Quakers had aroused much animosity in
the other sects and Anglicans alike, through their bigoted ideals and
religious pride. They, perhaps more so than the other faiths, believed that
they were the followers of the only Truth, and their attitudes towards
Protestant and Catholic alike were as intolerant as those towards them.

The crux of the matter was that before the authorities could allow religious toleration for all the sects, the dissenters would equally have had to tolerate other beliefs. But this was, and still is, an imperfect world. Although toleration had been granted, there were always those who were prejudiced in their thinking, and would act accordingly.

The staunch Anglican was, of course, the natural enemy of the Quaker. However, surprisingly perhaps, over the years even the extreme radicalism of High Laudianism had been defused, while among the moderate sections of the supporters of the Church the result had been an acceptance of those within their community who held dissenting views. In many cases, that acceptance had been borne with a reluctance characteristic of the period when traditional ideas and values were being uprooted wholesale, and conservatism was being regarded as outdated.

It would have appeared almost impossible in the 1660s that both Quaker and Anglican could live together in peace, and all the more undoubtful that they could be friends. Yet constant persecution of the Quakers had caused a reaction in their favour, and, even during the darkest days of their trials, there were many sympathisers among their neighbours. James Potter had many friends in all walks of life, and of varying denominations. The Greens of Baughurst, although staunch Anglicans, valued their associations with the Potter family, even having them as the witnesses to their wills. The Actons of Basingstoke, who held copyhold tenures in Baughurst, were particularly fond of the Potter connection. James Acton agreed to act as the guardian to James Potter's daughter in the event of the Quaker's untimely death in the 1670s. This was all the more unusual since Acton's brother was an ecclesiastic. Then there was Richard Baghurst, Potter's lessee. The list was endless.

Perhaps the most unusual acquaintance, it could never have been called friendship, was that between Potter and Woodward. Woodward had been the rector of Baughurst now for thirty-five years, and for all those years his most ardent opponent had been James Potter. They had viewed one another with a natural vehemence which was traditional and right for those times. Yet, although they continuously faced each other from opposing corners to do battle, they did feel a strong respect for each other — a respect which mellowed their attitudes over the years. They had needed each other, for the existence of their faiths depended upon the stimulus offered by the other. Since toleration they had been able to meet and discuss topics openly and without rancour, and their bond had strengthened, despite Woodward's invasion of James' lands for tithes debts, which was accepted as the natural outcome of the Quaker's refusals to pay. These tithe persecutions were now regularly performed without thought of malice on the one part, nor grudge on the other. Potter could easily afford the losses, but, as a prominent Quaker, could not afford to be seen paying the tithes directly to Woodward. Therefore, what now seemed to be the age-old game of strategy had to be played out in the traditional manner of Anglican versus Quaker. The persecutions were for the benefit of observers, where once the game had been for real.

Potter was one of the last remaining Quakers of the old school who could still play an effective part in the history of nonconformity. Before too long a new generation had grown up to take over control of events.

Likewise, Woodward was one of the few remaining in a diminishing group of Anglican die-hards, and his role in the system was all the stronger because, due to the traditional aspect of his incumbency, he held sway over his parish like a potentate. Baughurst had its own "Peculiar Court" of Probate, where Woodward held sessions concerning other administrative duties of the parish. In fact, he was the last rector of Baughurst to perform such powerful duties: no other since his death has been recorded as proving wills, etc., in this Court.

The autumn and winter of 1703 witnessed some of the most violent storms recorded to that date. It had been a wet year with a late harvest and, consequently, low yields.[46] Then the storms began. For eighteen days there was a period of very high winds, culminating in a hurricane on 26th and 27th November. Eight thousand people lost their lives in floods of the Severn and Thames.[47] Although the November gale was recorded as the most violent ever in England at the time, it was apparently surpassed in the south by another on 7th and 8th December.

Such extremely inclement weather would encourage rampant diseases. The common cold was a serious enough threat to health in those days, while influenza and pneumonia were fatal illnesses. The young were never guaranteed to survive either of these illnesses, while the aged proved to be early casualties, no matter how strong their wills.

As the violent gale of late December rattled around the roof of the Quaker meeting house in Baughurst, James Potter had eventually been confined to his bed, despite his weakening insistence on dealing with the business of the Monthly Meeting which he had in hand. For several days Margery tended her unfortunate husband as his fever raged, but as she unsuccessfully fought to bring it under control her own condition was seriously weakening. Before her husband finally expired she had been committed to bed in the throes of the disease which was extinguishing the light inside her husband.

James Potter was buried in his meadow at Town's End on 27th December 1703, during another violent gale which was causing havoc all over the south of England. Four days later, on 31st December, his wife was interred with him.

In another part of the parish the Anglicans were burying their late minister, the Reverend William Woodward. He had died at his Rectory of the same ague which had terminated the lives of his opponent and his wife. Woodward was laid to rest on the 30th December 1703, in the crypt beneath the parish church which he had served and had defended for so many years.

It was ironic, yet seemingly proper, that the traditional combatants should exit the arena together. It was as though fate had irrevocably closed the chapter, and indeed the book, on the history of Baughurst. The story would never again be the same without its leading characters. Whatever followed the zealous antagonists' battles for survival would have to be an anticlimax. Yet, the story was not over, for James Potter had left his people a legacy and, for a while, his life was a source of inspiration to them.

Although Potter and Woodward had spent much of their lives concerning themselves with the business of the other, and had died almost together under the same conditions, the contrast between them cannot be shown more vividly than in their interments. Potter and his wife were buried in a rough little meadow, in a communal crypt with no marking. The only record of their burial is in the Quaker register, which states briefly their names and dates of burial. Woodward, on the other hand, received a rather splendid farewell, and his last resting place is marked with a tablet which gives a rather flattering summary, in Latin, of his life. He was called ''a man of the old faith, the upholder of dignity and know-ledge'', he was ''benevolent to the poor and faithful to his friends and neighbours'', and was ''distinguished and influential''.[48] Would the Quakers have agreed with these sentiments?

They said little, if anything, of Woodward's death. The Quarterly Meeting was held at Alton on 28th December, the day after James Potter was buried.[49] It was attended by representatives from all over Hampshire who expressed their sadness over the loss of this distinguished gentleman. Potter's son-in-law was there, as the representative for Baughurst, and he was instructed to take the accounts book for the Quarterly Meeting, held by the late James Potter, and to deliver it up to the Alton Monthly Meeting, which would now be responsible for it. Baughurst had lost an important and influential voice at the Monthly and Quarterly Meetings.

Quaker Marriages at Baughurst 1695-1703

(8) JOHN HARRIS, of Gotaker, Psh of Hillmarten, in Co. Wilts, and MARY POTTER, of Baghurst, at Baghurst, 25th March 1696.

(9) JOHN BROWNE JUNR, of Basingstoke, and Mary Potter, at Baghurst 21st January 1697.

(10) JOGN WARNE, of Brimton, Co. Berks, and ANN SMITH, of Baghurst, at Baghurst 4th October 1702.

Quaker Burials at Baughurst 1695-1703

(33) JOHN GODDEN, son of John Godden, of Kingsclere, at Baughurst 2nd April 1697 (also recorded in the Parish Register as "John Godwin, buried in Potter's garden 2nd April 1697")

(34) SARAH BROWNE, buried in Potter's garden 30th October 1697 (recorded only in the Parish Register).

(35) ELIZABETH SPARROWBELL, of Itchingswell, buried at Baughurst 18th October 1698 (not recorded in the Parish Register).

(36) WILLIAM APPLETON, of Tadly, who died 10th November 1699, and was buried at Baughurst 13th November 1699 (also recorded in the Parish Register as "William Appleton, in Potter's garden, 13th November 1699").

(37) JAMES POTTER, of Baghurst, buried at Baghurst 27th December 1703 (not recorded in the Parish Register).

(38) MARGERY POTTER, wife of James Potter, buried at Baghurst 31st December 1703 (not recorded in the Parish Register).

[1] See p. 172 for a transcript of the deed.
[2] Sufferings, Hants.
[3] Now a museum near the Law Courts.
[4] Marriage Digest, Hampshire and Dorsetshire General Meeting.
[5] Men's Minutes, Alton Monthly Meeting.
[6] Victoria County History, Wilts.
[7] Sufferings, Wilts.
[8] Victoria County History, Wilts. (It is a pity that none of James Potter's letters from prison survived. K.S.)
[9] Sufferings, Wilts.
[10] Sufferings, Hants.
[11] Sufferings, Hants.
[12] Court Rolls, Cathedral Library, Winchester.
[13] Sufferings, Hants.
[14] Men's Minutes, Hampshire Quarterly Meeting.
[15] Men's Minutes, Aiton Monthly Meeting.
[16] Men's Minutes, Alton Monthly Meeting.

[17] Men's Minutes, Alton Monthly Meeting.
[18] Conveyance of the Basingstoke Meeting House and Burial Ground, 1788, H.R.O. Doc. No. 24M54/18.
[19] The burial ground was discovered and opened during the Redevelopment Programme of the town in the 1960s.
[20] Men's Minutes, Hampshire Quarterly Meeting.
[21] Men's Minutes, Alton Monthly Meeting.
[22] As there were normally six trustees attached to this meeting, Potter and Brown are assumed here.
[23] One of the founders of Wallis & Steevens, one of Basingstoke's more important industries.
[24] Conveyance of 1788.
[25] Now Wote Street.
[26] Conveyance of 1788.
[27] Conveyance of 1788.
[28] He was baptised at the parish church on 25th March 1646.
[29] Although they were probably married at the Whitchurch Meeting (not recorded), they were also married in the parish church of that town on the 19th June 1673, after their first child had been born in Basingstoke.
[30] George (born at Basingstoke the 4th December 1672. He is mentioned on p. 123), Elizabeth (buried at Alton the 10th December 1674), John (see note 35), Joseph (born at Whitchurch the 12th October 1676), William (buried at Alton the 25th October 1678), Mary (born at Whitchurch the 23rd March 1680), and John (born at Whitchurch the 25th August 1686).
[31] See pp. 142-4.
[32] Burial Digest, Hampshire and Dorsetshire General Meeting.
[33] Men's Minutes, Alton Monthly Meeting.
[34] Burial Digest, Hampshire and Dorsetshire General Meeting.
[35] He was born at Whitchurch on 29th September 1674.
[36] Marriage Digest, Hampshire and Dorsetshire General Meeting.
[37] Men's Minutes, Alton Monthly Meeting.
[38] Born 26th March 1703. His elder brother, John, was buried at Baughurst 7th March 1699.
[39] Men's Minutes, Alton Monthly Meeting.
[40] Men's Minutes, Hampshire Quarterly Meeting.
[41] Men's Minutes, Alton Monthly Meeting.
[42] Men's Minutes, Alton Monthly Meeting.
[43] Sufferings, Hants.
[44] Sufferings, Hants.
[45] Men's Minutes, Hampshire Quarterly Meeting.
[46] J. M. Stratton: Agricultural Records A.D. 220-1977, John Baker, 1978.
[47] According to Daniel Defoe, quoted in above.
[48] William Woodward's monumental inscription inside Baughurst Church.
[49] Men's Minutes, Hampshire Quarterly Meeting.

CHAPTER TEN
1704-1728

I

" Then John Harris of Baghurst brought a paper written by his Father James Potter signifieing his mind about the meeting house & burieng place with ye appertinances which he gave to moses neave Robert mercer Nicholas Gates Junr henery Streater Jn buy in trust for Freinds use & service the sayd deed being now in the hands of Nicholas Gates ye elder John Harris is now desired by this meeting to take care of the house & appertinances and manage things the best for Freinds advantage as he can & let Freinds know once in a yeare how the premises are "

*(Men's Minutes, Alton Monthly Meeting,
dated 10th January 1704)*

"Then an account was given that John Harris had delivered the book to Alton Monthly meeting & ye Monthly Meeting hath made theireof Andrew Andrewes to record the quarterly meeting busieness "

*(Men's Minutes, Hampshire Quarterly Meeting,
held at Alton on 29th March 1704)*

"Now: Paid in from John Harris ye Sum of Tenn Shilling being with Taxes and Reparations in full for the Rent Made of the Meeting Howse at Baughurst to the 21 day of Last 10th month "

*(Men's Minutes, Alton Monthly Meeting,
dated 14th March 1709)*

JAMES POTTER'S death left a great void which was never wholly filled by the Quakers in Hampshire. The immediate reaction to his sudden departure was one of misgiving. During the ensuing months the Quakers had to find able men who would undertake the responsibilities previously held by the late Potter.

Therefore, there was much work for those associates of James Potter to do. On 10th January 1704 John Harris travelled to Alton to attend the business meeting attached to that monthly gathering,[1] carrying with him a letter written by his father-in-law in respect of his wishes regarding the meeting house and burial ground at Baughurst. The members at Alton willingly abided by James' wish and gave Harris their formal assent to his occupation of the house, at a rent of 15s. 0d. per annum.[2] He was also provided with a certificate from the Quarterly Meeting allowing meetings at Baughurst,[3] thus signifying that, like his late father-in-law, he was the actual patron of that meeting.

The deed of conveyance to the trustees of the Baughurst Meeting, now fully realised with the occupation of the Harrises as tenants of those trustees, had dealt with the matter of the building itself. Yet the house itself stood on land owned by the Dean and Chapter of Winchester Cathedral, as Lords of the Manor of Manydown. The tenure of that copyhold estate was still officially in the hands of James Potter, and his heirs in reversion were his brother and his daughter respectively. Normally on the death of the tenant the land would revert to the late customary tenant's widow as her widow's estate for and during her term of widowhood (she would have to surrender her rights if she remarried). However, in this case Margery died shortly after James. Thus a procedure had to have been followed whereby the next in line would be admitted as the copyhold tenant on payment of a special fine known as heriot. The procedure was followed through the use of a solicitor, and the new admittance was duly recorded formally at the next Court in session, which was in the October of 1704, and was attended by John Harris as the representative of the new customary tenant. Richard Potter surrendered his interest in his late brother's estate, and James' daugher Mary was admitted as the copyhold tenant, with her husband as her proprietor. The following year the couple nominated their own daughters, Hannah and Mary, as their heirs in the copyhold lands centred upon the Quaker meeting house.[4] Thus the ambiguous situation had been created, due to the chaotic system of English land law which had its roots in the feudal manorial system dating back to the days of the Norman Conquest, whereby Mary Harris and her husband were the tenants of the trustees of the Baughurst Meeting, who, in turn, held a meeting house which stood on the land legally in the tenure of the same Mary Harris, as the customary tenant of the Dean and Chapter of Winchester Cathedral. At the same time the Quakers were entirely the customary and legal tenants of the Church.

While the meeting house and its lands were, in practice, at the joint disposal of the Church and the Quakers, the burial ground at Town's End was solely in the hands of the trustees as this had been freehold land which James Potter had bought.

Then there were the other lands held formerly by the late Quaker dignitary. Potter's will was proved on 14th February 1704 at the Prerogative Court of Canterbury in London[5] by the solemn declaration of Mary Harris before Dr Richard Raines. Immediately the conditions of her father's will were put into effect, with the exception of the gifts which James had willed to his loving wife, who was now dead.

John Harris was now the official head of the family and the community of Quakers, as well as the patron and representative of the Baughurst Meeting. Unlike his father-in-law, this gentleman aspired to greater affluence. James had even described himself in his will as merely a yeoman when, in fact, he was more of a lawyer and administrator, and farming was one of his lesser achievements. Even in 1704 the lease had not yet expired whereby the Baghursts were farming the vast Potter estate. Harris, however, had made his fortune in the clothier business and was now content in his living as a member of the lower gentry. His adherence to Quakerism was not as strong as that of his father-in-law, and his use of it was mainly inspired through his selfish aims towards power and wealth. In fact, the Harrises, although retaining their hold on the Baughurst Meeting and the Quaker community of that district in general, had now denied themselves of any responsibility towards the furtherance of the Quaker cause beyond the control of their local meeting and the occasional representation of Baughurst at higher level meetings. Consequently the Baughurst Meeting declined in importance immediately after the death of Potter, and the ensuing years were devoid of sufferings in that area as a general peace enveloped the community — to the extent that it appeared that the whole population were asleep.

II

"John Harris proposed unto this meeting That on Case Frds. Consent that the old Meeting house at Baghurst Be Conveyed to him etc. Baghurst Frds. will Erect a New Meeting house Near Leonard Coles in Hampshire and Settle on the following Trustees — Which this meeting agrees to and orders — James Hawkins to Deliver the writings of the said old Meeting house to John Harris — The Trustees are as under —

John Harris Junr. Robt. Applegarth Jun Tho: Kirton Henry Portsmouth Benja. Froud Junr. James Buy

Samul Waring John Curtis Robt. Baker and Sanders
Kirton - - - See the 15th of the 2d mo *P* 5th *1728*"

(Men's Minutes, Alton Monthly Meeting,
dated 18th January 1728)

"The Deeds of the new meeting house (mentioned p.
15th: 11 mo: 1727) Erected by Baghurst Freinds: Were
Brought to this Meeting and ordered to be Kept by
Samuel Waring = The Trustees Names therein the Same
(as nominated p. 15th: 11 mo 1727)"

(Men's Minutes, Alton Monthly Meeting,
dated 5th April 1728)

RICHARD POTTER, the last of the active members of the old generation of
Baughurst Quakers, died in his farmhouse in 1712, and was buried in his
garden plot, which was now reserved for the members of his own
particular family. The episode was noted only in the Court Rolls of the
Manor of Manydown.[6] His widow was duly admitted as the tenant for the
duration of her widowhood, which was formally recorded at the following
Court in the next year.

By this time Richard's son, Matthew, was already dead, and new grants
had to be made in respect of the continuation of the copyhold tenure of the
farm known as Potter's. It was now the turn of the late yeoman's
daughters to hold the future of their father's estate in their hands. Ann
Potter, spinster, and her sister Mary, the wife of John Brown junior of
Basingstoke, were, respectively, issued with warrants which gave them
title deeds to the farm after the deaths, surrenders, or forfeitures of their
mother and their brother, Richard Potter. Mary Potter, the widow of
Richard, died a few years later, and her son was thus admitted as the new
tenant.

Already the process had been initiated whereby the meeting house which
had been established by James Potter in 1696 was to be deprived of its
service to the local Quaker community. John Harris, the only son of John
and Mary Harris, was baptised in Baughurst Church on 25th January
1712.[7] Nine years later his sister, Hannah, married Samuel Payne, from
Weston Banfield, in that meeting house.[8] Then, in 1725, both the
daughters of John and Mary Harris surrendered their interests in the
copyhold estate which supported the house, and new warrants were
granted to John Harris junior and his unmarried sister, Mary, as respective
heirs to their mother in that estate. In 1727 John Harris senior began the

204

procedure of having the house released from the trusteeship of the Alton Monthly Meeting and having it conveyed upon himself as sole owner-occupier.

At the Monthly Meeting of 18th January 1728, Harris put forward his proposal to have a new meeting house erected near Leonard Cole's land at Inhurst[9] in order that the current meeting house be conveyed to him, thus terminating the Quaker ownership of his wife's copyhold farm.

The trustees of the new establishment had already been approached and all formalities had been more or less concluded at that point, with only the ratification of the business deal needed to make it legal and final. In the April of 1728 the deeds bearing the names of the new Trustees had been rendered into the hands of Samuel Waring, as the representative of the Trustees, and from that time James Potter's house became the property of John Harris and his family, with no benefits to the Quakers at all.

In its place Leonard Cole's house took over the responsibility of welcoming the Quakers to its weekly meetings of worship. John Harris, however, was careful to retain the patronage of the meeting, and, for the time being, the burial ground at Town's End remained open for public funerals. Yet, to all intents and purposes, the conveyance of 1728 was another episode in the decline of the faith in this rural setting. The establishment of Cole's meeting house was a major step on the road towards the demise of Quakerism in northern Hampshire. The new meeting would pass more directly into the hands of the community itself rather than be the tool of its patrons, the Harrises. In time even the heirs of James Potter would lose interest in maintaining that religion, and this was made all the more inevitable because the new meeting house was now remote from the former centre of Quaker activity.

Quaker Marriages at Baughurst 1704-1728

(11) JOHN WARNE, of Baghurst, and GRACE APPLETON, of Tadly, at Baugust, 20th May 1709.

(12) DANIEL WHITE, and MARY COALE, at Baughurst, 6th March 1720.

(13) SAMUEL PAYNE, of Weston Banfield, and HANNAH HARRIS at Baughurst, 14th September 1721.

Quaker Burials at Baughurst 1704-1728

(39) SUSANNA PARCHMOUTH, a Quaker, was buryed in woolen, 18th November 1706: witnessed by Alice Smith (recorded in the Parish Register only).

(40) CHARLS WHITTEKER, a Quaker, was buryed in wollen, 14th January 1707: witnessed by Anne Pescock (recorded in the Parish Register only).

(41) ANNE WARNE, a Quaker, was buryed, 18th January 1708: witnessed by El Silver (recorded in the Parish Register only).

(42) DAMERIS BURGES, of Brimpton, a Quaker, buryed, 3rd April 1708: witnessed by Alce Haskens (recorded in the Parish Register only).

(43) RICHARD POTTER, in 1712 (not recorded in either burial register: buried privately in his garden).

(44) MARY POTTER, widow, date not known (not recorded in either burial register: buried privately in her garden).

(45) PETER HINE, buried at Baughurst, 11th September 1726 (also recorded in the Parish Register as " Peter Hine, a Quaker, was buryed in ye place called ye Quaker's Burying-place ").

(46) LYDIA WHITACRE, widow of Alton, died at Brimpton, Co Berks, was buried at Baughurst 2nd October 1726 (not recorded in the Parish Register).

(47) MARY WHITACKER, buried at Baughurst 25th March 1727 (also recorded in the Parish Register as " Mary Whitaker, a Quaker, was buryed in ye place called ye Quakers' Burying-place, 25th September 1726 " — one or the other was erroneous).

(48) EDWARD BARNS, a Quaker, was buryed in ye place called ye Quakers' Burying-place, 26th June 1727 (recorded in the Parish Register only).

[1] Men's Minutes, Alton Monthly Meeting.
[2] Men's Minutes, Alton Monthly Meeting, dated 12th August 1706.
[3] Men's Minutes, Hampshire Quarterly Meeting, dated 25th December 1705.
[4] Manydown Court Rolls, Cathedral Library, Winchester.
[5] Public Record Office, Chancery Lane, London.
[6] Court Rolls, Manor of Manydown, Cathedral Library, Winchester. (See note 10.)
[7] All the children of John and Mary Harris were baptised in Baughurst Church, despite being Quakers.
[8] Marriage Digest, Hampshire and Dorsetshire General Meeting.
[9] Men's Minutes, Alton Monthly Meeting.
[10] At the Court for the Manor and Hundred of Crondall Richard Potter was admitted as tenant of " One messuage and one garden and one orchard and one virgate of land in Aldershott and one meadow containing by estimation four acres called Longcroft Meade ", for which he paid a fine of 8 shillings, on the Surrender of William Baker, gentleman, and his wife, Jane. Potter's admittance was recorded at the Court of the 31st August 1675, and he was represented at that 206 Court by Thomas Wheeler, gentleman, probably his brother-in-law, by virtue of a Letter of Attorney, dated that same day.

CHAPTER ELEVEN
1728-1770

I

"In the same year, on February 17th, there is a conveyance of land to trustees for the use of the Society of Friends in Baughurst, by Leonard Cole, a Quaker, for the purpose of building a Meeting House. The land conveyed is described as a parcel of land purchased by Leonard Coale, or Cole, from Richard Freeborn, containing about 15 poles (more or less) bounded on the east by a ditch adjoining the highway leading from Baughurst to Newbury, on the north by lands called Wildery Key, and on west and south by land owned by Leonard Coale. The outward walls of the Meeting House were to be a foot within the land bought. This land was left in trust for the people commonly called Quakers, to build a Meeting House for the aforesaid Quakers and for burying their dead. This land was to be used for no other purpose whatever, and the Trustees were to be all Quakers. The names include those of Sanders, Kirton, Froud (of Aldermaston), who were all buried in the burial ground in later years."

(Florence Davidson: "The Quaker Burial Grounds at Baughurst", P.H.F.C.J., Vol. 7, Part 2, 1915, p. 43)

" At the Request of Leonard Cole and the Appointmt of this Meeting, Saml. Waring Sends the Writings of Baughurst Meeting house to Leonard Coal by Robert Applegarth, and there, being a Doubt in the minds of Some Frds: respecting the Title Frds: has to the Burrying Ground at Baughurst, This Meeting Appoints Robert Applegarth and Henry Portsmouth to enquire into the

Title Frds: has in it, and Report the Same to our Next Meeting."

(Men's Minutes, Alton Monthly Meeting,
dated 10th February 1735)

"Robert Applegarth gave account that Frds: are entitulled to the Burying Ground at Baughurst, By a Settlement of it Contained in the Settlement of the New Meeting house there."

(Men's Minutes, Alton Monthly Meeting,
dated 10th March 1735)

". . . A special clause in the Deed requires that at no time hereafter are trees to be planted on this land used as a burial ground that might injure the land belonging to Mr. Coale which joined it.

With these deeds we have a note in Mr. Coale's writing of the money to be paid for making the burial ground in 1735. On the outside is this crude sketch of rather later date than the deed itself as is seen from the different style or writing to that inside the paper.

The charges for making the burial ground come to £17 14s. 9½d., of which £14 5s. 6d. was subscribed by and given to the trustees, and £3 9s. 3½d. extra, which was given by Mr. Coale to make up the amount. The burial ground at that time was carefully drained, and a brick wall put round it with a wooden gate as entrance, and the hedges planted. There is also a sum of four shillings paid "For the setting up of ye little house", which may have been a shed for the gravedigger's tools".

(Florence Davidson, op. cit., p. 44)

LEONARD COLE'S new meeting house stood alongside the turnpike road at Inhurst, separated from the latter by a ditch. Cole's lands adjoined the plot of ground set out for the meeting house and its stable and yard on its western and southern sides. The settlement had itself solved the more immediate problem of ownership of James Potter's house. Now Harris was free to make any alteration to the structure of the building as he wished. From that time onwards the former Quaker meeting house was to undergo several structural alterations which were fundamental to Harris' scheme of aggrandisement, with the end result that the building fitted neatly into the pattern of the smaller mansions which litter the English countryside and reflect the lifestyles of the former gentry class. The process was completed with the house being given the grand name of Baughurst House. Such a scheme would not have been practical if the house was still in the hands of the trustees, for the Quakers as a body could not have been seen to be associating themselves with trappings which were identical to those being utilised by the Anglican gentry. They were plain and quiet people who shunned ornamentation and attitudes which would make one appear as more than equal to the next man. Yet, individually, as in any faith and society, there were those who aspired for better things than their beliefs would allow. And among the Quakers there were many of gentry stock, and above.

At the same time, the nucleus of Baughurst was in fact shifting. The older limits of the parish had been extended to include the tithings of Ham and Inhurst, which were under the Greens of Inhurst. More and more the wastelands along the turnpike road from Newbury to Kingsclere were being occupied as the tenants of Inhurst were extending the boundaries of their fields, and cottages were being erected upon the roadside plots. While that part of the parish which was under the jurisdiction of Manydown comprised mainly farmlands, the hamlet of Inhurst had developed into a village populated by tradesmen and labourers. It was here in the northern limits of the parish that the Quakers were now more concentrated. John Harris had had the new meeting house[1] erected in the north-eastern corner of Leonard Cole's land. The lands belonging to Cole, a Quaker, were bounded in the south by the farm of John Buller, another Quaker. Furthermore Daniel White and John Warne, also Quakers, lived in the neighbourhood. On the eastern side of the turnpike road the common lands of Tadley stretched out for several hundreds of acres, where the homesteads of a few Quaker families nestled among the bracken. Therefore, it would have appeared that a wise decision had been made in favour of a new meeting house which was made more easily accessible to the majority of the common folk who attended the religious services there. And the new meeting house itself was more acceptable in the eyes of those common worshippers as it was no more than the humble dwelling of a labourer itself.

There remained only the question of the burial ground as a reminder of the past. This was still the plot of land at Town's End which had been conveyed by James Potter to the Trustees before the end of the previous century. But now it was fast becoming a bone of contention between the heirs of James Potter and the congregation of the Inhurst meeting. By the end of 1734 John Harris and Leonard Cole were in dispute over the ownership of the meadow at Town's End. Harris was maintaining that he was the legal proprietor of that piece of land, as the old meeting house had been conveyed to him by deed in 1728, and as the original deed of 1696 also included the meadow at Town's End within its scope then that very same parcel of land must have been included in the release of 1728. Cole, on the other hand, stated that there was no mention of the meadow in the 1728 deed. Therefore the burial ground at Town's End was still in the hands of the Trustees constituted by and with that deed.

The matter, thus, went before the Alton Monthly Meeting of 10th February 1735,[2] and, as a result the deeds were sent for and inspected by Robert Applegarth of Basingstoke as an independent arbitrator. Applegarth duly informed the Meeting that the members of the new meeting at Baughurst were entitled to the use of the burial ground at Town's End.

However, in order to prevent further disputes over this matter, it was agreed that a new burial ground would be established alongside the meeting house at Inhurst. A piece of land to the west of the meeting house yard was set aside and measured by Cole (whose land it was) and then it was drained before a brick wall was built around it. Finally a wooden gate was made to fit the entrance into the cemetery from the meeting house, and hedges were planted. The cost of the scheme came to £17 14s. 9½d., of which Cole handed over £3 9s. 3½d. of his own money — the rest had come from contributions of the regular members. Finally, a deed was drafted whereby it was stated that no trees were to be planted on the land which would threaten to disturb the adjoining land of Leonard Cole.[3] The trustees were the same as those who held the meeting house.

Thus, in 1735, Baughurst boasted no less than three actual Quaker burial grounds within its boundaries — at the farm of Richard Potter, at Town's End, and now next to Cole's meeting house. All three were still in use at that time. Harris had not denied the Quakers their rights pertaining to the little meadow at Town's End. He had merely wished to maintain his proprietorship over it. However, he was much the happier with the new arrangement as the Town's End cemetery could now be restricted for the sole use of his own family, much the same as the original burial ground had been reserved for the family of Richard Potter. If anything, the events of 1728-35 had widened the gap between the patrons of the Baughurst meeting and their humbler co-religionists. The Baughurst Meeting had become divided into two factions, which would further hasten its decline.

II

"Mr John Harris's will, which was proved in 1736, has this clause in it: "I give my son my little meadow at Townsend and after his death I give the same for the use and behoof of the People commonly called Quakers belonging to the Meeting of Baughurst and Brimpton for a burying ground for ever.""

(Florence Davidson: "The Quaker Burial Grounds at Baughurst", P.H.F.C.J., Vol. 7, Part 2, 1915, p. 45)

MARY HARRIS had died in 1729 and was buried with her parents in the crypt set aside for the Potter and Harris families in the meadow at Town's End. At the following Court Baron held at Manydown her son, John Harris the younger, was duly admitted as the customary tenant of that estate formerly in the tenure of his mother. At the same time the estate in its entirety had been assigned to him by his father, thus the elder John had relinquished all his rights to the house and lands. At that moment John, junior, was only seventeen years old.

John Harris, senior, died at the end of December 1736, and was buried with his wife on 2nd January 1737.[4] He had made his last will and testament on 9th December 1736, and this was proved at Prerogative Court of Canterbury in London on 1st February 1737, when the executor, his son John, made a solemn declaration before the Surrogate.[5]

Harris, in his will, had classed himself as "gentlemen of Baghurst", and had constituted his "brother" William Nicholls and Leonard Cole as the trustees of the will.

He left to his son, John, "all that my Mannor or reputed Mannor of Rushall lying and being in the severall Parishes of Bradfield and Standford Dingley, Berks, and Theale, Berks, with the appurtenances", etc.[6] He also bequeathed to John several other estates which he held in three countries. In Wiltshire were the leasehold estates at Lyneham and Goatacre in Hillmarten, which had belonged to his father before him; in Hampshire the copyhold messuage and lands at Tadley, Ashmansworth, and East Woodhay, the little meadow at Town's End in Baughurst where the Quakers buried their dead, Gentry Mead and Alderlands in the parish of Baughurst, and Colliers at Sherborne St John, of which the majority of these lands had been bequeathed to him by his late father-in-law; in Berkshire there were the freehold estate at Henwick, and the leasehold estate at Thatcham.

To his daughter, Hannah Payne, the testator left "the whole terme and leasehold therein" of Lyneham and Goatacre in consideration that she had agreed to the sale of her "fortunes" made to her by her husband. Samuel Payne and Hannah had separated by this time. Furthermore, Harris had left his unfortunate daughter a legacy of £500 to be paid to her in full within six months of her husband's death. In the meantime that sum was to be invested by her brother and he was to pay to her the regular amounts of the interest accrued, currently standing at four per cent.

To his daughter, Mary, Harris left his copyhold estate at Knightsbridge, which formed the border of Hampshire and Berkshire, just north of Headley in the parish of Kingsclere. He also bequeathed to her the copyhold estate which was then in the occupation of Widow Keswell, the copyhold estate which he had purchased from John Harris of Thatcham and currently in the occupation of Alexander Parsons, and a number of freehold estates occupied by Parsons. She was also given a legacy of £500.

Harris finally bequeathed to the poor of Baughurst £15, of which £10 had to be spent on bread to feed them, while the other £5 could be apportioned to them as money.

Thus, John Harris, gentleman of Baughurst, divided up his real estate, leaving his son and two daughters considerable advantages in order to face the uncertainties of their futures. In over thirty years he had prospered considerably and his influence over the tenants of Rushall, and the under-tenants and occupiers in his many estates, whether leasehold, copyhold or freehold, was tremendous. Yet his power was not contained and limited to his lands, for he ruled as a despot over the Quaker community of northern Hampshire through his hereditary patronage of the Baughurst Meeting. Therefore his influence was much stronger and his power covered a wider area.

Yet since his plans of aggrandisement had been fulfilled by the conveyance of 1728, his power had been waning. Now Leonard Cole contested the hereditary patronage of the meeting, as he was in the same position as Harris' father-in-law and Harris himself before that year. Cole's house was the meeting house of the district, and Cole wanted to end the stranglehold which the Harrises had on the community. He was attempting gradually to implement the beliefs and conditions of the early Quakers — the very same standards which James Potter had taken to his grave. Leonard Cole was trying to revive the democratic ideals of Quakerism, but was largely being thwarted by Harris' concern to retain his dominance over the community. They often clashed, but even to the end they remained good friends. Now that Harris was dead, Cole had his chance to alter the process, and instead of the Harrises at the helm of the

Baughurst Meeting, he would place himself there, simply acknowledging Harris' son as the nominal patron.

III

"Leonard Cole and Henry Portsmouth gave Account, found nothing to hinder the marriage of John Harris and Mary Gulson of Coventry."

(Men's Minutes, Alton Monthly Meeting, dated 9th July 1739)

JOHN HARRIS, junior, was not such a forceful character as his father. The latter had worked hard to expand his business and property schemes, while the younger John had little to do but to inherit the wealth and power which his sire had bequeathed to him. In 1737 he was one of the most influential persons in the district, at the tender age of twenty-five years. He had no need to press his advantage any further, and was, therefore, content to delegate his responsibilities to others.

Leonard Cole was the obvious choice in respect of the local Quaker meeting, and he had the further qualification of being the nominated overseer of the late John Harris' will. Therefore, the current tenant of the former meeting house preferred to remain the titular head of the Quaker community in his locality, despite his knowledge of Cole's attempts to alter the constitution of the meeting in order to embrace the more democratic attitudes of the membership, while, at the same time, denying Harris much of his inherited power. Harris himself was more relieved that somebody else would shoulder the problems which such a large meeting brought, leaving him free to play the role of the squire of the district.

Harris, however, would frequently attend the meetings at Baughurst, but allowing Cole to deal with the necessary business there. Occasionally he would allow himself to be elected to represent the Baughurst Meeting at the Alton Monthly and Hampshire Quarterly Meetings.[7] He was a fairly conscientious Quaker, but even then he was gradually emulating the Anglican squirearchy of those times, as were many of the other Quaker gentry of the eighteenth century.

In 1739 Harris travelled to Coventry to marry Mary Gulson. His ability to marry had already been investigated and cleared by Leonard Cole and Henry Portsmouth at the Monthly Meeting of 9th July.[8] John and Mary had, in all, nine children,[9] of whom only three died in infancy. Therefore, in the mid-eighteenth century it would have appeared likely that the Harris patronage lasted for a considerable number of years, especially as there were two surviving sons of this marriage.

Leonard Cole, meanwhile, was becoming a notable figure at the Monthly Meeting and a regular at the Quarterly Meeting. He represented Baughurst at Alton in October 1740, September 1741, June 1743, December 1743, and in July 1744, and at Basingstoke in July 1743, while his son was present there in January 1744. Yet he was the prominent representative of his meeting at the Quarterlies, where he appeared in March 1739, September 1739, March 1740, June 1740, September 1740, March 1741, June 1741, September 1743, December 1743, and for the last time in March 1744. At the Monthly Meeting of 14th November 1743 he was appointed to receive the County Stock collections.[10]

His last appearance to serve the interests of the Baughurst Meeting at higher level meetings was when he appeared at Alton in July of 1744. Soon afterwards he was dead. Cole was buried in the cemetery next to his meeting house on 15th August 1744, in the land which he had given to the Quakers nine years before. His death left a void in the ranks of the democratically-minded faction of the Baughurst Meeting, and would herald the clash of interests which was already undermining the existence of the meeting itself.

IV

" The traditional burial ground in the garden of Brown's Farm (Richard Potter's old home) is, and always has been, a grass-grown part of the regular garden, with an old yew tree and shrubs in it. It lies next the division hedge on the Baughurst and Newbury road. Confirmation of this being an old burial place has been the discovery of a bricked vault, by the present occupier, who dug to see if he could find traces of burial here. And there is an entry in the parish register on November 26th, 1742, which further confirms the fact of burial in the farm grounds: Ann Potter, a Quaker, was buried " in her brother's garden. " This may have been the grave she was buried in. "

(Florence Davidson: "The Quaker Burial Grounds at Baughurst ", P.H.F.C.J., Vol. 7, Part 2, 1915, p. 42)

WITH COLE'S DEATH, Harris now began to assert himself as the leader of the Baughurst Meeting more fully than he had done before. He had been encouraged in this by the realisation that the meeting might flounder over the question of its control. He was supported in his stand by his relatives, Richard Potter and John Brown, formerly of Basingstoke, but now resident at Baughurst. In opposition to him the democratic faction had found a new leader in John Buller, who aspired for a position among the gentry of Inhurst, and he was being supported by individuals such as Nicholas Marshall, Daniel White, and Joel West. Buller had indeed enhanced his position in the community since the death in 1741 of Sanders Kirton, one of the Trustees, who had been Cole's right-hand man, and had also received the favour of Benjamin Froud of Aldermaston, another of the local Trustees.

Yet again, Harris soon grew tired of the responsibilities connected with the Baughurst Meeting. He was willing to delegate these to his cousin, Richard Potter, and Potter, in turn, was leaving much of the business to his brother-in-law, John Brown. Therefore the impending struggle soon died down again and the Quakers went back to their "quiet" lives.

John and Mary Brown were frequent attendants of the Baughurst Meeting, and John was more than happy to act as the representative for that meeting at the Monthly Meeting. In October 1739, and again in the same month of the following year, he was at Alton discussing the businesses of the local meetings within the jurisdiction of that Monthly. His wife died in 1741 and was buried in the Quaker cemetery at Basingstoke, and soon afterwards John moved in with his son, Richard, who was then the miller of Baughurst. Richard had married Jane Leaver in the Anglican church in far-off Wantage (in order not to call down upon himself the wrath of the local Quakers) and the couple now had two children — John and Jane.

With his mother's death, Richard was nominated as the third life in his uncle's copyhold estate, after Richard and Ann Potter.[11] Meanwhile, John became a regular in Leonard Cole's meeting-house, and in October 1746 and January 1747 he again represented the meeting at Alton.[12] He died in 1747 and was buried in the garden of Richard Potter's farm.[13]

Ann Potter, Richard Brown's aunt, died in 1744 and was buried in the original burial ground at Baughurst attached to her brother's farm. This now made Brown the immediate heir to his uncle's copyhold estate. At that time he was still the tenant of Baughurst Mill.[14] Then, in May 1747, Richard Potter died, and at the next court session at Manydown House Richard Brown was duly and formally admitted as the tenant of that estate. At the same time he nominated as his heirs his own son and daughter. From this time the farm was to be called by its present name — Brown's Farm. The Potters had now become extinct in that parish where

215

their influence had generated a profound opposition to the traditional supremacy of the Anglican hierarchy. For more than eighty years now the Potter name had been associated with defiance and nonconformity. Now that name had expired, and its representatives were no longer the ardent supporters of Quakerism that their forebears had been, it would be completely forgotten in the ensuing years.

Ironically, though, even as the original Potter standards were being revived by those who were professing the more democratic ideals, they were being confronted with a similar revival from the Anglican traditionalists who were now seeking the means to oppress this nonconformist element in the parish. Tithe persecution had already begun as Richard Potter was being lowered into his grave. It was as if a signal had been fired, dictated by the recent changes in the personnel of the Baughurst Meeting.

V

" 1746. Daniel White of Baughurst had taked from him
in Kind by Order of
John Taylor Priest of Baughurst
in value .... £12 12s. 0d.
and Wheat, Barley, Beans & Hay
in value .... £ 3   8s. 0d.

£16   0s. 0d.

(Sufferings, Hants)

NOBODY IN THE Quaker community at Baughurst knew why the tithe persecutions had begun again so unexpectedly after so many years of apparent peace between the two rivals for the consciences of the local inhabitants. All they knew was that they had happened swiftly and suddenly before the Quakers had time to prepare themselves for the coming onslaughts against their privacy. It had been forty-three years since the last oppressive raid in the district.

During that period of peace the neighbouring districts of northern Hampshire had witnessed very few of these persecutions, and whereas once they had been regular occurrences, their irregular and isolated revivals had caused little concern among the Quaker communities in general.

George Wigg of Basing had suffered regularly during the years 1709-12. In the first year he had been deprived of hay, oats and barley to the total of £4 10s. 0d. on four separate occasions when his home had been visited by Thomas Evis, the servant of Thomas White, rector of Nately Scures, and by Thomas Mays, the servant of the Tithe Farm at Basing. In 1710 his losses were valued at £5 4s. 0d., in 1711 at £2 15s. 6d., and in 1712 at £4 2s. 0d.[15]

Twenty years had passed before the next oppression. This occurred in the town of Basingstoke in 1732 when Edward Jay, one of the church-wardens there, was ordered to relieve Robert Applegarth and George Eeles of some of their goods.[16]

Then, in 1746, it was the turn of Baughurst to experience the current revival of tithe visitations. On the order of the rector of that parish, John Taylor, the parish officers entered the fields of Daniel White and took away crops and goods to the value of £16 0s. 0d., an extraordinary amount of money for those times. The tithe oppressors returned time and time again to the farm of Daniel White. In 1749 his losses amounted to £10 5s. 0d., in 1750 they were £8 10s. 0d., and then £9 5s. 0d. in 1751, £9 0s. 0d. in 1752, £9 10s. 0d. in 1753, and £8 4s. 0d. in 1754. White died in 1755, leaving a widow, but even she was not exempted from the claims of the Church. She was relieved of goods worth £6 4s. 0d. in 1755, £10 0s. 0d. in 1756, £12 10s. 0d. in 1757, and £8 3s. 0d. in 1759.[17]

Meanwhile, the parish officers of Basingstoke were equally busy. In 1750, under the leadership of Richard Jayes the churchwarden, they visited the homes of Henry Portsmouth, Sarah Mitchell, Richard Wallis, and Thomas Hack, depriving those Quakers of such items as fourteen pewter plates, two bundles of paper, some bacon, spades, a shovel, and a whetting stone.[18]

In 1759, the last year of the Baughurst tithe persecutions, it was the turn of John Buller to suffer distress. He had barley and hay worth £2 14s. 0d. taken out of his fields in Inhurst.[19]

Then, as suddenly as the persecutions had begun, they died down. The mood had somewhat changed and Baughurst returned to slumber in tranquil sleep once more. Or so it appeared on the surface. The sleep into which the Quaker community was now allowed to settle was, in effect, a coma from which it would never recover as a fit and healthy body. The wounds it had inflicted upon itself over the years since the death of James Potter were gradually turning gangrenous. It suffered from constant pressures from both within and without, and these pressures were exerted more so because of the distresses caused by the recent tithe persecutions. The meeting was dying, but its members could not wholly recognise that fact — so engrossed with their own beliefs were they that they failed to appreciate the recent encroachments upon their domain. A decade later the more influential section of the Baughurst Meeting was about to desert their faith.

VI

" 1st : Baghurst Meeting have now sent their Collection towards County Stock being 3 " 3 s wch. is Order'd to be paid in to the Quarterly Meeting "

(Men's Minutes, Alton Monthly Meeting, dated 12th February 1763)

" As Baghurst & Winton have not Sent their Collection towards County Stock they are desir'd to do it. . . . "

(Men's Minutes, Alton Monthly Meeting, dated 11th May 1765)

" 5th : Our Public Stock being nearly Exhausted the Quarterly Meeting thought it Necessary to Order a general Collection to repair it this Meeting therefore Appoints following Friends to make same for our Monthly Meetings & are desired to get it Compleated by Next Quarter. "

(Men's Minutes, Alton Monthly Meeting, dated 12th December 1767)

QUAKERISM WAS now being undermined by a new enemy within its midst. The same evangelical spirit which had gained Quakerism its popularity among the lower and middle classes of the seventeenth century was now being used against the Friends. Since Toleration it had become a respectable faith and its " quietness " had now altered its appearance beyond all recognition. The former rebels were treated with the dignity and courtesy that they had earned over the years through their sheer honesty and willingness to work hard. Where Quakers had formerly been considered a threat, they were now regarded as prosperous assets to the community at large. They were peaceful and inactive, despite their refusal to pay the legal dues owing to the Established Church. They no longer represented the lower classes, for their prosperity in business appealed to the middle classes rather than the labourers and artisans. They were debarred from the higher classes of society because they were nonconformists and therefore legally restricted from the powers of the office-holders and parliamentarians. The faith suffered from these limitations, and, whereas the Anglican Church could more readily attract those with ambitions of grandeur, the lower classes would soon fall under the spell of the new evangelists.

John and Charles Wesley were regular visitors to Baughurst in those days. They were always made welcome at the home of George Whitfield, the former curate of Dummer, who now lived in a house in Inhurst situated between John Buller's farm and the Quaker meeting house. Whitfield supported the Methodism of the Wesleys, and would open up his home as a chapel for those converted to the new denomination. The combined forces of the Wesley brothers and Whitfield fired the imaginations of the local working classes, and before long many were deserting the meeting house of the Quakers for the chapel of the Methodists. In years to come Whitfield would in turn desert the Wesleyan cause in favour of his own brand of Methodism called Primitive Methodism, and his particular ideals found favour among the inhabitants of that district. Primitive Methodist chapels outnumber those of the Wesleyans in northern Hampshire.

As the membership of the Quaker meeting dwindled it quickly came to the notice of the representatives at the Alton Monthly Meeting.[20] John Buller was appointed to the Quarterly Meeting in the September of 1761, where he presented to the County Stock Baughurst's contribution of £2 12s. 6d. Three months later it had dropped to £1 11s. 6d. There were no further contributions until December 1762 when only 15s. 0d. had been collected.

On 15th August 1763 John Harris was appointed to collect the contributions of the several meetings under Alton and to deliver them to the Quarterly Meeting following.[21] However, Baughurst paid no contributions to the Public Stock for that year until the December when 3s. 3d. was paid in. Throughout 1764 and 1765 Baughurst was again negligent with contributions for the County Stock, and in March 1765 the members of that meeting were desired by the Monthly Meeting to send them to the Quarterly Meeting. But such pleas fell upon deaf ears. Although John Harris and John Buller were appointed as collectors in January 1766 the complaints against Baughurst continued. Finally, on 12th October 1767, the minutes of the Alton Monthly Meeting recorded the last notice of the Baughurst Meeting in respect of the contributions towards the Public Stock. It had been almost four years since that meeting had sent in its collection.

Yet the Baughurst Meeting still continued in existence, despite the continuous desertions and encroachments which it suffered. Those who remained to worship in the old way were the members of the older generation who supported the faith through thick and thin. Their children were not so charitable to the all-embracing institution. When they needed religious comfort they would go elsewhere, according to their station in life.

John Harris, despite his shortcomings, was a loyal supporter of the faith. As patron of the Baughurst Meeting he followed the traditional path, as had been dictated by his father and grandfather before him. His wife had died in 1755, and his last fifteen years of life were filled with his attempts to restore the faith to its former glory in Baughurst and the surrounding neighbourhood. But he was fighting a losing battle. Soon after his death in 1770, his son and heir dealt the final bitter blow to the Baughurst Meeting, when he deserted to the more influential Anglican Church. His defect encouraged the younger generation of the Brown family to do the same in the following year. Quakerism had now been deprived of its more affluent section in this parish.

Quaker Marriages at Baughurst 1728-1770

(14) THOMAS BURR, and ANN OGBORNE, at Baughurst, 22nd September 1731.

(15) RICHARD MATTHEWS, and MARTHA FROUD, at Baughurst, 22nd December 1732.

(16) JOHN HASKER, malster of Aldermaston, Co. Berks, son of William and Ann Hasker, of Silchester, and JANE WITHERS, of Baughurst, at Baughurst, 9th March 1736.

(17) EDWARD FERRIS, of Lynham, Co. Wilts, shopkeeper, and HANNAH OVERTON, daughter of Richard Overton, of the Forest, Co. Warwick, at Baughurst, 14th July 1752.

(18) THOMAS PEMBERTON, of Birmingham, and MARY HARRIS, daughter of John Harris, of Baghurst, at Baghurst, 16th March 1759.

Quaker Burials at Baughurst 1728-1770[22]

(49) ELIZABETH BLUNDING, wife of William Blunding, of Tadly, died 3rd December 1728, and was buried at Baghurst 6th December 1728 (also recorded in the Parish Register as "Elizabeth Blunden, a Quaker, was buryed in ye place called ye Quakers' Burying-place, 7th December 1728").

(50) ELIZABETH BLUNDON, buried at Baughurst 28th December 1728 (not recorded in the Parish Register).

(51) MARY HARRIS, buried at Baughurst 11th May 1729 (also recorded in the Parish Register as "Mary Harris, wife of Mr John Harris, a Quaker, buryed in ye place called ye Quakers' Burying-place, 15th May 1729").

(52) ANN BLUNDEN, at Baughurst 25th June 1732 (also recorded in the Parish Register as "Ann Blunden, a Quaker, buryed in ye place called ye Quakers' Burying-place, 25th June 1732").

(53) ALICE HASKINS, buried at Baughurst the 9th January 1734 (also recorded in the Parish Register as "Alice Hasker, a Quaker, buryed in ye place called ye Quakers' Burying-place, 9th February 1733").

(54) MARY KIRTON, infant, daughter of Sanders and Mary Kirton, buried at Baughurst 11th January 1735 (also recorded in the Parish Register as "Mary Kirton, daughter of Sanden Kirton, a Quaker, buryed in ye place called ye Quakers' Burying-place, 26th January 1735").

(55) JOHN HASKINS, buried at Baughurst 7th March 1736 (also recorded in the Parish Register as "John Haskins, a Quaker, buryed in ye place called ye Quakers' Burying-place, 7th March 1736").

(56) JOHN HARRIS, buried at Baughurst 2nd January 1737 (also recorded in the Parish Register as "Mr John Harris senior, a Quaker, buryed in ye place called ye Quakers' Burying-place, 7th January 1737").

(57) JOHN HASKER, son of John and Jane Hasker, buried at Baughurst 10th April 1738 (not recorded in the Parish Register).

(58) WILLIAM BLUNDEN,[23] buried at Baughurst 23rd March 1740 (also recorded in the Parish Register as "William Blunden, a Quaker, buryed in ye place called ye Quakers' Burying-place, 23rd March 1740". In pencil there is the annotation that he was considered "the strongman of Baughurst").

(59) SANDERS KIRTON, buried at Baughurst 24th December 1741 (also recorded in the Parish Register as "Sandon Kirton, a Quaker, buryed in ye place called ye Quakers' Burying-place, 29th December 1741").

(60) RACHEL THORPE, daughter of John Thorp, buried at Baughurst 1st January 1742 (also recorded in the Parish Register as "Rachael Thorp, a Quaker, buryed in ye place called ye Quakers' Burying-place, 3rd January 1742").

(61) LEONARD COLE, buried at Baughurst 15th August 1744 (not recorded in the Parish Register).

(62) ANN POTTER, buried at Baughurst 27th November 1744 (also recorded in the Parish Register as "Ann Potter, a Quaker, was buryed in her Brother's garden, 26th November 1742").

(63) MARY KIRTON, buried at Baughurst 10th May 1744 (not recorded in the Parish Register).

(64) REBECCA FROUD, senior buried at Baughurst 9th June 1745 (not recorded in the Parish Register).

(65)   JOHN HARRIS, son of John Harris, buried at Baughurst 21st April 1745 (not recorded in the Parish Register).

(66)   NICHOLAS MARSHALL, buried at Baughurst 5th October 1746 (not recorded in the Parish Register).

(67)   HANNAH HARRIS, daughter of John Harris, buried at Baughurst 9th January 1747 (not recorded in the Parish Register).

(68)   MARY HARRIS, daughter of John and Mary Harris, senior, buried at Baughurst 27th March 1747 (not recorded in the Parish Register).

(69)   RICHARD POTTER, buried at Baughurst 9th May 1747 (not recorded in the Parish Register).

(70)   JOHN BROWN, almost certainly buried in the garden of Brown's Farm some time in 1747 or soon afterwards, although his burial is not recorded in either of the sources. He last attended the Alton Monthly Meeting in January 1747.

(71)   JAMES HARRIS, son of John Harris, buried at Baughurst 22nd June 1749 (not recorded in the Parish Register).

(72)   SARAH MATTINGLY, buried at Baughurst 9th February 1750 (not recorded in the Parish Register).

(73)   REBECCA FROUD, junior, buried at Baughurst 5th May 1750 (not recorded in the Parish Register).

(74)   ELIZABETH HINE, buried at Baughurst 14th February 1751 (not recorded in the Parish Register).

(75)   HANNAH PAYNE, wife of Samuel Payne, buried at Baughurst 28th December 1752 (also recorded in the Parish Register as "Hannah Payne, buried at the Quakers' burying ground in Baghurst, 1st January 1753").

(76)   BENJAMIN FROUD, aged 85, of Aldermaston, Co. Berks, died 20th April 1753, and was buried at Baughurst 24th April 1753 (not recorded in the Parish Register).

(77)   MARY HARRIS, wife of John Harris, of Baughurst, buried at Baughurst 6th February 175 (also recorded in the Parish Register as "Mrs Mary Harris, wife of John Harris, Esquire, buryed at the Quakers' burying ground in Baghurst, 6th February 1755").

(78)   DANIEL WHITE, aged near 80, of Baughurst, sometime of Shillingford, Co. Oxford, buried at Baughurst in 175-[24] (not recorded in the Parish Register).

(79)   ANN COAL, sister of Leonard Coal, buried at Baughurst 14th January 1759 (not recorded in the Parish Register).

(80)   HANNAH HARRIS, wife of Robert Harris, of Reading, and daughter of Benjamin Froud, buried at Baughurst 17th February 1760 (not recorded in the Parish Register).

(81)   MARY WHITE, aged 75, widow of Daniel White, buried at Baughurst 30th January 1763 (not recorded in the Parish Register).

(82)   JOHN HARRIS, son of John Harris senior, of Baughurst, buried at Baughurst 11th February 1770 (not recorded in the Parish Register).

After 1735 there were three Quaker burial grounds in Baughurst, and all three were being used on occasions. From the above information it can be fairly safely assumed that the burials took place in the following cemeteries: the first burial ground in Richard Potter's garden (now Brown's Farm): Nos. 62, 69, 70, and 72; the second burial ground at Town's End: Nos. 49 to 54, 56, 65, 67, 71, 75, 77, and 82; the third burial ground near Leonard Cole's house: Nos. 55, 57 to 61, 63, 64, 66, 73, 74, 76, and 78 to 81.

[1] Now Rose Cottage, Baughurst.

[2] Men's Minutes, Alton Monthly Meeting.

[3] Quoted by Florence Davidson. The author has no knowledge of the whereabouts of the actual deed.

[4] The parish registers state 7th January.

[5] The will of John Harris is in the Public Record Office, Chancery Lane, London.

[6] "A nominal manor of Rushall or Rushall Court existed in the parish of Bradfield, owing suit and service to the main manor there." Victoria County History, Berks, iii, p. 397. In 1716 it was sold by Richard Bytheway and his wife Elizabeth to John Bowen and John Richards. In 1801 it belonged to the family of Bunny of Newbury.

[7] He was the representative at the Monthly Meeting in June 1739, March 1741, and in November 1755; and at the Quarterly Meeting in March 1739, March 1740, September 1740, September 1744, and March 1746.

[8] Men's Minute, Alton Monthly Meeting.

[9] These were all recorded in the Baughurst parish registers.

[10] Men's Minutes, Alton Monthly Meeting.

[11] Court Rolls, Manor of Manydown, Cathedral Library and H.R.O., Winchester.

[12] Men's Minutes, Alton Monthly Meeting.

[13] There is no record of his burial, but it can be fairly safely assumed that he was buried in the garden of Brown's Farm. It appears that burials here were now reserved for members of that family.

[14] Possibly Malthouse Farm, Baughurst, which was not under the Manor of Manydown.

[15] Sufferings, Hants.

[16] Sufferings, Hants.

[17] Sufferings, Hants.

[18] Sufferings, Hants. (See note 25.)

[19] Sufferings, Hants.

[20] Men's Minutes, Alton Monthly Meeting.

21 Men's Minutes, Alton Monthly Meeting.

22 Although Baughurst was rarely mentioned in this latter period in the minutes books of the Alton Monthly and Hampshire Quarterly Meetings, there must have been some representation in order that so many burials were being recorded for that meeting.

23 Florence Davidson relates the tradition (P.H.F.C.J., Vol. 7, Part 2, 1915, p. 42), that on one occasion Blunden was challenged to a fight by a boaster, who relied on his being a Quaker to ignore the insult. However, Blunden simply took hold of the man and tossed him over the nearest hedge.

24 The year was certainly 1755, according to the Sufferings Book.

25 Edward Jay was the son of Edward Jey (1663-1725), twice mayor of Basingstoke (in 1710/1 and 1719/20), and died in Basingstoke in 1738. His cousin, Richard Jayes (mentioned as churchwarden in 1750), the son of Richard Jey of Cliddesden (1661-1721), was born in 1695, and was a carpenter with his shop in Church Street, Basingstoke. His son, also Richard (1731-1790), was granted an allotment in the Basingstoke Enclosure Award of 1788, of which a portion is retained today under its original name of Jay's Close.

CHAPTER TWELVE
1770-1791

I

"2 December 1770: John Potter Harris Esq was baptized; He was born a Quaker December ye 13th 1745, as appears by this Register Book dated at that time"

(Baughurst Parish Register, Hampshire Record Office, Winchester)

JOHN POTTER HARRIS, the son and successor of the late John Harris, was publicly baptised in St Stephen's Church at Baughurst on 2nd December 1770, at the age of twenty-four years. After ten months as the titular head of the Baughurst Meeting, he had finally withdrawn the traditional patronage and had openly displayed his natural adherence to the Established Church as a member of the landed gentry. He could now alter his course and head towards more profitable goals in his ambitions to increase the wealth and political power of his family.

The desertion of John Potter Harris was naturally followed by those of his family. Although his brother, William, did not publicly announce his departure from the Quaker community in the same way as did John, his children were, nevertheless, christened into the Anglican faith.[1]

The Browns, likewise, followed the trend, as the restrictions imposed upon the landed gentry because of their allegiances to the nonconformist faiths were still hindering their activities. In fact, John Brown, the son of Richard the copyholder of Brown's Farm, had been a prominent witness to marriages in the parish church since 1759.[2] Now, on 29th July 1771, he was joined in holy matrimony with Mary Taylor in that very same Anglican establishment. Thereafter all their six children were baptised into the Church of England.

Furthermore, John's sister, Jane, who had witnessed the marriage of her brother, did herself marry John Spencer of Tadley in Baughurst Church. Much of the influence here had been determined by their mother, Jane, an ardent Anglican who had died at the family farm on 19th March 1770, and was laid to rest in the parish churchyard. She had carefully nurtured

225

her religious ideals through all her married life, and, although she had allowed her children to be raised in the Quaker traditions, she had also ensured that they had equal opportunities to study the ways of the Anglican community, stressing the benefits which they would gain by their adherence to the Established Church. By the time both children had grown up and were ready for marriage, the Quaker influence in the parish had already subsided and there was little left to attract those who felt no traditional ties to that faith.

So, at the end of 1772, there was only one member of the former influential descendants of the Potters remaining within the all-embracing benevolence of the Quaker community of the Baughurst Meeting. Richard Brown was an old man, who knew that his time upon this earth was now severely limited. Yet, with the inherited obstinacy of the Potters, he refused to desert the community and faith which had inspired and had comforted him all his years. If need be he would take his ideals to his grave alone, without the consensus of his family. He was old, and his ways were regarded as old-fashioned now, but he still held the respect of his family, neighbours and friends, who knew him as a kindly and hard-working gentleman. He would maintain his dignity to the end and would show the world that he would remain faithful to his beliefs, no matter how unpopular and how out-dated those beliefs might appear to the current generation.

Richard Brown attended the meetings at Inhurst as often as his health would allow, and even then his son would take him there, for John loved his father and was forever loyal to him, despite their religious differences. Richard did, on occasions, attend the Anglican services, especially the joyous occasions of his children's marriages. He was seventy-six when he died at his copyhold farm in April, 1779. He had left a will which determined the succession of Brown's Farm for two generations,[3] but had made no mention of God nor written instructions regarding his burial. These funeral directions had been made during his last hours, and naturally he had instructed his son, as his legal heir and executor, to have his body interred in the Old Quaker Burial Ground in their garden. The funeral ceremony was a private family affair, and thus was not recorded in the Quaker records. Richard Brown had passed quietly away at a time when his co-religionists were extremely quiet, almost to the point of utter silence, in their activities in this area. A few days after Richard's burial the Browns had a second tragedy when Richard's beloved daughter, Jane Spencer, died from the effects of the illness which her father had suffered during his last days. She was buried in the churchyard of St Stephen's. The Browns had finally ended their associations with the Baughurst Meeting.

The last of the Potter line to support the Quaker faith had now ended an association that had remained intact for almost a century and a quarter. As Richard Brown's body was lowered into the earth, near the farmhouse in which his forebears had lived for the last two hundred years or more, the twilight was already descending upon the Baughurst Meeting.

II

"Baughurst Meeting House & two Burial Grounds, one adjoining the Meeting House given by Leonard Cole, the other a Meadow including a Burial Ground situate at Townsend in Baughurst the Gift of Jno. Harris Senr. convey'd the 24th of the 6th Month 1778 from Henry Portsmouth and Benjn Froud to Alexr Neave, John Merryweather, Charles Heath (Andover), James Blose Junr, Benjn Constant Junr, Wm Heath — Jeffrey Junr, Henry Warner all surviving except Benjamin Constant —— "

(Deed of Conveyance, Baughurst Meeting, 24th June 1778, Hampshire Record Office)

THE BAUGHURST MEETING was last mentioned in the Men's Minutes, of the Alton Monthly Meeting on 29th September 1776, when it was declared (as per norm) that the members had not sent in their contributions to the Public Stock. This was almost nine years after the previous mention of that meeting in the accounts of business.[4]

Yet, the meeting was still in progress, and by the time the Alton Monthly Meeting had recorded this last mention of Baughurst in its minutes, a marriage had taken place at Leonard Cole's house and was duly recorded in the Quaker register.[5]

Even as late as 1778 there were strong signs that the Baughurst Meeting was merely slumbering, and that it might awaken yet again to become a thriving assembly. Of the original ten trustees constituted in 1728 only two were now living. According to the original deeds to the meeting, the trustees had the power to appoint new trustees to make up the number when the original number had been reduced to three. Therefore on the 23rd and 24th June 1778 a new deed was framed in order to constitute fresh trustees to make up the number. Henry Portsmouth and Benjamin Froude were thus joined by Alexander Neave, John Merryweather, Charles Heath of Andover, James Blose, junior, Benjamin Constant, junior, William Heath, William Jeffrey, junior, and Henry Warner.[6]

227

By 1788 Constant was dead, and by 1835 only William Heath was surviving. At this latter date there appeared to have been no sense of urgency recorded in order to constitute a new group of trustees. It was preferred to incorporate Baughurst with the Basingstoke Meeting for this purpose. It was as if Baughurst had now been forgotten as an individual community, yet this was probably expected as that meeting had failed to make contact with its monthly meeting for some years now. The only records of the occurrences at Baughurst were in the forms of marriages and burials, the latter hardly being recorded at all.

Meanwhile, encroachments had been made into the territory where the Quakers alone had held sway as the religious alternative to the Established Church. In 1791 Thomas Mayers was granted a licence by the authorities to establish a Baptist meeting house by the roadside at Loveday's Farm, just to the southwest of Brown's Farm, where the original Quaker meeting house had been. Then in 1795, after Primitive Methodists had been assembling unofficially in the parish of Baughurst for several years now, a licence was granted to William May to establish a meeting in the chapel-house formerly inhabited by George Whitfield at Inhurst.[7] The near proximity of the Methodist chapel to the Quaker meeting house was to prove disastrous to the latter congregation, and the granting of the licence to the Methodists was the final nail to be hammered into the coffin of the Baughurst Quaker Meeting. As Methodists began to pour into their newly-established chapel the Quakers could only watch with growing anxiety as the future of nonconformity in the area rapidly slipped from their grasp.

The years were passing swiftly, and the twilight was merging into total darkness under the swirling mists which were threatening to extinguish the old light which had shone like a lonely beacon in the wilderness of time. But before the darkness of night had totally obliterated the presence of this Quaker haven, the Baughurst Meeting had made one last effort to indicate to the world that it was still just about alive. The final record of this assembly was, ironically, a burial entry. Mary Barlow had no claim to fame at all, but was distinguised above all others as the vital proof that the Baughurst Meeting was in existence in 1791, albeit leading a very tenuous existence. She was Mary West, a widow, when she married Richard Barlow, a yeoman from Tadley, in St Stephen's Church at Baughurst in 1768. She was fifty-nine years old when she died on 5th November 1791, and she was buried in the cemetery adjoining the meeting house at Inhurst on the 9th of that month.[8]

The meeting did not end with the burial of Mary Barlow, but its life was now extremely limited. It was the Old Man of Baughurst. It had been in existence now for one hundred and thirty years, and had not been capable of adapting itself to modern life for at least the last forty of those years. Its membership was old and conservative. Those who would adapt and show more progressive spirit had, by this time, moved to the towns, leaving behind them the contemporaries of Leonard Cole, Richard Brown and John Harris, who merely dwelt upon the reminiscences of the past glories.

The darkness of night deepened to allow the Old Man of Baughurst to fall into his last undisturbed sleep. As he slept time hurried on. That night was very long indeed, and during it many old souls, who had been comforted by the words of George Fox, were to pass away without fitting memorials to their very existence.

The Baughurst Meeting had expired, and before long it would appear that the Quakers had never been associated with this northern Hampshire village. They did not leave behind memorials which would advertise their prevalence in any of the districts where they lived. They left only the houses in which they assembled for worship and the cemeteries in which they were buried. Therefore, when such a community as was entrenched at Baughurst finally died out there was never anything much remaining which would provide a souvenir of their associations — except their own records and their bones which were buried in the earth which they honoured. They had forsaken all the trappings and ceremonies which had been the prime memorials of their Anglican rivals, and preferred the anonymity of the simple and virtuous ways. Therefore, because of their self-denials, they remain almost unknown as individuals. Their lives — their very existence — can only be found in their own records. Fortunately, some traditions survive to allow us the clues of their existence in the first place. Despite the death of the Baughurst Meeting, the tradition of Quakerism in Baughurst is still very strong to this day. In fact, there is some pride attached to their existence in that parish among the local inhabitants today. That pride is now proved to be justified. Not many places can boast connections with a Quaker meeting which had endured the longest persecutions against Protestant nonconformist sects. Not many parishes can boast a Quaker meeting-house and burial ground. Still fewer districts can boast that they have had three Quaker meeting houses and three Quaker burial grounds. Baughurst can. It can also boast that it had a very important Quaker dignitary who had begun it all, and that the meeting had been visited — and approved — by Fox himself.

Quaker Marriages at Baughurst 1770-1791

(19) RICHARD GILKES, of Whitchurch, clockmaker, son of Thomas Gilkes, of Sibford, Co. Oxford, and LETITIA

GILBERT, daughter of Benjamin Gilbert, late of Newbury, at Baughurst, 1st November 1774.

(20) JEFFREY WALLIS, of Hartley Row, and ANN BONNY, of Hartley Row, daughter of Thomas and Frances Bonny, of Reading, Co. Berks, at Baughurst, 12th September 1776.

(21) EDMUND FRY, of Worship Street, Psh of St Leonards, Shoreditch, Co. Middx, letter-founder, son of Joseph and Anna Fry, of Bristol, and JENNY WINDOVER, at Baughurst, 19th April 1785.

Quaker Burials at Baughurst 1770-1791

(83) RICHARD BROWN, buried at Brown's Farm, Baughurst, in April or May 1779 (not recorded).

(84) MARY BARLOW, aged 59, of Tadly, who died 5th November 1791, and was buried at Baughurst 9th November 1791 (recorded in the Quaker records only).

There were several other burials in the period, especially after 1791, but were not recorded. Therefore they cannot be ascertained, and must remain anonymous.

[1] William and Mary Harris' son, John Potter Harris, was baptised at Baughurst at the age of six in 1782.

[2] Baughurst Parish Registers.

[3] Dated 6th November 1775, proved at Winchester on 12th May 1779. It is now at the Hampshire Record Office.

[4] Men's Minutes, Alton Monthly Meeting.

[5] Marriage Digest, Hampshire and Dorsetshire General Meeting.

[6] Deeds of Conveyance, Hampshire Record Office.

[7] A. J. Willis: "Hants Miscellany III".

[8] Burial Digest, Hampshire and Dorsetshire General Meeting.

EPILOGUE
1791-1892

O N 27TH MARCH 1835, new trustees were constituted for the burial grounds at Baughurst. On that date the surviving trustee of the previous constitution, William Heath, handed over his responsibility to the combined forces of Henry Crowley, William Curtis, William Holmes, Newton Bransley, James Curtis, David Bransley, Francis Ashley Wallis, Thomas Benjamin Horne, Thomas Edward Heath, Josiah Neave, Samuel Thompson, Samuel Clarke, Edward Westlake, and Henry Evans, who were thus proclaimed as the new trustees of the Quaker properties in Basingstoke, Baughurst, Bramshott, Alton and Whitchurch.

Then on 25th October 1849, the Alton Monthly Meeting appointed a committee to visit and to survey the properties within its compass, and to report their findings to the full General Meeting. The committee had this to report of the Baughurst visit:

> " The burial ground at Baughurst is the Committee believe quite gone out of the possession of Friends, it is occupied as Garden grounds without any boundary marks to seperate it from contiguous garden ground: the Committee believe that any attempt to regain it would be useless, as the present possesser disputes the right of Friends and he has had undisturbed possession for more than 20 Years. "[1]

The Quakers had lost possession of this once vital area because of their own lapse of concern. The warning signs had been apparent now for several decades, but the Alton Monthly Meeting was so completely wrapped up in its own particular problems that it turned a blind eye towards the shortcomings of the Baughurst Meeting. When action was finally decided upon it was much too late. " The present possessor disputes the right of Friends and he has had undisturbed possession for more than 20 Years ". In fact, his undisturbed possession was very much in excess of those twenty years.

In 1827 the Inhurst Enclosure Act, combined with those of Ham and Pamber, was passed and put into practice. At that time the house which belonged formerly to the Baughurst Meeting was in the possession of Daniel Tyler, the carpenter, and he was granted the right by his tenure of

231

that cottage and another to the north to enclose the waste ground between the road and his properties. Tyler had, therefore, been in possession of that cottage for at least twenty-two years when the Quaker committee from Alton visited him in 1849. His ownership had probably extended for several years before the Enclosure Act was made legal, as his right to the property would have had to have been examined thoroughly by the Enclosure Commissioners. It would appear that Tyler had gained possession of Leonard Cole's house some time after it had become vacant and seemingly deserted by the Quakers themselves.

Tyler was still the proprietor of the former meeting house in 1839, when the Tithe Commissioners visited Baughurst for the business of surveying the parish as condition of the Tithe Commutation Act. The occupier, at that time, was Samuel Thorngate, the baker. Thorngate was still inhabiting the cottage when the Quaker committee arrived ten years later, although the property was now in the hands of a person surnamed Dicker.

Meanwhile, the burial ground itself which was attached to the meeting house was also the property of Daniel Tyler, and later of Dicker, but in 1849 it was being tilled by William Cowderey. The Quakers also had difficulty detecting where the boundaries had been, and it is highly likely that the cemetery itself spilled into the lands formerly owned by Henry Flower, but by 1839 were in the possession of John Hawkins of Oak House, the Duke of Wellington's tenant farmer at Ewhurst. In 1854 Hawkins was granted the lease to farm Wellington's Manor Farm estate after the previous tenant, Ann Woods, the widow of Farmer Joshua Woods, had been evicted for bad management. Therefore all the interested parties concerned were in no mood to hand back the lands and buildings which the Quakers were now claiming as theirs by right.

The final word in the dispute was the Quakers'. Unhappily, in order not to prolong their distress, a pencilled note was added to the record of their loss — "This property cannot now be identified". Yet, if they had really dug into the records and had investigated the property carefully, they would have found that the cottage was what is today known as "Rose Cottage" in the village of Baughurst, and that the burial ground was situated to the west and south of the above-mentioned building.

The old burial ground at Townsend was also abandoned by the same committee. In 1839 the meadow was owned by the Duke of Wellington, as part of his Wolverton Park Estate, and was in the occupation of John Arnott. The Quaker claim to this property was as tenuous as that in Inhurst.

Today the meadow incorporating James Potter's burial ground is attached to the property known as "Forgefields". The present owner well remembers an incident in that meadow when he had not long purchased it. He had placed a horse in there for grazing, and was alarmed to see it gradually begin to disappear as the earth opened up beneath it. The accident exposed a vault in which three skeletons were found in a reclining position. The owner did not investigate further, preferring to leave the burial ground as undisturbed as possible. He had trees planted around the area soon afterwards.

John Potter Harris died in the June of 1797 and was buried at Baughurst Church on the 28th of that month. He was fifty-two years old and a confirmed bachelor. His inheritance, therefore, passed to his brother, William, who was married and the father of one son and two surviving daughters.

Harris was an absentee landlord. For many years he and his family lived at Coventry, until he purchased an estate at Thatcham, in Berkshire, from the Rev. Lovelace Bigg-Wither of Manydown House, and moved there with his family. In the meantime he had placed tenants at Baughurst House. Until 1801 the mansion house in Baughurst was occupied by John Miles, and that year he was replaced by John Christopher Rideout, esq.[2]

Harris, therefore, had little concern for the farmlands surrounding and attached to Baughurst House, for these were rented out to individual farmers. In 1804 he began a series of land transactions which would dramatically reduce his holdings in that Hampshire parish.

He sold off nine acres of the copyhold lands attached to Baughurst House to Thomas Bates, the farmer of Little Ham Farm in the north of the parish. Then in 1806, he released a further twelve acres of the estate situated near Browning Hill to Thomas Faulkner.

The year 1806 was a tragic one for William Harris, for in that year his only son and heir, John Potter Harris, died unmarried, at the age of thirty. The father was completely destroyed by this sudden tragic change of events and it would appear that he began to suffer a gradual decline in his health. He had made his will in 1805, but had failed to alter it after his son's death (with the exception that he added a codicil in 1809 to grant full power of management of the will to his wife).

In 1810 Harris was obliged to sell off two more portions of the Baughurst estate to Peter Knight and Joseph Taylor. All that remained of the original lands were the immediate grounds surrounding and containing Baughurst House itself. And this he sold in 1813 to Henry Randell of Yateley for £2,010.

William Harris died at Reading in February 1817.[3] His will was proved at Oxford on 17th January 1820, on the oath of his widow, the sole executrix. However, a dispute over the will arose in 1829, as to which court had the power and jurisdiction over its probate. Subsequently it was removed to the Prerogative Court of Canterbury on 1st August that year.[4]

William Harris left two daughters — Mary, the wife of John Adams a wharfinger of Farnham Wharf and of Basingstoke, and Sarah Harris, spinster of Reading. Therefore, the name of Harris and its connections with Baughurst House would soon die out. Mary Adams died in 1828, and her sister never married. It was the conclusion of the line which descended from the illustrious James Potter.

Richard Brown was succeeded by his son, John, in 1779. John and Mary Brown had, in all, six children — three sons and three daughters. John was particularly prosperous as a farmer of his copyhold lands, and had earned himself the title of " Mr Brown " by the time that he died, aged sixty-four, in 1801.

According to the custom of the manor, and to the conditions of Richard Brown's will, John's widow was admitted as the tenant of Brown's Farm after her husband's death. In reality, however, the estate was being farmed by her eldest son, Richard, a confirmed bachelor.

Mary died in 1822 and Richard was admitted as the tenant in her place. He became the most prosperous of that family, owning over seventy-five acres of land in Baughurst in 1839, including Loveday's Farm which he had purchased for £300 in 1828. By 1839, however, he had retired from farming and was living in a cottage on Silchester Common, while his farmlands were being occupied by William Reader the barrister of the Middle Temple in London, who owned Baughurst House. Reader had leased out his mansion house and Brown's Farm to the Carter family as his undertenants.

Richard Brown died in 1849, leaving Brown's Farm to his nephew, John Brown, the son of the second son of John and Mary Brown.

John Brown, the brother of Richard, had despaired of any chance of inhabiting his ancestral home at Brown's Farm. At the same time he probably wondered if he was suited to the life-style of that of a yeoman-farmer. Instead of remaining at Baughurst to watch his inheritance pass to his eldest brother, he decided to search for pastures new. He wandered into Surrey, where he gained a position as the gardener for Mr Andrew Drummond of Gifford House, at Putney. John was married by that time and was to sire eight children. He led a rather unadventurous life, which ended in 1832, at the age of fifty-eight, when his claim to the inheritance of Brown's Farm passed to his eldest son, John Brown, farmer at Roehampton.

234

It was this latter John Brown who finally succeeded to his uncle's farm in Baughurst in 1849. He did not enter into his inheritance until after 1851 when the lease granted by Reader to John Carter had expired. When he did finally take over his hereditary farm he worked it as the owner-occupier, employing labourers to till the soil and to feed the livestock, etc. John Brown never married, so when he died in 1865, at the age of sixty-two, he bequeathed the estate to his married brother, Thomas.

Thomas Brown was born at Putney in 1804. By 1835 he had married Mercy Miles of Cobham, in Surrey, and the couple had produced two daughters and two sons. Thomas took up the occupation of carman, which was the equivalent of today's self-employed lorry-driver. However, when his brother had left for Baughurst, Thomas took over the small farm at Roehampton, until John's death in 1865. In 1865 the widowed Thomas Brown entered into his family inheritance at Baughurst, leaving the Roehampton farm in the capable hands of his younger son, Thomas.

Thomas Brown, junior, married Maria Thirza Richards, a carpenter's daughter, at Reading in 1867, and soon afterwards the Browns sold off the Roehampton lands. The son, with his new bride, moved in with the old farmer, and there the last generation of the Browns of Brown's Farm were born between 1868 and 1883.

Thomas Brown, senior, died of heart disease while working in his fields on 22nd July 1872. He left the farm to his younger son, and in 1874 his son was recorded in the Register of Landowners as holding over sixty-three acres of land there.

Time was fast running out for the last of the descendants of the Potters of Baughurst. Crisis after crisis afflicted the farming communities during the latter quarter of the nineteenth century. If it were not the adverse weather conditions which affected both crops and livestock, then it was the cheaper imports of grain and frozen meat which were endangering the businesses of the British farmers. Then there were the attitudes of the farmers themselves. They were rather a conservative breed, who had failed to recognise the need for expensive improvements in the years of prosperity preceding the so-called "Great Depression". Everybody who lived in the countryside suffered in one way or another, and the economic disasters of the 1880s and 1890s forced labourers and farmers alike to migrate to the towns *en masse*, where living conditions were so much better.

The Browns remained at Baughurst for as long as possible, but as time passed it was becoming increasingly impossible to sustain a living from the land. Finally, in 1892, the truth had to be faced. Thomas Brown found a charitable purchaser in Mr Singleton of Baughurst House, whose ambition it was to amalgamate the lands and to use Brown's as the home farm of the whole estate. Therefore, in the first two weeks of September 1892 the following advertisement appeared under the Auction notices of the *Hants and Berks Gazette*:

> "Mr A. W. Tyrrell is instructed to SELL by AUCTION on the premises, on FRIDAY, SEPTEMBER 16th, 1892, at One o'clock prompt, the FARMING STOCK, comprising Bay Cart Horse, Cow with Calf, Prime Fat Devon Heifer, 20 Hampshire Down Lambs, 4 Porkers, 7 Stove Pigs, Hay-making Machine, Horse Gear, Harrows, Ploughs, Carts, Wagons, and other Effects.
> At the same place and date will be sold a quantity of HOUSE-HOLD FURNITURE, comprising Dining Room Suite, Tables, Bedsteads, Bedding, etc., the property of the late Miss Wellesley, removed for convenience of sale."[5]

On Michaelmas Day, 29th September 1892 the Brown family moved out of Baughurst to take up their new home in the New Forest. Thus ended tragically the associations of the last of the descendants of the Potter family with the Quaker properties in Baughurst. The Browns were to return to their native parish in later years, but not to Brown's Farm. They would view this historical building with a sadness that can only be recognised by those who had lost something extremely valuable in their lives, and have no chance to recover it.

There is nothing left but a few dusty documents which contain any evidence at all that James Potter lived. It is likely that even these papers will rarely see the light of day again, unless some enquiring mind may wish to research one of their Quaker ancestors who lived in Hampshire so many years ago. Then that person may see the name of James Potter liberally adorning a few pages of the Sufferings Books, or mentioned in the minutes of the Alton Monthly Meeting and Hampshire Quarterly Meetings. They will possibly pay little attention to the name at all.

On the surface of it all, there was nothing substantial which James had left to posterity. He does not even have a memorial to his name. He died almost as anonymous as he was born.

Considering all things, it does appear that he had nothing worthwhile to leave future generations. Having read his history, it would also appear that he was eventually a failure, for even the meeting which he had established perished within a hundred years of his death.

Yet, the failure of his meeting did not necessarily indicate the failure of the man. He had left to his successors a prosperous and influential meeting, and it was they who had failed him eventually. The demise of the

Baughurst Meeting began when the standards which Potter had set were being abandoned for the mere principles of power. The well-being of the assembly took second place to the personal ambitions of its elected leaders. In this, pure Quaker beliefs were forgotten. And James Potter was a true Quaker.

James Potter, however, did leave a memorial. A man who had worked so hard and conscientiously for his faith must be congratulated for helping that faith to survive its worst ordeals. The spirit of James Potter, and others like him, were later revived in order that true Quakerism would not perish throughout the nineteenth and twentieth centuries. The ideals which were entrenched in the first flushes of Quakerism and other nonconformist sects became, in time, inherent in modern society. The struggles were, therefore, not in vain if regarded over a wider period.

The concepts of James Potter and those of his ilk became the basis of the modern Welfare State system, which developed from such traditional institutions as the Quakers' Public Stock and personal contributions for the sake of charity and communal benefit. These people had already founded a system of education for their children centuries before one of their kind, W. E. Forster, introduced in 1870 the Elementary Education Act for all children between the ages of five and ten. Their stand in defence of religious toleration had produced many changes in the law of the land. The Toleration Act was just one such, while the Quakers' refusals to swear oaths caused the act of 1696, whereby we now have a choice between oath or affirmation. Prison reform was another development from the Quaker camp (remember Elizabeth Fry?), as were their seventeenth-century protests against slavery and the exploitation of working children. Currently the trend is towards unilateral or universal disarmament, based upon the age-old Quaker doctrine of resistance to the destruction of human life.

Yet all these things were not necessarily the results of Quaker pressure alone, as other nonconformist and conformist groupings share the responsibility for bringing about the successful development of our modern society. However, the Quakers did help to lay the foundation stone of the Welfare State system, with their major stand against the prejudices of the majority or ruling classes. They were fearless of the consequences of their actions to the point that they actually recorded their business, despite the fact that the authorities could and would use such records as evidence against them.

And James Potter was more fearless than most. While the moderate Quaker stood aside and gave little to the cause other than that required of him, all major decisions and actions were taken by the leaders of the communities, which meant that they also accepted the responsibilities of these decisions. James Potter was definitely not a bystander, but an actual participator in the struggle for the minority classes. He was a leader because he held that certain quality which made him outstanding among his fellows. He had an intelligence which was probably remarkable in a countryman of those times, and of such a degree that he could communicate with judges and lawyers, and put up a strong argument for his case. Perhaps his arguments, which were controlled, possessed little more than simple logic, but they were normally successful. His weapons were always words, and these he found adequate, for he could do battle with anyone he chose if he thought that the cause was right. And his opponents knew that James' words could be dangerous. They knew this from the early days, for why would he spend five years in prison when his fellow Quakers would remain in that dank cell for just over a year at worst? Why was James often persecuted more than his friends and neighbours? He was recognised as a troublemaker of the greatest degree. Yet his stand, and those of his kind, brought us certain benefits which would not have been granted freely by Parliament of its own will.

Parliamentary historians state, with some pride, that all our civil liberties have developed from that ancient assembly. Yet this is not totally true because that noble institution attempted to suppress certain liberties during the course of the seventeenth century, and it took a handful of men and women, who were debarred from that assembly, to challenge its persecuting policies and to create enough opposition against it for it to reconsider its views and to amend its policies. The true heroes were, of course, the stubborn defenders of religious toleration, for many of our civil liberties stem from that ideal. And James Potter was a prominent defender of that cause. He suffered imprisonment and persecution for his right and those of his fellows to worship as they pleased.

It is true that he left nothing tangible. It is true that he is unknown outside this history. It is, therefore, about time that his story was told. He would not tell it himself. He was humble and modest about his deeds, unlike Richard Baxter the so-called Presbyterian leader who wrote his own autobiography as a tribute to his deeds, and Potter's hero, George Fox, the founder of Quakerism, whose journal was an attempt to set an example for his followers. Potter wrote only minutes of meetings and sufferings and deeds to meeting-houses, and witnessed wills. His personal letters did not survive the ravages of time, although it is known that he did often write. He would not have attempted a self-glorifying life-history as he would have felt that there was little to write. At the same time he was too busy with other businesses. Enough, however, has survived among the original Quaker records to give us a fairly reasonable account of his life.

Therefore, James Potter did leave behind him a memorial that time could not taint. We have to search hard for it, though. In the end we can certainly distinguish that here was a remarkable man, who could not have been swayed from his purpose in life — a dissenter, whose dissent was for the common good and not for very personal ambitions of wealth and fame. His history was the history of English dissent, and therefore not a narrow biography. He was not remembered because his foundation had eventually failed. Yet the failure and extinction of the Baughurst Meeting must surely be considered as a tribute to the man himself. When Potter died the Quakers of Baughurst had lost the strength which had united them. So much had been concentrated in the character of a single man. Just as the Republic had crumbled after the death of Cromwell, then, on a smaller scale, the Baughurst Meeting had begun to expire on the decease of Potter. Yet Quakerism survived in northern Hampshire and much of the credit must be placed at the door of James Potter and his friends. Baughurst had nurtured the faith in this area during its darkest days of persecution, when it was virtually non-existent in the towns. When the danger had passed newly-constituted meetings sprang up in Basingstoke, Whitchurch, Newbury and other urban areas under the influence of former members of the Baughurst Meeting. The founders of those meetings had a source of inspiration in Potter. Those meetings still function and they are probably Potter's most enduring memorials — yet the present members have not heard of him.

James Potter was, therefore, a major contributor to our history in one way or another. He personified the English dissenter, whether on religious or purely social grounds. He was both typical and untypical of that kind. He was outstanding without being renowned outside his sphere of influence. He did a great deal for his people, without receiving the gratitude of posterity. He was, above all, the unsung hero of whom everybody talks but knows hardly anything of him. There were many James Potters in this world whose reputations have been cast into oblivion by a thankless multitude of generations. Perhaps one day some of them will be researched and their stories told.

AN ACCOUNT OF THE QUAKER MEETING HOUSES AND BURIAL GROUNDS IN BAUGHURST

A LL THAT IS needed to complete this book is a thorough revision of the article submitted to the Hampshire Field Club by Florence Davidson in 1915. Until now this had been the only attempt to give an account of Quaker activities in Baughurst. Unfortunately, because of its unique standing, Davidson's article has gained the reputation as the last word on this particular subject.

It is time that the article was shown up for what it really was — an amateurish attempt to write a vague history on a subject which needed a great deal more research undertaken than was actually given. Florence Davidson's essay was based upon about ninety per cent hearsay evidence and tradition, and perhaps only ten per cent documentary evidence. She could have been excused if the majority of the sources available today were in private hands at the time of her research. But the Quaker records have never been privately owned, and were, even then, accessible. She even quoted from a series of them — the birth and marriage digests of the Hampshire and Dorsetshire General Meeting. Yet she did not bother to pursue the matter and search out further Quaker records. She handled the whole affair as an amateur researcher — which indeed she was — and the trouble is that there are so many of her kind about even today. There are many (not all) who write local history or trace their family or the history of their house in a slap-dash fashion, disregarding the normal and lengthy business of proving their case. This is fine if the results are not published, but there are a few who then write articles or even books based upon such meagre findings, and then add their own unfounded conclusions to the work. In this way history becomes fiction instead of fact, and the reader believes what did not happen instead of what did. Newspaper reporters who turn their attentions to local history easily fall into this class. Hearsay evidence and tradition form a major part of the histories written by these people. They normally attempt to take all the credit for their writings, while not acknowledging their sources of information.

It is high time that the record was set straight regarding the Quaker properties in Baughurst. In the first place tradition was correct when it pointed to Brown's Farm as the first meeting-house in that parish. This fact, also affirmed by my grandmother — herself a Brown — is borne out by several documents relating to different sources. The mention in 1669 of episcopal returns of Richard Potter's house, and in the Quaker marriage and burial registers, as well as Richard's constant tithe visitations in the early years, indicate beyond doubt that here was the meeting-house established in 1662, while the Manydown Court Rolls, when traced back to that period, show that Richard Potter's house was Brown's Farm.

The burial ground at Brown's Farm — "Richard Potter's garden" in the parish registers — which is traditionally set beneath the yew-tree by the road, is again proven by the fact that a brick vault was uncovered there in the lifetime of Florence Davidson (here she is reliable, for part of that brickwork still remains exposed). There is another tradition, although less known, that there was an even older burial ground within the limits of the farm. This is extremely logical, for I doubt if the Quakers at that stage would have planned a communal burial ground near the roadside, for fear of discovery. The paddock is regarded as the traditional site of the first burial ground. It probably was, for a field was more easily disguised than the garden approach to the farm. Yet this is merely a local tradition and cannot be proved.

The second meeting house was Baughurst House. This is more readily proved by James Potter's deed of conveyance to the Trustees, and by John Harris' receipt of the property from the Quakers in 1728, and sub-stantiated once again by the Court Rolls of Manydown. Davidson makes no mention at all of James Potter — which is remarkable, considering his position in the history of the Quakers — and hardly anything of Baughurst House (she said that Harris had it built).

The second (or third if one considers the traditional cemetery in the paddock field at Brown's Farm) burial ground was located in a meadow at Town's End. That meadow is now part of the estate of Forgefields. There is enough mention of the cemetery at Town's End in the records of the deeds held by the trustees of the Baughurst Meeting, and in the wills of James Potter and his son-in-law, John Harris. There is also the recent proof of the exposure of a vault in that meadow. It is also recorded on the Ordnance Survey map of the area, as are the other cemeteries. Davidson mentioned the burial ground but not in the right context. She assumed that, according to the will of John Harris, it was established in or after 1770!

The third meeting house has since proved the most troublesome to identify. Davidson makes no indication at all of where she believed it was situated, yet the Ordnance Survey map, probably based upon her

241

assumptions, record the burial ground attached to it in the wrong place altogether. The Schedule of Deeds relating to the properties of the Quakers in Baughurst describe the premises as:

" All that piece of Land at Baughurst in the County of Southampton (formerly enclosed out of the Land purchased by one Leonard Coale of John Freeburn the son and Heir of one John Freeburn) containing by estimation 14 or 15 perches (more or less) formerly bounded on the East by a Ditch adjoining the Highway leading from Baughurst to Newberry (but which said Ditch is now filled up and forms part and parcel of the said piece of Land) on the North West and South by the Land formerly of the said Leonard Coale but now of Dicker partly in the occupation of Samuel Thorngate & William Cowderry. And also All that piece or parcel of Land part also of the Lands of the said Leonard Cole and purchased by him of the said Richd (sic) Freeburn containing by estimation 6 poles (more or less) and which was added to the last mentioned piece of Land for the purpose of enlarging the said Burial Ground bounded on the East by the Highway leading from Baughurst to Newberry on the North and part of the West by Lands heretofore of the said Leonard Coale but now in the occupatn of the said Samuel Thorngate and William Cowderry on the remaining part of the West by other Lands purchased by the said Leonard Coale of the said Richard (sic) Freeburn aforesaid and on the South by the above mentioned piece or parcel of Land with the Messuage and Tenement (formerly a Meeting House) and other buildings thereon."

The Schedule of Deeds was dated 1835, when the last group of trustees were constituted for the Baughurst Meeting. Only one of the former trustees was surviving at that time, and if there were problems of identification then he would surely have known the location of the last meeting house. Furthermore, there was the original deed quoted, surprisingly enough, by Davidson, although I am afraid I could not locate it (perhaps it had disappeared between 1915 and 1985) which would have identified the land.

The description of the property tallies exactly with that of the original deed quoted by Davidson, and the planned extension of the burial ground. The meeting house stood in the south-western corner of the estate, while the burial ground was situated alongside its western and northern limits. In 1835 Samuel Thorngate was mentioned as one of the occupiers, with William Cowderry, and the property was owned by someone named Dicker. In 1839, according to the tithe map and apportionment, Thorngate was still residing in Baughurst, but there was no mention of Cowdery

242

nor a Dicker in that precise area. The Dicker may very well have been Daniel Tyler, with Dicker entered in error or wrongly copied from the original document instead of Tyler. In 1839 there was such a cottage and garden in the Inhurst hamlet of Baughurst where Thorngate, a baker, lived as the occupier under Daniel Tyler, a carpenter, who actually lived in a cottage to the north of the baker's residence.

The cottage in which Thorngate lived in 1839 was precisely the one now named "Rose Cottage". This building is the residence of two spinster sisters, the Wigleys, and is actually situated in the south-western corner of their plot, with the majority of their land running along the northern and western sides of the land. Furthermore, one of the sisters remembers the time when the main sewer was being installed to replace the old cesspit in the garden. Excavation there had exposed some brickwork a little distance below soil-level. This could very well have been a vault, part of the Quaker burial ground.

The cottage itself, however, is believed to have been built during the nineteenth century. This does not disprove its claim. The last Quaker meeting-house in Baughurst was obviously in terrible disrepair when Tyler took it over, for the Quakers would not have used it for several years before that time. It probably remained a tumbled-down affair for several more years after, until such a time when major repairs or complete renovations had to be made. It was probably rebuilt from the original bricks, while its windows and doors were replaced and the roof slated instead of thatched. This was definitely the site of Leonard Cole's meeting-house, with the burial ground surrounding it on two sides.

The Ordnance Survey location of the burial ground must now be revised. Misinformation has led to its siting near the Methodist chapel and Buller's Farm — a considerable distance to the south of the actual burial ground. Perhaps their siting was based on the information that it was situated near the forge. I have not seen any deed relating to the forge, but, apparently, the owners of the meadow at Town's End have. If this is the reason why the Ordnance Survey sited the burial ground near Buller's Farm then it must have been for the fact that John Treacher, blacksmith of Inhurst, held property near there. Yet Treacher also held lands by copyhold tenure to the south of that area, within the confines of the Manor of Manydown. He also held substantial property to the east of the road from Baughurst to Newbury, in the parish of Tadley, at a point not far from Rose Cottage, and it could be possible that he had his smithy there. The owners of the meadow at Town's End have used this mention of the proximity of the forge to assume that they live in the meeting-house because Forgefields is situated near the forge at Town's End. They also took into account that the burial ground was attached to the meeting-house and have believed that they have lived in a particularly important historical residence for some years now. Unfortunately, history is fact and the fact is that the three meeting-houses of Baughurst were situated at Brown's Farm, Baughurst House and Rose Cottage respectively, though at least some of the glory can be claimed as the burial grounds were at Brown's Farm, Forgefields and Rose Cottage. It has taken seventy years for the record to be made straight, simply because of improper research.

At this point I wish to make this plea on behalf of the owners and occupiers of the old Quaker properties. These people are rightly anxious that their privacies may be invaded through the publication of this book. They are indeed proud that they have the fortunes to be able to dwell in such places of real historical interest. This does not mean that they have to bear crowds of visitors or merely curious spectators to roam their grounds at will. Probably their fears will be unfounded, but at the least their wishes should be respected. After all, the Quakers themselves believed in peace. Allow them to have their last wishes.

[1] Schedule of Deeds pertaining to the Baughurst Meeting, Hampshire Record Office.

[2] Land Tax Assessments, Hampshire Record Office, and the will of William Harris, Berkshire Record Office.

[3] Attested by his daughters, Mrs Mary Adams and Miss Sarah Harris, 30th December 1819 (Oxford).

[4] By mistake granted in the Archdeacon of Berkshire's Court on 17th January 1820, but seized upon by the P.C.C. on 18th July 1829 on the threat of a fine, and then transmitted to London on 1st August that year. The will was dated 26th December 1805, the codicil 6th September 1809. Richard Brown was a witness.

[5] Hants and Berks Gazette Library, Pelton House, Basingstoke.

INDEX

Surnames in capitals: Quakers denoted by
*, Anglican clerics by †, Justices and Assize
Judges by ‡
Pedigrees (between Author's Note and
Prologue) which include indexed persons
are denoted as follows: [B] Brown, [H]
Harris, [P] Potter

Baptists, 34, 161, 228
BAREFOOT, 110, 116; Margery*, [P], 110, 116 (see also POTTER, Margery)
BARLOW, Mary (1732-91)*, 228, 230; Richard (fl 1768), 228
BARNES, Edward (d. 1727)*, 162, 206
Barrow, 32
Basing, Hants, 216-7
Basingstoke, Hants, [B], 13, 40-3, 47, 52, 65-6, 68, 80-1, 120, 131, 136, 149, 163, 165-6, 169-71, 175, 179, 185-90, 192-3, 196, 199-200, 204, 210, 214-5, 217, 228, 231, 234, 239
BATES, Thomas (1775-1845), 233
BATT, Robert (fl 1700), 183
Baughurst, Hants, [P, H, B], 13-5, 21, 45-50, 52, 55, 57-61, 66-9, 75-91, 94-100, 102, 104-5, 109, 111-2, 115-6, 121-7, 129-37, 142, 144, 147, 149-50, 152, 154, 157-9, 162-4, 167-8, 170, 172-80, 182-6, 188, 190-217, 219-36, 239-44
BAXTER, Richard, 238
BEAUFORT, Margaret (1443-1509), 153
BEAVIS, Stephen (fl 1657)*, 63
BENCE, Martin (fl 1661)*, 64, 66; Philip (fl 1660)*, 64
BENNER, Richard (fl 1671), 102
BENNET, Gervase (fl 1650)‡, 32
BENTHALL, Edward (fl 1662)†, 21, 45-9, 52, 55, 66-70, 75, 77-8, 80, 84
BENWELL, Thomas (fl 1788)*, 187
Berkshire, 43, 52, 81, 97-9, 101-3, 107, 109, 127, 131, 142, 163, 186, 191-2, 199, 206, 211-2, 220, 222, 230, 233
BERKSHIRE, Harriet, [B] (see also BROWN)

BIDDLEWORTH, Robert (fl 1661)*, 63, 65
BIGG-WITHER, Lovelace (1741-1813), 233
Bighton, Hants, 60
Bill of Rights (1689), 160
Birmingham, Warws, 81, 220
BISHOP, John (fl 1660)*, 64; Richard (fl 1683)‡, 145
Bishop's Waltham, Hants, 110, 116
Bishops' Wars, the (1640), 59
BLAMSHOTT, William (fl 1661)*, 65
Blasphemy Act (1650), 21, 32
Bloodless Revolution, the (1688-89), 160
BLOSE, James, junr (fl 1788)*, 227
BLUNDEN, Ann (d. 1732)*, 221; Elizabeth (d. 1728)*, 220; Elizabeth (d. 1728)*, 220; William (d. 1740)*, 176, 191-2, 220, 224
BLYTHE, Richard (fl 1671), 101, 103-4
BONNEY, Ann (fl 1776)*, 230; Frances (fl 1776)*, 230; Thomas (fl 1776)*, 230
BOWEN, John (fl 1716), 223
Bradfield, Berks, 211, 223
Bramshott, Hants, 63-4, 171, 176, 194, 231
BRANSLEY, David (fl 1835)*, 231; Newton (fl 1835)*, 231
Bridport, Dorset, 43
BRIGGS, Thomas (fl 1670)*, 94-5, 97
Brimpton, Berks, 49, 58, 68, 81, 95, 98-9, 101-5, 115, 121, 123, 125, 127, 131, 141-2, 155, 163, 176, 186, 192, 199, 206
Bristol, Glos, 37, 81, 230
Brixton, Isle of Wight, 63
BROCAS, Thomas (fl 1683)‡, 145
BROWN, [P, B], 13-5, 89, 220, 225, 235-6; Ada (1878-1966), [B]; Ann (1786-1820), [B]; Ann (b. c1815), [B], (see also MARLOW);

249

Enclosure Act for Pamber, Ham and Inhurst (1827), 231-2
English Reformation, the, 34
Episcopal Returns (1669), 81, 241
Equality, 16, 22, 35, 55
Established Church, the: see Anglicans and Anglicanism
EVANS, Henry (fl 1835)*, 231
EVELYN, John (1620-1706), 37
Evingar, Hundred of, 145, 147
EVIS, Thomas (fl 1712), 216
Ewhurst, Hants, 232
Exclusion Bill Crisis (1679-1681), 139, 153
Excommunication, Writ of, 66, 98
Exmouth, Devon, [B]

FAITHFUL, John (fl 1682)*, 140, 143
FAULKNER, John (fl 1702)‡, 182-3; Mr (fl 1675)‡, 121, 124-6; Thomas (fl 1671), 103; Thomas (fl 1810), 233
FEEL, Margaret (fl 1652)*, 34; Thomas (fl 1652)‡, 34
FERRIS, Edward (fl 1752)*, 220
Fifth Monarchists, 65
FINKLEY, Nicholas (fl 1661)*, 65
Five Mile Act (1665), 78-80, 131, 185
FLOWER, Henry (1765-1833), 232
FOLKINGHAM, Nicholas (fl 1649)†, 32
FORD, Mark (fl 1681)*, 146-7
Fordingbridge, Hants, 170
Forest, the, Warws, 81, 220
FORSTER, W. E., 162, 237
FOX. George (1624-1691)*, 21, 31-30, 43, 47, 57, 62, 66, 75, 82, 86-7, 94-7, 99, 107, 131, 176, 229, 238
France and the French, 138-9, 157
FREEBORN, John, 242; Richard, 207
FREWIN, Mr (fl 1655)‡, 42
Friends: see Quakers and Quakerism
Friends of the Truth, 32

FROUD, Benjamin (1667-1753)*, 222; Benjamin, junr (fl 1788)*, 203, 207, 215, 222, 227; Martha (fl 1732)*, 220; Rebecca (d. 1745)*, 221; Rebecca, junr (d. 1750)*, 222
Froyle, Hants, 81, 88, 127
FRY, Anna (fl 1785)*, 230; Edmund (fl 1785)* 230; Elizabeth*, 162, 237; Joseph (fl 1785)*, 230

GAMMON, William (fl 1682), 140, 143
Gatcombe, Isle of Wight, 64
GATES, Nicholas (fl 1704)*, 120, 128, 132, 145, 151, 201; Nicholas, junr (fl 1704)*, 171, 173, 176, 189, 201
GEALL, William (fl 1680)†, 132
GIDDING, John (fl 1682)*, 121, 125, 142
GILBERT, Benjamin (fl 1774)*, 230; Letitia (fl 1774)*, 229
GILKS, Richard (fl 1788)*, 187, 229; Thomas (fl 1774)*, 229
GILL, Jane (fl 1687)*, 163
GILPIN, Joseph (fl 1692)*, 176
Glorious Revolution, the (1688-1689), 160-1
GLOSS, Stephen (fl 1661)*, 66
GLOVER, Hannah (fl 1692)*, 176; John (d. 1686)*, 164
Goatacre, Wilts, [H], 81, 180-2, 199, 211-2
GODDARD, John, [B]; Richard (fl 1682), 141-2; Sarah (b. 1807), [B], (see also BROWN)
GODDIN, Ann (d. 1685)*, 163; Daniel (d. 1684)*, 163; Jeremiah, alias Jeremiah Godwin (fl 1692)*, 163, 177; Jeremiah, junr, alias Jeremiah Godwin (d. 1692)*, 177; John (fl 1697)*, 199; John, junr, alias John Godwin (d. 1697)*, 199; Joseph, alias Joseph Godwin,

alias Joseph Greene (d. 1684)*, 163; Joseph (d. 1686)*, 164
GODWIN, see GODDIN
GOSMORE, Thomas (fl 1675), 121, 123-5
GRANTHAM, Francis (fl 1701), 183; Lawrence (fl 1675), 122, 126
Great Depression, the (1872-1898), 13, 235
Great Plague, the (1665), 80
GREENAWAY, Ann (d. 1684)*, 115 (see also BURGIS)
GREENE, 196, 209; James (fl 1671), 102; Joseph: see GODDIN; Richard (d. 1741), 194; William (fl 1675), 122, 124-6
GUEST, Robert (fl 1671), 102
GULSON, Mary (d. 1755)*, [H], 213, (see also HARRIS)

HACK, Colonel (fl 1656), 37; Hugh (d. 1665), 60; Thomas (fl 1750)*, 217; William (fl 1775)*, 187
Halifax, William Savile, Earl and Marquess of (d. 1695), 157
Ham, Hants, 209, 231
HAM, Thomas (fl 1661)*, 66
Hampshire, 38, 43, 64, 81, 87, 94, 107-8, 110-1, 129-32, 142, 146, 151, 166, 169-70, 189, 193, 198, 201, 203, 205, 211-2, 216, 219, 229, 233, 236, 239
Hampshire Genealogical Society, 14
Hampton Wick, Surrey, 81, 188-9
Hannington, Hants, 52
Hants and Berks Gazette (now Basingstoke Gazette), 236
HARMSWORTH, Edward (d. 1730), 183; Ralph (d. 1728), 182, 184; Thomas (fl 1597-1641), 59
HARRIS, [H], 190, 205, 211; Anne (b. 1750)*, [H]; Anne (d. 1794), [H]; Elizabeth (1786-1804), [H]; Hannah (fl 1680)*, [H]; Hannah

(1700-1753)*, [H], 194, 202, 204-5, (see also PAYNE); Hannah (1746-1747)*, [H], 222; James (1748-1749)*, [H], 222; Joan (d. 1704)*, [H], 181-2, (see also RICHMOND); Joan (fl 1680)*, [H]; John (d. 1693)*, [H], 181; John (1674-1737)*, [P, H], 180-2, 190, 193, 195, 198-9, 201-6, 208-12, 221-3, 227, 241; John (1712-1770)*, [H], 204-3, 211, 213-5, 219-20, 222-3, 225, 229, 241; John (1744-1745)*, [H], 222; John Potter (1745-1797)*, [H], 225, 233; John Potter (1776-1806), [H], 230, 233; Mary (1676-1729)*, [P, H], 182, 193-4, 202-4, 206, 211, 220, 222, (see also POTTER); Mary (fl 1680)*, [H]; Mary (1697-1747)*, [H], 194, 202, 204, 212, 222; Mary (d. 1755)*, [H], 222, (see also GULSON); Mary (1740-1761)*, [H], 220, (see also PEMBERTON); Mary (fl 1800), [H], 230; Mary (1787-1828), [H], 234, (see also ADAMS); Sarah (fl 1680)*, [H]; Sarah (1742-1802)*, [H], (see also PLOWDEN); Sarah (fl 1820), 234, 244; William (1752-1817)*, [H], 225, 230, 233-4
HARRIS, Hannah (d. 1760)*, 222; John, of Thatcham, 212; Robert (fl 1760)*, 222
HARRISON, William (fl 1683)‡, 145
Hartley Row, Hants, 230
HARVARD, John (fl 1661)*, 65
HASKER, Alice: see HASKINS; Ann (fl 1736)*, 220; Henry (d. 1705), 183; Jane (fl 1738)*, 221; John (fl 1738)*, 220-1; John (d. 1738)*, 221; William (fl 1736)*, 220
HASKINS, Alice (d. 1734)*, 206, 221; Joan, alias Joan Hoskins (d.

252

Monmouth, James Scott alias Crofts, Duke of (1649-1685), 139, 151, 154
Monmouth's Rebellion (1685), 154
MONTAINE, Richard (fl 1683)*, 140, 143-5, 147-8
MULLINS, Henry (fl 1661)*, 66
MUSGRAVE, Elizabeth (fl 1668), 82-5; George (d. 1666)†, 79-84
Muster arms, 16, 22, 36, 38
MYHILL, Richard (fl 1671), 101, 103-4

Nately Scures, Hants, 52, 216
NAYLOR, James (1617-1660)*, 37
NEAVE, Alexander (fl 1788)*, 227; Josiah (fl 1835)*, 231; Moses (fl 1697)*, 128-9, 132, 186, 191; Moses, junr (fl 1704)*, 171, 173, 176, 201
Nether Wallop, Hants, 143
Netherlands, 72
New Amsterdam, America, 43
New Forest, the, Hants, 236
Newburgh of Fife, Lord (d. 1644), 149
Newbury, Berks, 43, 81, 102, 104, 142, 207, 209, 214, 223, 230, 239, 242-3
NEWMAN, Winifred (fl 1658)*, 63
NICHOLAS, Mr (fl 1657)‡, 45, 54-5
NICHOLLS, William (fl 1737), 211
Nonconformists and Nonconformity, 21-2, 31-3, 46, 48, 65, 70, 73-4, 78-80, 84-5, 90-4, 111-7, 122-3, 126, 131, 135, 137-8, 140-1, 145-7, 151, 153-61, 181, 186, 195-7, 216, 218, 225, 228-9, 237, 239
North Warnborough, Hants, 120
NORTON, John bt (fl 1683)‡, 145; Richard (fl 1683)‡, 145
NOTT, Lawrence (fl 1628), 59
Nottingham, Notts, 31-2

NOYCE, Robert (fl 1682)‡, 140, 142-3

OATES, Titus (fl 1689), 138
Oath of Abjuration, 36, 41-2, 52, 55
Oath of Allegiance, 36, 64-5, 141-4, 147, 159, 161-2
Oath of Non-Resistance, 74, 80
Oath of Supremacy, 141-4, 147
Oath-taking, 16, 22, 36, 38, 64-5, 70, 144-5, 147, 157-9, 237
Odiham, Hants, 120
OGBORNE, Ann (fl 1731)*, 220
OGG, David, 156
Old Alresford, Hants, 116
Orange, Willem III, Prince of (1650-1702), 113, 160, (see also William III, King of England)
Orkneys, Scotland, 14
OVERTON, Hannah (fl 1752)*, 220; Jeremiah (fl 1692), 167-8; Richard (fl 1752)*, 220
Oxford, Oxfs, 36, 139-40, 233
Oxfordshire, 81, 176, 222, 233

Padworth, Berks, 95
PAGE, Christopher (fl 1668)*, 87-8; John (fl 1661)*, 63-5
PAICE, John (d. 1668)*, 88; John (fl 1673)*, 120; Mary (d. 1668)*, 88
Pamber, Hants, 81, 153-4, 163, 177, 231
Papists: see Catholics and Catholicism
PARCHMOUTH, Susanna: see PORTSMOUTH
PARK, Elizabeth*, [B], 188-9, (see also BROWN); James (fl 1675)*, 121-2, 124-6, 129, 132
Parliament, 35, 45-7, 51-2, 59-60, 63, 70-3, 75, 78-80, 86, 92-3, 112-4, 116, 137-40, 155-7, 160-1, 218, 238; Cavalier P, (1661-1679), 73-4, 114, 137-9; Conven-

255

257

Somerset, 81
SOPER, Ann (fl 1650), 60
SOUTH, Mary (d. 1685)*, 163; Robert (d. 1692)*, 153-4, 163, 177
Southampton, Hants, 65, 110
Southwark, Surrey, 121, 124
Southwich, Hants, 63
SPARROWBELL, Elizabeth (d. 1698)*, 199
Speenhamland, Berks, 142
Spelmonden, Kent, 149
SPENCER, Agnes (d. 1630), 60; Jane (1740-1779)*, [B], 226, (see also BROWN); Joan (d. 1678)*, 60-1, 75, 88, 91, 95, 109, 116, 133-6, 148; John, [B], 225; Margaret (d. 1688)*, 164; Mary (fl 1628), 59; Ralph (fl 1629-1641), 60; William (fl 1565-1590), 60
SPICER, William (fl 1682)*, 142
SPRINGER, Bartholomew (fl 1676)†, 132
Standford Dingley, Berks, 211
STEPHENS, William (fl 1683)‡, 145
STEWKELEY, Hugh, bt (fl 1683)‡, 145
Stoke Poges, Bucks, [B]
Stoney Heath, Hants, 50
STEVENS, C. J. (fl 1893), 89
STREETER, Elizabeth (fl 1661)*, 63; Henry (d. 1661)*, 63, 65; Henry (fl 1704)*, 171, 173, 176, 194, 201; Robert (fl 1674)*, 117-9
STUBBS, John (fl 1655)*, 40, 42
Subsidies, 59, 138
Sufferings, 15, 45, 66-7, 82-3, 89-90, 98, 101-2, 106, 121-2, 126, 133, 140-2, 144-5, 150-1, 154, 165, 167, 178, 182, 191, 193, 203, 216, 224, 236
Surrey, 107, 109, 234-5
SWAINE, Edward (fl 1683)*, 142; Sarah (d. 1681)*, 148; Thomas (fl 1681)*, 148

Swallowfield, Berks, 81, 87-8
Swanmore, Hants, 129
SWANN, Walter (fl 1659), 67, 69
SWANSON, Mr (fl 1671), 106, 110-1
Swarthmore Hall, Cumb, 33-4, 39

Tadley, Hants, [B], 67, 69, 78, 81, 88, 97, 103, 105, 125, 127, 130, 147-8, 163, 176, 191-3, 199, 205, 209, 211, 220, 225, 228, 230, 243
TAMPLING, James (fl 1661)*, 65
Tangier, 56
TANNER, Valentine (fl 1682), 140, 143
TARLTON, Abraham (fl 1682)*, 143
TAYLOR, John (fl 1746)†, 216-7; Joseph (fl 1814), 233; Mary (1744-1822), [B], 225, (see also BROWN)
TERRY, Joan (fl 1668)*, 87-8; Robert (fl 1661)*, 65
Test Act (1673), 138, (1678), 138
Tetherton, Wilts, 181
Thames, River, 197
Thatcham, Berks, 81, 132, 163, 211-2, 233
Theale, Berks, 211
THOMPSON, Samuel (fl 1835)*, 231
THORNGATE, Samuel (fl 1849), 232, 242-3
THORPE, John (fl 1742)*, 221; Rachel (d. 1742)*, 221
Tithe Commutation Act (1836), 232
Tithes, 16, 22, 38, 63-4, 66-9, 76, 82-6, 90-1, 122-3, 126, 129, 131-2, 134, 136-7, 147, 150-2, 156-8, 162, 167-70, 178-9, 182-4, 192, 196-7, 216-7, 241
Toleration, 16, 46, 70, 72-3, 80, 82, 113-7, 121, 123, 139-40, 156-61, 169, 186, 196, 218, 237-8
Toleration Act (1680), 161, (1689), 158-62, 167-8, 185, 237
TONGE, Israel, Dr (fl 1678), 138

258